VISUAL MERCHANDISING AND DISPLAY

VISUAL MERCHANDISING AND DISPLAY:

The Business of Presentation

Martin M. Pegler, ASID and ISP

FAIRCHILD PUBLICATIONS · NEW YORK

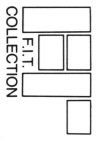

F.I.T.
COLLECTION

Other Titles by the Author

Language of Store Planning and Display
Dictionary of Interior Design
Store Windows that Sell (Vols. I & II)
Stores of the Year (Vols. I, II & III)

Victoria Arthur, Designer

Copyright © 1983 by Fairchild Publications
Division of Capital Cities Media, Inc.

Second Printing 1984
Third Printing 1986
Fourth Printing 1987

Standard Book Number: 87005-434-1
Library of Congress Catalog Card Number: 82-84000

Printed in the United States of America

Preface

Long gone are the days of unrestricted budgets and crepe-paper streamers suffocating a display window with swirls, twirls, and shirred fantasies. There was a time, and it was not so very long ago—only a decade or two—when windows were filled with props and backgrounds, overgrown with paper and plastic posies, a literal forest in which one could not see the merchandise. It was a time when trimmers "decorated," and the epitome of a successful window was how fanciful, how pretty, how unusual it was. The trimmer spent hours pinning, padding, and primping the garments, and then proceeded to lose them amidst palms, crystal chandeliers, gilded chairs, and champagne coolers.

Today's visual merchandiser still uses potted palms, chandeliers, and gilded chairs, but only to enhance or back up the merchandise. The test of a good display today is: *Does it sell?*

With every recession, depression, or financial crunch, the display budget gets another chunk taken out of it, and store owners put more money into media advertising. However, radio, television, and print ads are worthless, unless there is some follow through at the store. Here, at the point of purchase, is where display or merchandise presentation becomes absolutely necessary. With changes in retail shopping patterns, with the growth of malls and giant shopping centers, and the subsequent decline of much of "Main Street" and "in-town" shopping, the display windows that face out to the street, are stepping back in favor of display on the selling floor.

Some store managers feel that the cost of maintaining a display window simply does not justify the expenditure of staff, space, and materials. It is not only the cost of the props, mannequins, backgrounds, and energy for lighting; it is more than the wear and tear on the merchandise and the adverse effects of sunlight and heat; it is more than the decline of pedestrian traffic. It is also the value of the up-front real estate, which can be converted to valuable selling space rather than be used to show a few select pieces of merchandise.

Some stores have removed their window walls and

opened up the floor space for fixtures and counters. Others have masked large, full-sized windows into much smaller shadow boxes which require a lower budget and less trim time and upkeep. The balance of the window can be used for storage, dressing rooms, or, possibly, for additional floor selling space. Happily, however, many store managers still feel that window display is very important. It is in the window that the store puts its best foot forward in order to sell its "image" and its "uniqueness." With the recent growth of urban redevelopment and the apparent increase in pedestrian traffic, in-town stores may experience a renaissance—and so will window display.

The indoor mall concept has opened the whole store to perusal. Interior store display has increased in importance over the past few years since many potential customers rush from the parking lot into the store with nary a glance at the exterior display windows. Open-back windows allow the shopper to look right into the store, and suddenly it is no longer just racks, counters, and fixtures. The emphasis in store design is on "ambience," and the concern is for the creation of a selling "environment." High ceilings are coming down, departments are being converted into shops, and specialty areas are becoming boutiques.

Today's store plan hardly ever has a central aisle directing the shopper from the entrance door to the elevator or escalator and then quickly up to a particular area or type of merchandise. Getting around in a store is, or should be, an experience. It is "theater"! There is an "overture"—a merchandise presentation upon entering. Sometimes, it is set up on a stage or platform or on a rug. Sometimes, it takes the form of a vignette setting. The mood is established and the customer is immediately involved with the merchandise and the accessories that go with that merchandise. The lights go up, and the lights go down. Spotlights are used to dramatize and highlight the displays and some of the merchandise, and there is low lighting to lead the customer on to the next scene or setting. Sometimes, there is music; the aroma of perfume and cosmetics may enhance the moment. Wherever the customer wanders, he or she finds merchandise on display: on counters, on ledges, on and off columns, on back walls, over

hang-rods, hanging down from the ceiling, spread out on the floor, or raised up on platforms.

The displayperson today is a salesperson. He or she is a merchant who must know the "whys" and "wherefores" of what is being shown to be sold. The world is now almost totally visually oriented. People have television, and are accustomed to seeing images. The printed word has become a less important vehicle of communication. International travel has made the world so small that department stores are now filled with the sounds of many languages, and the graphic presentation of merchandise must take the place of signs and printed or spoken explanations. The displayperson can, in one vignette setting, in one "picture," speak thousands of words in a dozen languages.

Display did not die, but it has changed! The job of the merchandise presenter has become more involved, more exciting, more challenging, and more stimulating. Display and fashion are so closely intertwined that the health of one depends on the well-being of the other. Fashion is capricious, ever-changing, always new and exciting. Similarly, display must always change, be always different, be always new.

This book is written for the person who is interested in merchandising—presenting merchandise and selling merchandise. That individual is a store owner/manager who wants to make a fashion statement, breaking away from the rank and file of neighboring merchants and the confines of the store's building line. He or she wants to say something "special" to the shopper about the store, the merchandise, and himself. Or that individual is someone hired to present the store's merchandise and to create or reinforce the store's image.

A fashion awareness is necessary. A creative talent is a great advantage. A sense of professionalism can be developed. An artistic flair is a plus. But, "You've got to know the territory." You—the presenter—have to know *what* is to be presented, to *whom*, and *why* and *when* it is to be shown or displayed.

This book explains the *how* of effective merchandise presentation. It is written for the merchant, the artist-designer, the student, and the salesperson. It is for anyone who has merchandise to sell, who cares for the merchandise, or who is concerned about the concept to be sold or the image to be projected.

This book is filled with "basic truths" of visual merchandising and display—the concepts, ideas, and suggestions on how to use them. There are few rules, however, but there are many concepts and ideas that will work if the displayperson understands them and knows how to adapt them to his or her needs. In display, one does not say "always" or "never." It is too definite, too limiting, too inhibiting. A good displayperson should occasionally break a rule, knowing in advance what breaking that rule might mean—how it might affect the merchandise, the customer, and the store's image. If it still seems like the thing to do—to startle, to surprise, to obtain a new awareness from "jaded" customers—then go ahead and do it!

Someday, perhaps, all of retailing will be display. We may come to a time when a retail operation will consist exclusively of display settings without any stock. Encased in a square glass bowl, the customer will find several mannequins beautifully dressed and accessorized, posed in a contemporary room setting. A keyboard and screen, connected to a computer somewhere in the bowels of the operations, will take questions and supply answers concerning price; sizes, colors, and fabrics available; delivery; and so on. The customer will then punch in the order, giving his or her name and account number as well as the desired color, size, etc.; and the package with the purchase will be waiting when the customer leaves the store. Meanwhile, he or she might have a robot serve a lunch that was punched into a computer keyboard. While dining, the customer may witness a "sensoramic," electronically projected fashion show, or perhaps have an old-fashioned beauty parlor experience. Things may change, but the displayperson will still be around. No matter what else changes, one must still *show* in order to sell.

Acknowledgments

I wish to acknowledge with special thanks:

Hugh T. Christie and my co-educators in the Display and Exhibit Department at the Fashion Institute of Technology, State University of New York, for their helpfulness and their suggestions; and to all those other persons who are trying to create a place in academe for visual merchandising.

Fred Howard of Howard-Marlboro Displays, Incorporated, for his interest, his expertise, and the photos he so graciously provided for the chapter on point-of-purchase display.

All the countless students who have sat through my countless lectures while I tried and tested what appears on these pages.

All those visual merchandisers, displaypersons, merchandise presenters, store planners, and display manufacturers and suppliers whose work and imagination made such a deep impression on me that many of their precepts now appear in this book. My thanks to all the above for making the merchandising scene more exciting, more glamourous and more fun, and for putting more entertainment into this "showing business."

Angelo Virgona, my editor, for his patience and smiling good humor in the face of my wrath over adjectives removed and dashes changed to commas. Thanks for leaving in most of my concepts, some of my idioms, and even a little of my bombast.

Suzan, my wife, for her love, her faith, her willingness to pre-edit and type my manuscript, and her courage for correcting me and my errors.

And all of you who want to know more about this business of presentation.

I am greatly indebted to Laurence Fuersich and his capable staff at the Retail Reporting Bureau ("Views and Reviews") for the many pictures he allowed us to reproduce in this book. A very special "thank you" to Sanford Litwak, the photographer.

Contents

ix

VISUAL MERCHANDISING AND DISPLAY

1 Why Do We Display?

We show in order to sell. Display or visual merchandising is "showing" merchandise and concepts at their very best, with the end purpose of making a sale. We may not actually sell the object displayed or the idea promoted, but we do attempt to convince the viewer of the value of the object, the store promoting the object, or the organization behind the concept. Though a cash register may not ring because of a particular display, that display should make an impression on the viewer which will affect future sales.

The displayperson used to be the purveyor of dreams and fantasies, presenting merchandise in settings that stirred the imagination and promoted fantastic flights to unattainable heights. Today's displayperson, however, sells a "reality." The shopper can be whatever he or she wants to be, simply by wearing garments with certain labels having a built-in status. The displayperson dresses a mannequin (possessing a perfect figure) in skin-fitting jeans, for example, flashes the lights, adds the adoring males or females, and reinforces the image of sexuality and devastating attractiveness that is part of the prominent name on the label. Wearing Brand-X jeans, whether size 8 to 18 for her or size 28 to 42 for him, makes the wearer feel special. She imagines herself to be that slim, sensuous femme fatale she has seen on television, surrounded by gaping admirers. He feels as special when he is wearing television-advertised hip-hugging jeans.

Today's mannequin often resembles the shopper on the other side of the glass; it may have a flawless figure, but far from perfect features. This prompts the customer to think, "If that mannequin can look so great, why not me?" That's reality! That's selling! The visual merchandiser, therefore, presents more than the merchandise. He or she presents the image of who or what the shopper can be when using the merchandise displayed.

It has been said by presidents and vice-presidents of large retail operations; it has been uttered by experienced shoppers and by conscientious consumers: "There is very little difference between the merchandise sold in one store and that sold in another." Many department and specialty stores carry the same name brands—the same nationally advertised lines seen on television and in *Vogue* magazine. Often the real difference is in the price of the merchandise being offered for sale.

Why, then, does an individual shop in Store A and pay more for the same item selling for less in Store B? Why does a shopper tote the shopping bag from Store C rather than an equally attractive bag from Store D? Why does the shopper tattoo herself or himself with garments branded with a store's name on pockets, patches, shoulders, and hips? It has to do with the store's image! If everyone believes that people who shop in Store A are "young, smart, sophisticated, amusing, clever, trendy, and fun to be with," then a shopper who buys clothes at that store can also be young, smart, sophisticated, and so on. The displayperson reinforces that belief with the merchandise display, with the type of mannequins shown, and by the manner in which the mannequins are dressed, positioned, and lit. In this way, the displayperson promotes the store's image and fashion trendiness. Although, in the case of Store A, the visual merchandiser is not selling any one piece of merchandise, but the whole idea that any purchase from A will guarantee social success and the stamp of the "right" taste level, he or she is still *selling*. We shall return often in later chapters to the concept of image and image projection in merchandise presentation.

In addition to selling actual merchandise, display can be used to introduce a new product, a fashion trend, and a new "look" or idea. The display may be the first three-dimensional representation of something the consumer has thus far only seen in sketches or photos. Display can be used to educate the consumer concerning what the new item is, how it can be worn or used, and how it can be accessorized. The display may also supply pertinent information, the price, and other special features.

The visual merchandiser may create a display that stimulates, tantalizes, or arouses the shopper's curiosity to such a degree that he or she is "challenged" to enter the store and wander through it, even though the shopper is not motivated by the displayed product itself. This is still a victory. It gives the displayperson and the merchant many more opportunities to sell that shopper once he or she is inside the store. To make a shopper a *stopper*, and a "walk-in" rather than a "walk-by," is a commercial achievement. And always, as mentioned earlier, the purpose of visual merchandising is to promote the store image; to let people know what the store is, where it stands on fashion trends, what one can expect inside the store, to whom it appeals, the price range, and the caliber of its merchandise and merchandising.

The displayperson always puts the best "face" forward; but like Janus (the two-faced Roman god who looks back to what has been and at the same time ahead to what will be), the displayperson looks to the street to bring the shopper in and, at the same time, keeps an eye inside the store to be sure that the interior presentation is in keeping with what has been promised on the outside.

Recapping, the thrust of display, and why it is necessary, include the following:

- To sell by showing and promoting
- To introduce and explain new products
- To answer questions on the use and accessorizing of a product or fashion trend
- To encourage the shopper to enter the store
- To get the customer to pause and "shop" the selling floor
- To establish, promote, and enhance the store's visual image.

2 The Exterior of the Store

How and where we display depends largely on the architecture and fenestration (window placement) of the structure, the physical layout of space, and the fixtures inside the building. First, let us consider the facade of the building and the arrangement of the display windows in the store-front design. We will follow with an in-depth survey of the various types of display windows used in retail operations, as well as the advantages and limitations inherent in each type of window.

SIGNS

The store's sign, on the outside of the building, makes the first impression on the shopper. It sets the look and image of the store. How the sign is lettered, the materials used, the style of the lettering, the color—all are important. Its size and scale, in proportion to the store's facade, the size of the building, and the signs around it, can make points for or against the store's image. Unlit or missing light bulbs are definitely minus points. Flaking paint; cracked, peeling backgrounds; outrageous, highly luminous colors can be minuses also. The sign should be the store's "signature"—personal, original, and recognizable. It should make a statement.

MARQUEES

Some older stores as well as some of the very newest have marquees, or architectural canopies, extending out over their entrances. The marquee, a *permanent* awning for protection from the elements, is an integral part of the building facade. It is often cantilevered out over the street, in front of the main entrance to the store. It is similar to the porte-cochere (a porch at the door of a building for sheltering persons entering and leaving carriages) of the last century, or the big sign-boards with running lights that used to identify movie houses and theaters in the 1940's and 1950's.

The marquee can be an exciting place to start the display of a store-wide event or promotion. A "change of seasons" can be announced here. The fact that the marquee protrudes from the building line offers the advantage of increased visibility and greater prominence compared to all the other store signs from the surrounding operations. If the marquee is so designed, it could have changeable announcements (like the change of movie titles). A flat-topped marquee is an excellent place for the grouping of seasonal plants and foliage as well as larger than life-sized props. It is a perfect location for a giant Santa or even his sleigh and eight clamoring reindeer.

OUTDOOR DISPLAY

Outdoor Lighting

There is a whole industry involved in creating and installing outdoor lighting displays. The use of hundreds and hundreds of lights on building facades and canopies can be most effective for some holidays and store events. The lights can be draped or swagged or wired to frames to form recognizable symbols or letters. However, this type of display does require an extra expenditure of electrical energy, and the effect of the lighting is limited to the twilight and evening hours when the store may not be open for business. In suburban operations, however, with their later operating hours, the use of lights in the evening may be especially worthwhile. Very often, the strings of lights or the framed light unit are wrapped or covered with tinselly, shimmering materials that reflect light during the daylight hours. This provides some degree of decoration to the store exterior during those hours when the lights are not on or when they are barely visible.

Banners

Outdoor fabric banners are inexpensive and expendable, but they are colorful, eye-catching and eye-filling devices that flutter and flap in the wind. They can be and should be changed with the seasons or the store events. A few holes, worked into the design, will allow the wind to sweep through without tearing the fabric. The banners can be hung from flagpoles, projected from the building, or hung flat against it. The same banner design, reduced in size and scale, could be hung from the marquee, between the display windows, or projecting from or against the columns inside the store. To be truly effective, however, the idea should not be overused. If there always is a banner flapping overhead, after a while the shopper won't even look up. He or she will just assume it is the same "old" one that was flapping there the week before. When a banner is used, it should be different in color, size, or shape from the one previously flown, and it should be introduced only after a decent interval has passed, e.g., another season, a new promotion, a sale event.

Since logos and graphics are so important in today's scheme of image and identification, the designs used for the banners could be based on the special wrap or store bag design that was created for the season or promotion. The store's window displays could, in color and concept, reiterate the same graphic theme—but with a difference. If, for example, at Christmas, a store is using an irregular gold star on a cerise and white peppermint-striped ground as the store's wrapping paper and gift box, that motif would appear on the banners, and the window might have a cerise background, a peppermint-striped floor, and the display space would be filled with dozens of cascading gold stars of assorted sizes, invisibly suspended. All through this book, we will constantly refer to the advantages of displays that tie in with and enhance what is going on inside the store, in the newspaper ads, on television and radio, and in the store mailings. In order to work, display should not only attract and excite; it should reinforce an idea and present dimensionally what was until then a flat representation.

Planters

Planters, flower boxes, and plants outside a store add to the general ambiance of the store, especially if the store is on a "concrete and glass" Main Street, with nary a leaf or blade of grass in sight. This is a social amenity, a way the store can show its good neighborliness, its friendliness, its being part of a community.

The planters can become a part of the display scheme, with changes in the varieties and colors of the plants to go with promotions or seasons. Red geraniums could call attention to a "country-casual" display, or add an extra dollop of color to a "red" promotion—anything from fashion—to housewares—or even a spring-into-summer story. White flowers would certainly enhance any bridal setting, and mums and asters speak colorfully for fall and back to school.

Planters, set below and in front of a display window, actually dramatize the window presentation by adding greater depth to the setting. Artificial flowers and plants will do, but the real thing is so much nicer.

Awnings

Awnings add another gracious touch to the exterior of the store. Not only do they supply shelter for the shopper during inclement weather, but they also make viewing a window display more pleasant during the heat of the day. Some displaypersons use the awning as a device to cut down on the glare and reflection that turn show windows into giant mirrors. However, more and more awning users are now relying on them to add color and eye appeal to the store front. The awning can become part of a seasonal display or announce a store-wide promotion. The use of awnings is also discussed under "Closed-Back Windows" in Chapter 3.

WINDOWS IN STORE-FRONT DESIGN

The Straight Front

Straight front windows run parallel to the street. The entrance to the store may be a break between a pair or

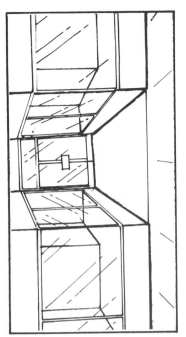
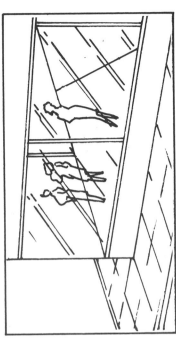

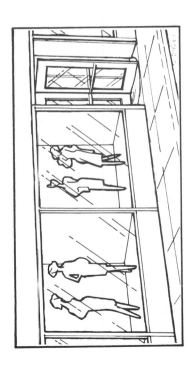
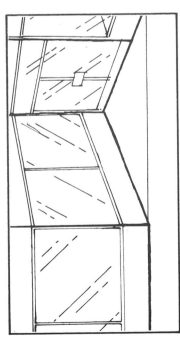

Figure 2-1, *top*. This straight store front consists of the entrance and a bank, or series, of display windows.

Figure 2-2, *bottom*. An angled store front.

Figure 2-3, *top*. An arcaded store front.

Figure 2-4, *bottom*. A corner window.

a run of windows, or to one side of a single window. The windows themselves may be closed back, open back, or elevated.

The Angled Front

With the angled-front design, the store entrance is recessed from the street and the display windows lead back from the street to the entrance, creating an aisle for the shopper. The windows may go back at an angle to the entrance, thus becoming wider in the back than they are in the front. The back end of the window is actually on the same wall as the entrance; that wall can be completely closed, partially closed, or open backed. Usually, in an angled front (and the arcaded front, which follows), the display windows are under some kind of enclosure, cutting down appreciably on glare. These windows may also be rather shallow to allow an unimpeded entrance into the store, and more walk space for shoppers and potential customers.

The Arcaded Front

The arcaded front consists of a series of windows with backs and three sides of glass, coming forward from the entrance wall which is set back from the street. The windows are "peninsulas" of glass attached to the store and are usually under some kind of overhead cover. The shopper can meander through a circuitous route to an entrance between these protruding display windows.

The Corner Window

The corner window is a window that faces two streets which are perpendicular to each other. It is a window with a double exposure and double traffic. The corner window may be the sole display showcase for a store with an entrance near the corner of a street, or it may be the end of a run of windows.

Usually, this window will have two adjacent panes of glass, meeting at right angles. The back may be open or closed. Most stores convert this type of window into a triangular plan. The two glass fronts are the "legs" of the triangle and the long back wall is the "hypotenuse." The space that is cut off from view becomes valuable storage space. Because the two windows are at right angles to each other, the viewer can almost always see the overhead and side lighting—as well as a view of other stores and signs beyond the display area. Customers can find themselves distracted by viewers looking in from the other side of the window and by mirrored backgrounds which reflect traffic lights and the signs from other stores.

3 Display Window Construction

CLOSED-BACK WINDOWS

A closed-back window is the typical display window with a full back wall, sides, and a large plate-glass window facing the pedestrian or street traffic. It is also known as an *enclosed window*.

A noted visual merchandiser, discussing trends in display, has stated, "For real drama and excitement in display, there is nothing to compare with what you can do in an enclosed display window." In the familiar and traditional giant, plate-glass fronted "fish bowl," which some merchants and store planners feel is extinct, the displayperson can arrange tableaux and vignettes from life, in idealized settings. Here, under perfectly arranged lights, the cast of characters stay where they are placed; remain smiling through sleet, rain, snow, and slush; and wear the garments with nonchalant ease and grace.

The displayperson is the stage designer, the lighting designer, the prop person, the director, and the producer. The only thing the displayperson does not have to produce is the merchandise, although he or she may be responsible for the accessorizing. This is the "fun" and "creative" part of the job. That same visual merchandiser, who was quoted, predicts that the enclosed window will be brought into the store. These oversized shadow boxes will become a part of the show and spectacle of interior display.

In order to understand what can or cannot be accomplished in a display window, it is necessary to understand the physical construction of the window and the limitations imposed by that construction.

A smaller store may have a single display window, or a pair of windows, often separated by the entrance into the store. Larger stores, some specialty stores, and in-town department stores will often have a "run" or group of windows (called a *bank*)—maybe two, three, or four windows—and then a physical divider between the windows like a doorway, a wide area of masonry (*pier*), or even a small shadow box. The windows in the group or bank may be separate entities, completely framed and delineated from each other by a heavy molding or pier.

The display window may also be one very long, "run-on," window of 20, 30 or more feet. The only visible divider in this run-on window is the thin metal band that retains the plate-glass windows. Often, the visual merchandiser will add dividers, inside the window, to separate the one long stretch of glass into two, three or four individual display areas. In the case of the single long window, the displayperson does have greater flexibility and control over the presentations. He or she can, at times, have a mass scene with five or more mannequins arranged in a realistic grouping in a

Figure 3-1. A long, run-on, closed-back window, separated by metal mullions which hold the plate-glass windows. Each area is treated individually and together become a "bank" by carrying through a single idea, promotion, or decorative motif. *Liberty House, San Francisco.*

setting that continues through the length of the long window; and at other times, divide the run into small, separate presentations where a single mannequin is "starred" in a solo and very concentrated performance.

This flexibility makes a change of pace possible. Some shoppers are so used to seeing the same physical arrangement of window and mannequin that they no longer "see" the window or the display. A shopper who becomes over-familiar with the same type of display setup, week after week, after a while will not notice that the merchandise has been changed. But, if one week the mannequin is gone and replaced by a dress form—or the merchandise is draped from a chair—it can be the change itself that will stop the shopper.

Where the architecture of the store is such that the size of each window in a group is predetermined, and the displayperson cannot move dividers to make the windows wider or narrower, there still are options open to the creative window dresser. We will discuss those options, shortly, when we consider proscenia and the masking of windows.

One of the greatest problems the visual merchandiser has with a display window is the glare in the glass that blinds the shopper and cuts down on the visibility of the merchandise presented. Another problem is reflection. The shopper gets a better view of what's going on out in the street and in the shop across the road than in the window in which he or she is looking.

In some newer stores, architects have experimented with tinted glass, angled sheets of glass, curved glass, and even deeply recessed windows. Tinted glass affects the color of the merchandise and requires more energy to light the window properly. Curved windows can be even more disastrous than flat glass when it comes to reflections. Deeply recessed windows leave costly pockets of space which might be otherwise used for storage or selling. In the past, manufacturers have come up with yellow or green transparent vinyl window shades that look like oversized fly-catching strips. Although they do prevent sun fading, they do not cut down much on glare or reflection; and they also distort the color presentation of the merchandise. Some merchants have added blinds, but it has been reported that some shoppers feel like voyeurs when they look through the slats.

Many stores, in conjunction with their visual merchandisers, have used decorative awnings to shield their windows, thus cutting down on the glare. Reflection is still a problem, but some visual merchandisers have found that the use of lighter colored backgrounds in the window creates better balance with the light coming from outside as well as minimizing the reflection somewhat. The awnings are changed seasonally, or for holidays, or store promotions. This affords the store an opportunity to enhance its exterior appearance, to promote a special event, and also to provide a degree of comfort to the prospective customer who would like to "do" the windows before entering the store.

Displaypersons have also found that placing the merchandise and the lighting further back in the window, away from the glass, makes it possible to see the merchandise in the proper light and setting. The shopper's eye is drawn past the glare and reflection. The major problem, however, in setting and lighting the

Figure 3-2. A straight store front with an open-back window on each side of a dramatic entrance. The angled plate-glass windows are used to cut down on glare and reflection as well as to accent the unusual store front. *Battaglia, Boca Raton, Florida.*

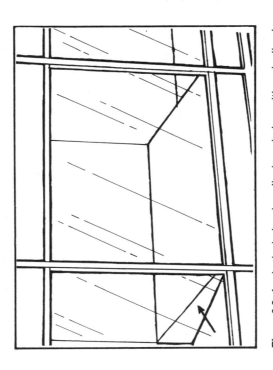

Figure 3-3. A raked window is a display window with an inclined floor (indicated by the arrow). It is also called a *ramped window.*

merchandise back in the window is that the storefront may appear unlit or dimly lit until the viewer is directly in front of the window. The viewer can only look at the merchandise from 5 or 6 feet away instead of getting a really close-up view. Display manufacturers have been experimenting with optical devices, mirrors, and odd-shaped panels of glass in order to overcome the glare problem.

The Floor

Once past the plate glass and into the window proper, the floor must be considered. Most display window floors are raised anywhere from 8 or 9 inches to 24 inches from street level. Rarely is the floor of a standard 8 or 9-foot-high window raised more than 2 feet—that would place the mannequin too high above eye level.

Raising the floor does make it possible to dramatize an object by forcing the viewer to look up to it. The elevated position adds prestige and also makes it possible for passersby to see over the heads of window shoppers. Even though the entire window will not be seen over the street traffic, it is possible to glimpse some of the presentation. Hopefully, it will be enough to make the viewer want to come in for a closer look.

Some stores have installed raked floors where the back of the floor is several inches higher than the front, creating a ramp effect. When merchandise is displayed on this inclined floor, small objects like shoes, handbags, cosmetics and such, when placed at the back, are more easily seen. Some visual merchandisers rely on platforms and risers to elevate groups of merchandise or mannequins for greater visibility, separation, or dramatic impact.

A few stores, like Lord & Taylor in New York City, have elevator-type windows. The floor is actually an elevator platform that can be lowered to the basement level where the "window" is prepared and set, and then raised to the desired level. Sometimes, the floor is below street level, and the shopper is invited to come in really close and look down into the setting. At other times, it might be raised above the usual floor level for a special effect.

Most display-window floors are finished with parquet wood tiles or carpeted in a neutral and subtly textured broadloom. The displayperson may use floor boards, cut out of fiberboard (Homosote and Masonite are two popular trademarks), to cover the existing floor. These floor boards can be painted or covered with fabrics, decorative papers, scattergrass, etc., to change the look of the floor without damage to the permanent floor. This padded floor also permits the displayperson to use pins and nails without affecting the finished floor. Where the floor of the window has been left unfinished (concrete or rough wood), the visual merchandiser may have two sets of floor boards: one in use in the window, and a second set in the display department, where it is available should a different "floor" be required for the next window change. Regular vinyl floor tiles are also frequently used by the displayperson to create color and style changes. They are simply laid down, perhaps with double-faced masking tape, and easily removed and stored for future use.

The Back of the Window

The back of the traditional display window goes from floor to ceiling and is usually fully constructed. Some stores have removable panels closing their windows so they can, when they wish, change from a closed-back window to an open-back window, or convert the display space into selling space. The part of the constructed window back that faces into the store may be part of the main floor interior. It may be shelved, hung with merchandise, or be a backup for a counter area. In some stores, there is a storage area between the back of the display window and the actual selling floor.

In any case, where there is a constructed back, there is usually a door or sliding panel that allows for the passage of merchandise, mannequins, and trimmers. The size of the back opening and the angle of entry can affect the size of the props and what will or will not get into the window. It may necessitate making backgrounds and props in sections which can then be assembled inside the window. The back wall itself, unless it is wood paneled or an especially good quality surface (marble, travertine, brick, etc.), is often painted

a neutral color, and special drapes, appliqués, graphic panels, or decorative props are placed in front of it.

A ceiling track that accommodates drapery to cover the back wall may work effectively to promote different looks, seasons, or types of merchandise. All the displayperson need do is change the fabric to suit the particular need. Where there is ample depth to the window, it may be possible to use photo projection techniques—either from the front or the back. Where the window is very deep, and the merchandise being featured is small and requires close-up viewing, the depth of the window can be cut down with the use of screens or panels that are brought in toward the glass line.

The Ceiling

The ceilings in the windows of most older stores are quite high and often made of concrete or some other impenetrable material. The lighting equipment for the display window is often located in the front of the window, just above the glass line, though newer stores and renovated windows have grids in the ceiling and lighting tracks further back in the window. Ceiling grids are metal frameworks secured into the ceiling by means of vertical supports, allowing the grid to hang down to 9 or 10 feet above the floor of the window. The grid facilitates the hanging of drapes, panels, streamers, and so on, in the middle of the window.

The displayperson can secure spotlights to the grid when he or she wants light in a particular spot, and feels that a regular light source just won't work. The ceiling and the grid, if there is one, are usually painted a dark, "disappearing" color so as not to be too conspicuous.

The Side Walls

Where the display windows are constructed as "rooms" (with three side walls, a window wall, a floor and a ceiling), the side walls may be "painted out" or used as part of the display theme. Even with side walls, the displayperson may opt for panels set against the front glass and angled in toward the center of the window. These panels are similar to flats or "teasers" used in stage design. They limit the view of what is on the sides and concentrate the viewer's sight line on stage center.

Side-lighting strips or panels may be masked behind these dividers or "teasers," making it possible to bring lights further back in the window, yet keeping the source of light hidden. The angled panels also add a feeling of depth to the window by creating an aspect of forced perspective to the merchandise presentation.

These panels or "fins" also work to divide the run-on or overly long, nondivided window into smaller viewing areas. Self-standing screens, dividers, flats, or

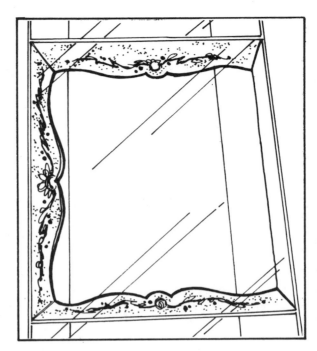

Figure 3-4. The mannequin on the far right is leaning on the angled plane, or "teaser," which cuts down the width of the window and hides the side lights. The mannequins are held erect by means of wires which are secured to the floor. *Macy's, New York.*

Figure 3-5. The proscenium is a masking valence, or frame, usually around the top and sides of the window glass of a display window.

hung drapery will separate one display group from the next, yet allow the continuous flow of a theme or promotion.

Proscenia

Some stores take the theatrical quality of their display windows seriously and enhance the theater-like setting by using proscenia (the plural of *proscenium*) around the window glass. The proscenium, from the Greek "before the scenery," is the structural arch, usually rather ornate, often seen in a theater surrounding the curtain.

In the display window, the proscenium consists of a top valance, which masks the lighting across the top of the window, and side valances, which separate one window or display grouping from the next and also hide any side-lighting devices. There are displaypersons who use the valance as a decorative frame for the window and will use different colors, perhaps enhanced with branches, lights, or other decorative motifs for Christmas or special store-wide events. In some instances, the valance or proscenium is structurally fixed, unchangeable, but definitely a part of the store's architecture and its image.

Masking

As previously mentioned in this chapter, there are options available to the displayperson with the large plate-glass window and a small merchandise presentation. One option is masking the window and turning a large area into a small shadow box (see page 14). The

Figure 3-6. This full-sized window is masked off by means of felt-covered panels into a long, low rectangular space in order to place greater emphasis on the sweater sets and matching hats. No special backgrounds or props are required, and the lighting is "right on target." *Lord & Taylor, New York.*

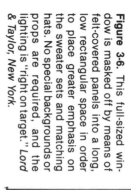

Figure 3-7. This open-back window is actually part of the selling space of the store. A platform raises the "display" area. The track lighting, above, is used to dramatize and spotlight this area. The merchandise shown on soft-sculptured mannequins in the window, is enhanced by having the same type and color merchandise as is shown in the selling space immediately behind it. *Courrèges, New York.*

plate glass can be painted out with an opaque paint or partially covered by panels set against the glass inside the window. A small constructed box can then be set into the opening that remains.

Stores that do not want to change large windows too often, or are limited in staff, find it expedient to mask off these windows and do small shadow-box presentations of accessories and separates. This is especially effective on side streets or in windows facing parking lots or low-traffic areas. Even an occasional change on the main traffic street can have special value. It is the surprise, the jolt, the change from the norm or the traditional which can attract attention and bring the shopper closer to the store and, hopefully, into it.

The displayperson may also find it effective, at times, to mask off the window opening of a full-sized window, and though the window is still dressed and treated as a full window, it can only be viewed through the limited opening in the window mask: It is like the "peephole" in the construction barrier that always draws the curious. There is something about looking through a keyhole or a slit that makes the viewer feel as though he or she is in on something special. When used with care and with the appropriate merchandise—but not overused—this "knothole in the fence" technique works particularly well.

OPEN-BACK WINDOWS

An open-back window has no back wall, but offers a direct view into the selling area beyond. Much of what has been written about the closed-back window is relevant to the open-back window. The open back creates particular problems for lighting and background presentations, and extra effort is demanded of the displayperson to maintain a sense of excitement in the window, while at the same time, the "in-store" merchandise and lighting are competing for the viewer's attention. It need not be a losing battle, and neither area has to suffer or take "second place." The open-back window does, however, require special handling.

Glare and reflection in the window are still problems. Approaches to lighting the open back must always be balanced with the effect that the window lighting will have inside the store; lighting the back of the window may also mean lighting up the selling floor. Spotlights that are used to light the window merchandise may be irritating to the customer as he or she approaches the open-back window from inside the store. When possible, the displayperson might use a panel, screen, drape, or ribbon curtain to block partially the view of the store interior and, at the same time, create a positive background for the merchandise fea-

tured in the window. The panel or screen can supply the desired color and texture to complement the merchandise and possibly deliver the seasonal or promotional message as well. The displayperson must then divert the attention of the viewer to the area in front of the panel, toward the window foreground.

Some displaypersons will take advantage of the view of the store interior and "dress" the area directly behind the window to enhance the merchandise being presented. This is especially successful in smaller stores and boutiques where the shop owner has greater control over what is being shown and what is being sold. If the color red is being promoted and only red garments and accessories are being displayed in the open-back window, it is an effective display and merchandising technique to bring the red merchandise on the selling floor up to the front of the store. Thus, the interior selling story reinforces the window story and, at the same time, provides a compatible backup for the window display. The message becomes stronger and more emphatic. (When we discuss store interior display in Chapter 4, we will again refer to the effectiveness of placing the garment displayed next to the on-floor stock of that garment.)

Where a panel, screen, or fabric curtain is used to separate the display area from the selling space, but not completely close it off, the decorative device should be finished on both sides. While the side facing the street is usually decorative and appliquéd, the side facing the selling floor may or may not be. Using one panel, it is possible to use one kind of fabric on the front to complement the merchandise in the window and a different fabric or treatment on the back of the panel which will blend with the decoration or the merchandise seen inside the store.

Sometimes, plants are used as dividers and, depending on the merchandise and the store image, these can be very effective. At other times, semisheer curtains, fine metal mesh, security grids, or beaded chains have been used as dividers. Most of these will allow some daylight into the store, permit a view in as well as a look out, and, in the case of the smaller store, provide a feeling of greater openness.

ISLAND WINDOWS

An island window, also called a *lobby window*, is a window that has glass on all four sides, allowing the merchandise presentation to be viewed from any angle and from any direction. Paraphrasing theatrical terminology, it is "display in the round."

Since there is no back in an island window, the display techniques required for this type of setup are specialized and very different from those used for the standard three-wall display window.

Presenting the merchandise is a major problem. The displayperson cannot gather, pin, or tuck away anything in the back because there is no back. Unless the window is equipped with a turntable floor, there should be something interesting and attention-getting from whichever direction the window is approached.

Usually, there is some distinct traffic pattern, and the displayperson will play up one view and play down some other view or approach. For example, if an island window is located directly in front of a store, it would be more important to emphasize the view from the street. It is safe to assume that the side opposite the main entrance is the one seen by the customer as he or she leaves the store, while the face fronting onto the street should entice the shopper to walk around the island window and come into the selling space proper.

The turntable floor, or a turntable set on the floor, is an excellent device that can be used occasionally to get special action or reaction. The turntable supplies motion in the window (almost always an attention-getting device), and makes the entire presentation viewable while the shopper stands in one place.

If a single suit or garment is presented in an island window, it can be accessorized in four different ways—four different colors or four different attitudes, for example. Each view gets a different accessory story. A three-dimensional, full-round prop (a statue, a plant, a flower-filled vase, etc.), raised up on a platform or riser, can be used to supply a centralized high point or focal point in the window. The merchandise groupings might then be fanned out around that prop so that they

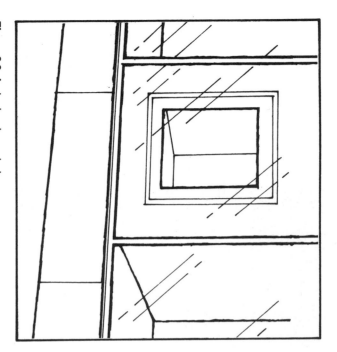

Figure 3-8. A shadow-box window.

blend into each other without losing their individual fashion message.

Lighting is a serious problem in an island window. The overhead lights will be visible from some direction, no matter how they are positioned. Some will strike a passerby full in the eye. Care should also be taken to get the light on the merchandise and off the glass as much as possible. Light on the glass can actually create a "barrier," preventing the merchandise from being seen!

In addition to the problems stated above, is the inevitable one of glare and reflection. In the island window, the probability is multiplied by four. Like the open-back window, the conflict and confusion of what is going on around and behind the glass is compounded. If not properly lit and demarcated, the all-glass unit can become a store liability with prospective customers walking into the glass. (This sometimes happens with unlined or unbanded all-glass doors.)

In older stores, the island display window unit is often located under a marquee or in an enclosed foyer, with closed-back display windows on either side of it and the store entrance behind it. By minimizing the overhead lighting in this area and keeping the walk-around space in semidarkness, the lighting in the island window and the other display windows will be more effective and more dramatic. Glare and reflection will be minimized and the visibility beyond the island window greatly reduced.

SHADOW BOXES

A shadow box is a small, elevated window used for the close-up presentation of special merchandise or accessories. The size varies, but it is usually about 3 feet by 5 feet, either "portrait" (vertical) or "landscape" (horizontal). Besides having a smaller window surface, the shadow box is often shallower (18 to 24-inches deep) and higher from the street level than the standard display window. All of this tends to bring the merchandise nearer eye level and the closer scrutiny of the shopper. Since the space is so confined, merchandise is shown sparingly. It can be tacked onto the back wall, which is not very far away, or stepped up with platforms or risers.

Lighting is usually limited to a very few minispots or pinpoint spotlights, and the lights are generally directed right at the merchandise. Some stores, selling only small, precious merchandise (jewelry, shoes, belts and ties, cosmetics, small leather goods), may have more exciting lighting installations, including back and side lighting, atmospheric or wash lighting, and high-lighting of the merchandise.

Since the glass surface is smaller and the sight line

Figure 3-9. Two seated mannequins are used in this elevated but low window. Together they form a perfect triangular composition. They sit comfortably in the window and are at the right eye-level for the viewer on the street. *Jaeger, New York.*

funnels in, dramatic effects and strong color contrasts are required to attract the shopper's eye. Shadow boxes often appear on side streets (they sometimes are full-size windows that have been masked off to create small feature windows), or on either side of an entrance to a store. Where the store has a foyer or some area of separation between the street doors and the doors into the selling floor, one will often find shadow box display cases to brighten up the area and to "sell" the persons waiting to go inside. (Shadow boxes may also be incorporated in the interior design of the selling floor; this is discussed in Chapter 4.)

SPECIAL WINDOWS

Elevated Windows

An elevated window may have its floor raised up to 3 feet above street level. It may be only 5-feet tall and the display area may be much shallower than is necessary to show certain kinds of merchandise. This higher but shorter and shallower window does present problems, but none are insurmountable. They do require different treatments and nonstandardized solutions.

A regular, full-size mannequin—be it realistic or abstract—will not be able to stand up in this window, but it can sit, kneel, or lie down. There are many fine mannequins designed to be used in just those positions. This is fine when a horizontal or diagonal presentation (see Chapter 7) will work with the merchandise and the store's fashion attitude. If the informal and rather relaxed mannequin will not do justice to the

garments, then a dressmaker form or suitform might do the job. A shorter, headless and possibly legless form may also fit in the low-ceilinged window.

Another technique for showing merchandise in these shallower, elevated windows, without the use of a three-dimensional form is called *flying*, by which the garments seem to be in movement, soaring through a display window controlled by invisible wires, pins, and tissue-paper padding. Many boutiques also make an "art" of shaping, draping, and dimensionalizing clothes against walls, on panels, and from furniture.

In an elevated window, the floor is higher and thus closer to the average viewer's eye level. It is a good window in which to do a lay-down presentation of the merchandise and the accessory groupings with an occasional buildup for special interest. Some stores prefer this type of display setup because it creates a boutique-like atmosphere and gives the store the opportunity to show more merchandise, especially if the merchandise is separates and related fashion accessories. (These techniques will be discussed more fully in Chapter 10.)

Deep Windows

A very deep window, even if it is of standard height and width, presents another type of problem. It may require too much merchandise, too many mannequins, and too much electric energy to light the back of the cavernous window. Also, the back may be so far from the front glass that showing merchandise in the rear may be worthless. The viewer cannot really see that far back and misses the details of the merchandise and nuances of the display.

If the deep window has an open back, a screen or drape with a finished back can reduce some of the depth of the window as well as providing a setting for another display, this one viewable from the inside of the store. Thus, by cutting the depth, the displayperson can create two display areas, tell two different merchandising stories, and provide shopping interest inside and outside the store.

If the deep window has a closed back, the displayperson may build a new back wall, closer to the glass line, and utilize the space between the existing back wall and the new back wall for the storage of props, fixtures, and/or mannequins.

A self-standing screen or drapery hung from a ceiling track will also work to cut down the depth of the window.

Tall Windows

Where the window glass soars—well above the usual 9 or 10 feet in height—the displayperson has several problems with which to contend. The simplest solution, it would seem, would be to add a valance or top proscenium. Either of these devices will visually cut down the window size, but may be at odds with the architectural look of the building. It may destroy the sweep of the line or the repetition of shape and pattern intended by the store's architect.

In a very tall window, the overhead lighting, which is usually attached to the ceiling above the front glass line, is so far away from the merchandise or mannequin on the floor that it is almost worthless as a strong accent light. The displayperson will either have to rely on side lighting for the emphasis and use the overhead lamps for atmospheric wall and floor washes, or possibly drop the ceiling lights down to a better, more useful level, making the equipment completely visible to the street viewer. This may prove to be distracting, or it might, in fact, add a theatrical quality to the setup. Some stores feel that the display lighting is an honest and integral part of the display; they see nothing wrong in showing the lighting equipment as part of the window construction.

In such a window, the displayperson can elect to take full advantage of the extra height and raise the mannequins onto pedestals, piers, or columns. The merchandise can soar, if the architecture and style permit, to create new and startling effects. Instead of a horizontal lineup of mannequins, they can be staggered on different levels. The assorted heights will tend to separate the mannequins from each other and, though part of the same composition, each will be individualized and highlighted. If it is right for the store's fashions, or if a bit of whimsy is desired, a mannequin can be made to float, fly, or just be suspended in midair à la Mary Poppins—umbrella and all! The magic of suspended forms or gravity-defying feats is certain to gain window attention.

4 Store Interiors— Where to Display

Once a shopper has passed through the air screen or the foyer, he or she is on the selling floor. In older stores, including those built in the 1960's, there were usually massive departmental identification signs hung from overhead, or secured and bolted, immovably, to the perimeter wall. The problem of designating what is being sold, and where, is now part of the displayperson's job. Rather than using strong, quickly dated signs, which could not be easily changed, the displayperson combines fashion and color, not only to let the shopper know which department he or she is approaching, but also to make a definite contribution to the ambience of the whole store and the specific area.

The signage used today is coordinated to the look and architecture of the store and is part of the overall "texture" of the selling floor. Signs identify an area, but the actual selling is left to the merchandise presentation. By showing the merchandise, properly accessorized, on the right kind of mannequin, form, or hanger—with the right props and decorations—the displayperson invites the shopper in to peruse more of the treasures only suggested by the display setups.

ISLAND DISPLAYS

In newer mall stores, where the windows are played down and the interior is played up, the shopper will be greeted immediately on entering the store by an island display, a featured display space viewable from all sides. This is an important area, well-lit and clearly identified by a raised platform, a change of flooring material, or an area rug. An abstract construction may highlight the area.

In an island display, the store presents a special story—be it a color, a style, an event, or a storewide promotion. If a color trend is recommended in the island display, the displayperson will usually follow through on the rest of the selling floor by playing up the same color in related merchandise (accessories) or even nonrelated merchandise (throw pillows, luggage, china and glass, etc.). An island display that is on a slightly raised platform can be more effective and get more attention than an on-the-floor display, but whatever the "architecture," it should be changeable or rearrangeable, just as the merchandise and the promotions change.

When an island display is laid out on the store's floor plan, effective lighting for that area should be planned. The displayperson may still find it necessary to supplement the lighting in this area for more drama and emphasis. As in the window setup, some kind of ceiling grid would be desirable for the suspension of props and/or lights. Though the presentation is

Figure 4-1. A group of modular platforms and cubes are combined to create a multilevel, architectural setting (an island display) for a major fashion statement as proclaimed by the silk-screened signs suspended overhead. The merchandise on the selling floor, surrounding this grouping, is the same as that worn by the female mannequins. G. Fox & Co., Ingleside, Massachusetts.

thought of as full round, the view from the entrance is the most important aspect of the "show."

Platforms

A riser, or platform, set just off the aisle and spotlighted from above, will also serve to identify an area and promote a particular piece of merchandise. If a shopper sees a mannequin raised up on a platform for better visibility, over the traffic on the floor, wearing a robe or a nightgown, would it not be logical to assume that robes and nightgowns were being stocked next to or behind that figure? That is merchandising and that is display.

In Chapter 11, "Fixtures," we will discuss this concept of selling and also go into more detail on the many free-standing floor fixtures that are available not only to hold and sort garments, but to present a display of that merchandise to the prospective customer. We will explain the use of kiosks, easels, drapers and costumers, outposts, and so on.

COUNTERS AND DISPLAY CASES

There are many places on the selling floor where the displayperson can use his or her own special blend of fashion "know-how" to affect the selling environment. Counters and display cases are two such areas.

A counter is a major area for merchandise presentation. It is truly the "point of purchase"—the place where the merchandise is presented and the sale is

concluded; the money or credit card is taken and the bagged or boxed purchase is delivered to the shopper. Some store planners are predicting the demise of the "counter," calling it obsolete, unduly and unnecessarily expensive to purchase and maintain. It must be staffed and it does take up a specific amount of floor space. More often than not, it is fixed in place. For the counter to be truly effective in producing sales, specific fixtures, beneath and/or behind it, to hold and show the merchandise being sold, are required. There are many different types of counter fixtures available. Many are designed to do specific things; counter fixtures will also be discussed in Chapter 11.

The counter itself may be no more than a table top or ledge on which a sampling of the merchandise can be displayed or presented to a potential customer. The counter may be the top surface of a piece of furniture which stocks merchandise on shelves or in drawers below, or it can be an all-glass or partially glass case for a below eye-level display. Today's most common, basic display case design has a glass or transparent plastic top, and at least three sides of glass. This enables the shopper to see the merchandise displayed for sale, while at the same time, protecting the setup from "touch, feel, and steal." The unit is usually raised off the ground on a pedestal, and seems to "float," in keeping with the trend for lighter, more open, and less "nailed-down" looking interiors. The bottom, or floor, of the display case, if not part of the interior architectural scheme (made of marble or bronze or fine wood), can be equipped with floorboards of cardboard or fiberboard and covered with various fabrics and decora-

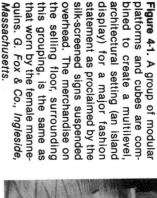

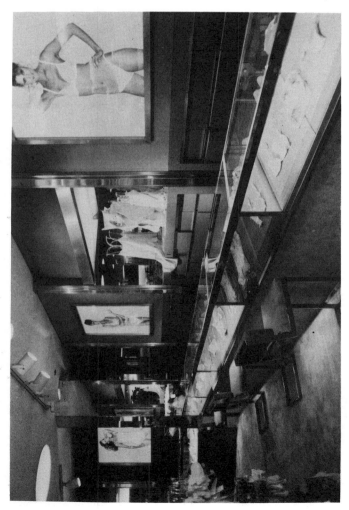

Figure 4-2. The merchandise inside the cases is carefully displayed on color-coordinated boards and lit by lamps inside the cases. Other merchandise is shown on the ledge (center of photo); the backs of the garments are reflected in the mirror that lines the semienclosed ledge. The backlit colored photos show the merchandise "in use." *Macy's, New York.*

tive papers which can be changed with the seasons or the color of featured merchandise.

Since display cases are often about 2-feet deep, it is advisable to use risers and saddles (see "Counter Fixtures" in Chapter 11) in the case in order to raise some of the merchandise closer to the shopper's eye level, or to make interesting setups of assorted merchandise at different levels. Small groupings can also be shown as individual collections by varying the viewing levels. It is possible, then, for Valentine's Day, for example, to cover the floor of the case with red felt or red satin, use assorted risers covered in the same red fabric (perhaps edged with paper lace doilies) for a display of cosmetics, costume jewelry, and/or any other small accessories to stimulate a point-of-purchase sale for that particular gift-giving time.

If the all-glass-fronted case/counter is used for stocking merchandise, the stock should be arranged in neat, orderly, color- or pattern-coordinated groupings contained in see-through boxes or trays. A seasonal or promotional touch can still be added: a red ribbon tied about a group of scarves; a cluster of Christmas ornaments and a spray of greenery tucked in with some sweaters; the top shirts (of stacks of shirts) accessorized with bright green ties for St. Patrick's Day; or violets scattered over a case filled with handbags when the store has decreed that violets mean spring.

Museum Cases

The museum case is primarily a display case that can, on occasion, serve as a counter or demonstration area.

As the name implies, the case is similar to those found in museums and consists of a column or pedestal (usually rectangular) with a five-sided glass case on top. It is often taller than a counter, and the merchandise, precious and special, is raised up closer to the viewer's eye-level. Again, the base of the case or floor pad should be coordinated with the merchandise presented and/or the seasonal theme. The museum case is approached and viewed from all sides, and small platforms, risers, or saddles can be used to enhance the presentation and to help delineate the assorted pieces of merchandise in the same case.

Demonstration Cubes

Demonstration cubes are rug-upholstered, laminate-covered, or wood-finished blocks found on and about the selling floor. These cubes are prepared in various sizes (3 feet by 3 feet by 3 feet is a popular size), and they can be grouped and clustered, or used individually. The cube can be used as a mannequin platform, a display surface for a "laydown" of accessories with a single suit or outfit raised on a costumer or draper (see Chapter 11, "Fixtures"), or as the name suggests, for demonstrations. A salesperson for anything, from skin-care lotions to toaster-ovens, can set up for business on one of these cubes. The raised surface can be used to show, to explain, and to sell an item. These cubes are particularly popular as midtraffic islands to gain attention for a special product, or used right off the aisle as a "draw-into-the-department" device. Shoe departments will often use them in clusters or in an echelon forma-

Figure 4-3. Fine accessories and cosmetics are shown in these mirror-pedestaled museum cases, while mannequins in three-sided glass enclosures add other "untouchable" displays to the selling floor. *Macy's, San Francisco.*

Figure 4-4. These "cubes" can either hold stock, be used for display, or serve as demonstration counters. The modular units are all rearrangeable and can easily be formed into new combinations, creating new floor patterns. *Goldwaters, Tucson.*

Figure 4-5. An island ledge rises up behind the encircling counter, and sweaters plus plants are displayed on it. Garments are also shown in the corner element of the counter and in the shadow-box-like setting, on the far left, above the shirt bins. *Barney's, New York.*

tion, along an aisle or as a low divider, to show sample shoes. Low cubes—17 or 18 inches tall—also double as seats or benches.

LEDGES

The traditional ledge is raised about 5 feet from the floor and is often an "island," i.e., free-standing on the selling floor. The ledge is usually the top surface of a backup storage unit behind a selling counter. In most stores, that would be a two-sided storage unit, about 3 or 4-feet deep by 5-feet tall, with bins, shelves or cabinets, surrounded by counters. The length of the ledge would depend on how many storage units are lined up together on the floor, the type of merchandise being sold, and the size, design and nature of the department itself. The ledge can also be the top surface of a storage unit that is set flat against a perimeter wall with a counter set in front of it. This type of ledge would be viewed only from the front.

In the department and large specialty stores built before the mid-1970's, it was not unusual to have soaring ceilings on the main floor—anywhere from 18 to 25 feet above the ground. With this great openness above the level of merchandise and customers, the ledge displays were the major focal display areas inside the store. It was here that fantasies grew to unprecedented heights. Each new season or promotion was greeted with fully dressed and accessorized mannequins, often in groupings, in settings complete with budding trees or towering flower and foliage arrange-

ments. In this elevated location, above the traffic of the floor, the ledge display was an eye-filling spectacle.

By lowering store ceilings, budgets and rising energy costs have also simplified the type of ledge displays in use today. The newer selling floors and stores that are actively renovating their selling areas are bringing the ceilings—and thus the lights—closer to the merchandise. Some of the mall stores being currently designed use a dropped ceiling for emphasis as well as for economy in heating, air-conditioning, and illuminating the floor. The lower ceiling brings and focuses the shopper's attention onto a particular spot. It also creates a more intimate feeling. Shops within shops, or boutiques, use this technique to separate the special area from the rest of the floor or department. Though some ledges will still accommodate standing mannequins, more stores are using kneeling, sitting, or reclining figures on their ledges; the scale, in relation to the lower ceiling, is better.

Customers cannot and should not be able to handle merchandise displayed on ledges, but since it is space that is very visible, the displayperson should not lose any opportunity to use the ledge for seasonal or promotional displays which may include merchandise and props.

A ledge that backs up onto a wall may have colored panels or drapery backgrounds behind the merchandise presentation. Headless forms or torsos, as well as drapers or costumers, may work well in these areas to show the garments dimensionally.

By the nature of their location, ledges are usually lit from overhead by wall washes or by fluorescent lights hidden behind fascia boards (see the following page). The displays will probably need more definition and brightness, and a few well-aimed spots, from overhead, could achieve that.

SHADOW BOXES

As previously discussed in Chapter 3, shadow boxes are miniature display windows—or elevated display cases. Very often, however, they are worked into the design of the selling floor. They may appear above and behind counters, when the counters are situated in front of floor-to-ceiling walls or partitions. They are usually at eye level, shallow, and offer possibilities for limited lighting effects. Small merchandise and fashion accessories are commonly shown in shadow boxes.

Every effort should be made by the displayperson to keep the shadow-box displays fresh and current, in keeping with the store's promotions and seasonal changes. They should be changed frequently. The colors and textures of the floor, background, and riser should be varied. Arrangements should be altered. In keeping with the seasonal theme, props should be used to complement the merchandise and the department. If the interior design of a shop or area dictates a monochromatic color scheme, the clever displayperson can still work wonders with patterns, textures, and unusual materials within the restrictions set by the store architect or designer.

If the lighting inside the shadow box is limited to a thin-line fluorescent tube or an incandescent "sausage" lamp (a long, pencil-like lamp often used to illuminate

display cases or below-counter areas), the displayperson may attempt to introduce a minispot in the shadow box. There are many compact and attractive highlighting fixtures available on the market today; if the lamp is in keeping with the decor, it can be integrated into the shadow-box presentation. Let the lamp show! It might even become an attention-getting device and add to the interest of the presentation. Small, high-intensity lamps also fit into the scale of small shadow boxes and, at the same time, do a big accent lighting job.

ENCLOSED DISPLAYS

Larger than the shadow box, an enclosed display is usually a fully glassed-in island platform that can hold a mannequin or two. They may be located at the entrance to a department, line an aisle, or be part of a perimeter wall. In size and construction, an enclosed display may be very similar to a closed-back display window found in the front of a store. The purpose is the same: to show the merchandise in a protected area.

With the increasing incidence of in-store theft and the soaring cost of merchandise, merchants not only want to protect their displayed wares from "walking off" the selling floor, but they want to cut down on eventual "as-is" sales. Who wants to buy a $300 dress that has served as a "hand towel" for hundreds of people? Who wants a negligee snagged by the ring or bracelet of a passerby? Inside the glass display window, on a mannequin or form, the garment can be shown at its best and can get an assist from some well-chosen and expensive accessories. The merchandise can be prop-

Figure 4-6. Two raised and well-lit shadow boxes with displays of fashion accessories flank either side of a "shop-within-a-shop." Thus, this boutique is set apart from the rest of the selling floor. *Neiman Marcus, Beverly Hills, California.*

Figure 4-7. A column, located in the center of this department, has been converted into a floor-to-ceiling tree, and it becomes a focal point of the whole area. An octagonally shaped, dropped ceiling frames and contains the area. The matching octagonal green carpet becomes a "grassy plot." The picket fence camouflages the clothes racks and adds to the decor of the area. *Diamonds, Phoenix.*

erly lit and come out a week or two later as crisp, fresh, and saleable as it was when it went in. And all the accessories will still be there—including the mannequin's hands! This is one way to add drama and excitement inside the store, especially when there are no display windows out front. (See Figure 4-3.)

COLUMNS

Columns are an integral part of a store's construction. They hold up ceilings, support the weight of the roof, and are an excellent place to hang decorative props. Columns often delineate a department's beginning and end. They may be lined up on either side of a major aisle, adding vertical highlights on a horizontal floor. That is where the column shines in the display scheme of things: Banners can hang from them, wreaths can adorn them, garlands can entwine them or be swagged from them. Arches can spring from them and cross over aisles and ledges for dramatic effects. Store-wide event posters can illuminate them, and if need be, a column can be a directory or signboard for a shop or area. The column can be a background panel for a mannequin on a platform. It can be a four-sided mirror which adds the illusion of space to a department or supplies the necessary reflective surfaces into which most customers want to look.

Columns not only can hold merchandise, they can also be used to show merchandise decoratively. Some ledges are adjacent to columns, and the combination of ledge and column can offer interesting display possibilities. Columns can be covered with panels, painted, or camouflaged, but the wise displayperson will take advantage of the rhythm and repetition of columns in the floor plan of the store—and their obvious verticality—and of their visibility above the traffic, and use them creatively whenever possible.

FASCIA

A fascia is a band—a horizontal board or panel. In stores, the fascia is often found 6½ to 7 feet off the ground, above the bins, shelves, or clothing rods that are attached to a wall or partition. It can be used to conceal lights and as a background for merchandise displays.

Any ceiling lights that are directed down to the merchandise on the selling floor will lose intensity because of the distance. Therefore, it is a common practice and good merchandising to bring a light source closer to merchandise that is to be inspected. These lights are often placed 7 feet above the ground and are extended out from the wall or partition. The fascia covers the light fixture from the shopper's view and also helps to focus the light down onto the merchandise.

In the past, a broad expanse of fascia (starting at 7 feet off the ground and often reaching up to the ceiling) was the area that carried department identification—either in permanently attached letters or supergraphic symbols. Today, with departments in flux, expanding and contracting as merchandise and seasons dictate, big signage and permanent wall decorations are virtually "out" as elements of store design.

Figure 4-8. The "flying" jeans, in the upper left, move along the angled fascia and are lit by the high hats in the ceiling directly in front of them. The merchandise on the wall below is partially lit by a hidden fluorescent fixture (under the fascia) and from the incandescent high hats above. A raised platform, set in front of the mirror-covered column, becomes the main display area for this shop. *Rich's, Union City, Georgia.*

The fascia is a wide panel, 4 or more feet wide. It is close to the ceiling lights and is usually visible from across the floor and certainly from the aisle. It has become a popular place to pin up merchandise and seasonal decoratives: jeans, shirts, sweaters, accessory groupings, and so on. The display on the fascia is used as both a merchandising and decorating technique. The fascia still functions to identify the merchandise in the department and, at the same time, calls the customer to come over.

As the type of merchandise sold in a specific area changes (i.e., from skiwear to swimwear), the display can change the identity and ambience of the area. Colored panels can be superimposed over the wide, flat face; decorative appliqués, photo blowups, forms, or figures can be used; or garments may be pinned up imaginatively or arranged in geometric patterns. The seasonal or promotional events that take place in the store can be tied in with the fascia trim. A spotlight should be directed at the above-eye-level display to attract more attention to the display and to the area below.

If properly used, the fascia will tell what is being sold below, suggest the variety, and also specify the time of the year or the "look" that is in vogue.

T-WALLS

Often one area or department will be separated from another by bins or double-sided, open-faced "closets" hung with merchandise. These two-sided walls or partitions will extend from the back or perimeter wall out to the aisle. The flat end of this unit, on the aisle, can be converted into a valuable display space. A panel to cover the end of this unit makes the top stroke of the "T." The merchandising wall is the upright of the "T."

A platform can be placed on the aisle, in front of the panel, to highlight the merchandise stocked behind the display. A fully dressed and accessorized mannequin, a prop, a piece of furniture to hold another garment or complementary outfit, a plant, a colored panel to emphasize the outfit on display, or a seasonal device—all can add to the importance of this wall, which is often only 4 to 6-feet wide and 8-feet tall.

ONE-HUNDRED-PERCENT TRAFFIC AREAS

There are locations throughout the store that get very heavy traffic, and they are referred to as "100 percent traffic areas." These areas are in front of and around escalators or elevators, at entrances or exits, and near major featured spots like restaurants, atriums, and central meeting areas. Displays in these areas are, and should be, changed frequently, and they are often combined with a salesperson or demonstrator plus a certain amount of stock for quick, "impulse" shopping. Low-priced, easy-to-sell merchandise is promoted in these locations, and the displays serve as flags to catch the attention of and slow down shoppers long enough to get them involved in what is being offered. Color, motion, and even sound can be effective here.

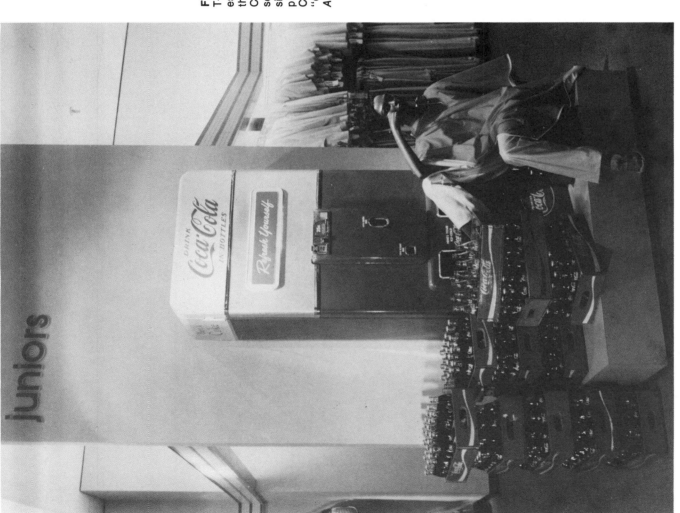

Figure 4-9. A quite ordinary T-wall suddenly becomes the essence of the "junior" look thanks to the ever-popular Coca-Cola machine and the cases of soda bottles. The mannequin sits rather than stands on the platform since the elevated Coke machine makes the big "come-on" statement. *Rich's, Atlanta.*

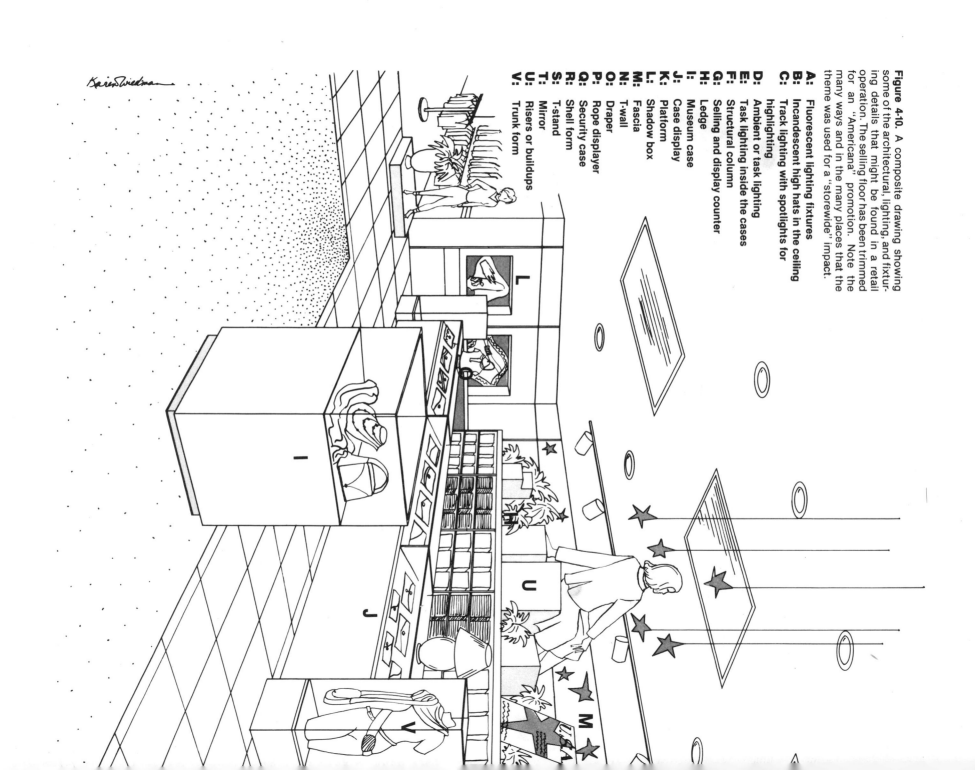

Figure 4-10. A composite drawing showing some of the architectural, lighting, and fixturing details that might be found in a retail operation. The selling floor has been trimmed for an "Americana" promotion. Note the many ways and in the many places that the theme was used for a "storewide" impact.

A: Fluorescent lighting fixtures
B: Incandescent high hats in the ceiling
C: Track lighting with spotlights for highlighting
D: Ambient or task lighting
E: Task lighting
F: Structural column
G: Selling and display counter
H: Ledge
I: Museum case
J: Case display
K: Platform
L: Shadow box
M: Fascia
N: T-wall
O: Draper
P: Rope displayer
Q: Security case
R: Shell form
S: T-stand
T: Mirror
U: Risers or buildups
V: Trunk form

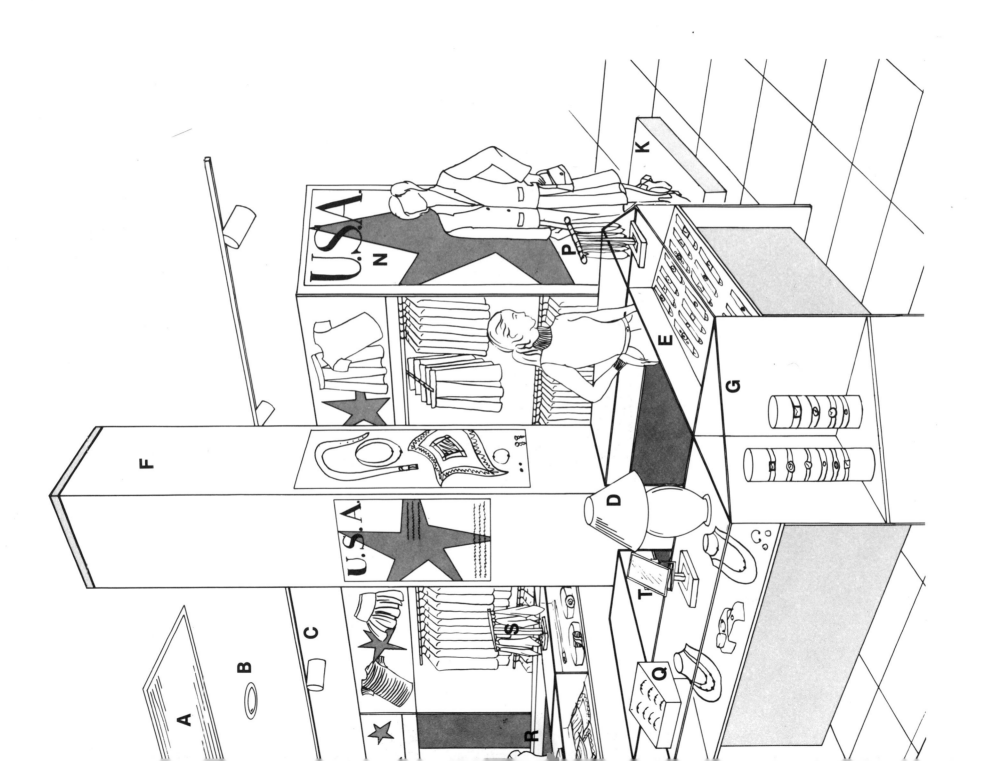

5 Color and Texture

Color sells! It is what is shown and what the shopper sees first. For many customers, it is actually more important than the size, the style, or the price tag. From infancy, people see colors and are affected by and react to them. Many books have been written about color and the psychology of color: which colors expand or go forward, which contract or withdraw, which will "raise the roof" (or the ceiling at least), and which will seem to bring the ceiling down. Some colors make the viewer feel warm, expansive, generous, full of good feelings, all aglow—responsive enough to buy anything. Some colors will make the viewer feel cold, aloof, unresponsive, moody, and impossible to reach.

To add to the color confusion, everyone does not react in the same way to the same color. A happy childhood, for example, surrounded by a loving family, and associated with a pink and pretty bedroom, pink and frilly dresses, just pink and pampered all the way, can make "pink" a joyful, loving color. But, if the pink room were forced on the person, the pink but not so pretty dresses were hand-me-downs, and pink evoked the memory of medicine and sickness, then "pink" will certainly not be a "turn-on" color. The displayperson/store planner will not be able to provide the ideal setting for each and every customer, but it is possible to satisfy the vast majority while alienating only a few.

PHYSICAL AND PSYCHOLOGICAL REACTIONS TO COLOR

Based on current research (Faber Birren, *Color in Your World*, and Dr. Max Lüscher, *The Lüscher Color Test*), the following reactions and images are most often produced at the mention of the basic colors.

YELLOW: It is sunshine and gold; happy, bright, cheerful, vital, fun-filled, and alive; daisies, marigolds, and lemons. It is optimism, expectancy, relaxation, and a wide-open-armed acceptance of the world, suggestive of change, challenge, and innovation. It is spring, summer, Easter, and when it "turns to gold," it is autumn.

ORANGE: A friendly, sociable color; agreeable, overt, glowing, and incandescent. It is exciting, vibrant, and filled with anticipation. It is fire and flame, a rising sun in the tropics or a setting sun in the desert; Halloween and autumn leaves.

RED: Exciting, stimulating, loving, powerful, and sexy—these are some of the words used to describe red. It can be assertive, demanding, and obvious, possibly even cheap or vulgar. Generally, it comes across as warm, stirring, and passionate. Red is Valentine's Day and Christmas. It is carnations for Father's Day and patriotism—one part of the flag and firecrackers. It conveys "sale," "clearance," a warning, a fire, and a fright. It is a popular color.

PINK: Pink may be regarded as sweet, lovely, pretty—little girl complexion, rosebuds, and ribbons and lace. Or it may connote something fleshy, raw, undercooked, and underdeveloped. Pink is also flowers for Mother's Day, for Easter eggs, and bunny ears; nightgowns and lingerie; and an elegant approach to Christmas.

GREEN: An alive, cool, and "growing" color. It is springtime and summer—lawns, bushes, trees, and forests—the perfect accent to almost any setting, especially if it is alive and growing. It is St. Patrick's Day and the other half of a Christmas color scheme. Various shades of green can also be bilious, sick, and stomach-turning—or reminiscent of khaki and war.

BLUE: Always a popular color choice and the favorite of most. Cool, calm, comfortable, and collected, it speaks of soft, soaring skies, serene lakes, gentle horizons, and the security of hearth, home, and flag. It is quiet, but can become cold, moody, or even depressing. It is always right for spring and summer skies, shadows on snow, and patriotic celebrations.

BLUE-GREEN: The happy "marriage" of blue and green. It is a cool, tasteful color—sensitive and restful, but alive, vital though quiet. It is water, sky, and grass, peaceful and growing, a great summer color to complement white and glowing tan complexions.

PEACH: Suggests the warmth and happy excitement of orange (toned down) with none of its grating qualities. A smiling, glowing color, it is easy to be with and delightful to be in. A new "neutral," a pastel "earth-tone," a friendly color that will go with almost anything.

RUST: The other end of the orange scale, it is deep, rich, earthy without being earthbound. Rust is a full-bodied color with the warmth of orange, but with none of its obvious, blatant, or irritating qualities. It is the "earth" color that goes with other colors, but is neither invisible nor intruding. The personification of autumn.

VIOLET/PURPLE: Regal, aloof, cool, and standoffish. This is a color of taste, distinction, discretion, and definitely not for the run-of-the-mill, average customer. A high-fashion color that has to be sold, it is aesthetic and "different," but can come off as overbearing, pompous, or even funereal. Lavender may convey "old-fashioned charm," Victorian and Easter trim. Purple can be wine, grapes, and autumn.

GRAY: The neutral barrier that makes separations, but no statements. Dr. Max Lüscher, the noted colorist, says, "It is neither subject nor object, neither inner nor outer, neither tension nor relaxation." It exists—and exists well—with other colors that have more to say. Gray may be either a depression, "down-in-the-dumps" color—or a super-elegant and sophisticated color that suggests fine jewelry, silver, furs, and designer salons.

BROWN: The earth, hearth, and home; the family and the farm; the simple things, wood, clay and other natural materials. It steps back to let other colors go forward, but unlike gray, it does not disappear. Brown is warm, a warm neutral that does cast a glow. From the lightest off-white beige to the deepest charcoal brown, it is relaxed, unexciting, in no way unnerving. The deep color for autumn.

WHITE: The blankest of the blank, but a strong and able supporting player which makes every other color, by comparison, turn in big, bold, and brighter performances. It is innocence and hope, angels and religious celebrations, a wedding gown, and the blinding brilliance of clear light. Cotton-puff white can be a sparkling accent, a sharp highlight, a crisp delineator, or an unpleasant comparison by which other "whites" may come off as dingy or unhappily yellowed. White can also be sterile, antiseptic, bleak, and harsh.

BLACK: Connotes night, a vacuum, and an absence of light. It is mystery, sex, and death as well as the color of intrigue and sophistication. Ultra-chic or ultra-depressing, it also can be ominous and threatening or downright dull. It can be as sensuous as satin, as deep as velvet. Black is a neutral, but a neutral that requires careful handling.

The Color Families

In the descriptions of reactions to the colors listed above, certain adjectives appeared over and over again. Some colors were described as "warm and glowing," while others were "cool, calm, aloof." Still another group of colors could be categorized as "neutrals." Thus, most colors are grouped into ambiguous but convenient "families."

Red, orange, yellow, pink, rust, and peach can all be classified as warm, aggressive, spirited, advancing colors. Blue, green, violet, and blue-green are regarded as a group of cool and receding colors. That leaves white, black, gray, and brown to band together as the "neutral" color family.

By personal preference, people of certain age and social groups will respond more readily to one family over another. Young children and nonsophisticates, however, commonly delight in and respond to bright, sharp colors: yellow, red, green, brilliant blue, shocking pink, and clear turquoise. Casual, outgoing, fun-loving, high-spirited people who want fashions and settings to match are drawn to the warm colors. Sophisticated people are supposed to appreciate subtlety: the slightly off-colors, toned down and neutralized without being neutered. Elegant and big-ticket merchandise seems to make a better showing and get a better customer response in a "cool" environment. "Serenity" sells silver, furs, and other choice merchandise.

COLOR MIXING

In working with color, it is wise to have a basic idea about what color is, how it works, and what it can do. If we accept the long-established theory that there are three basic pigment colors from which all other colors can be mixed, we are well on the way to understanding color.

Red, yellow, and blue are called *primary colors*. By mixing red and yellow, we get orange. Blue and yellow combined will produce green. Equal parts of red and blue make violet, or purple. These resulting colors—orange, green, and violet—are *secondary colors*. Furthermore, mixing yellow (a primary color) with green (a secondary), and depending on the quantity of each color used, the result would be a yellow-green or a green-yellow. This is a *tertiary color*. All those romantic, exotic names with which fashion and decorating abound, are actually selling names for these tertiary colors: shrimp, mango, avocado, chartreuse, peach, plum, pumpkin, and so on.

Value refers to the amount of light or dark in a color. Add white to any of the full-value colors (primary, secondary, or tertiary), and depending on the amount of white added, the result will be a *tint*, or *pastel*, of that color—a lighter, more gentle variation of the original color. The addition of black to a color will produce *shades*, or deeper, richer, more full-bodied versions of the color. Thus, the addition of white to red could result in a pretty, soft, baby-sweet pink, while the addition of black to red could produce a masculine, heady garnet, dubonnet, or maroon.

COLOR SCHEMES

The *color wheel* graphically shows the relationship of colors to each other. The location of colors on the wheel is relevant to the following discussion.

Analogous or Adjacent Colors

Colors that exist harmoniously next to each other on the wheel, because of shared characteristics (and pigments), work together in a display area to create specific effects. Yellow, yellow-green, green, and green-blue are examples of "neighboring," adjacent, or analogous colors, as are yellow, yellow-orange, orange, and orange-red. Adjacent colors reinforce each other; they are compatible and usually can be counted on to create a close harmony. Thus, when used in close groups or clusters, they can create an *analogous color scheme*; for example, blue sky and green grass to make an aqua or turquoise outfit appear cooler and crisper.

Complementary Colors

Complementary colors are found opposite each other on the color wheel. Red is the complement of green (and vice-versa); blue and orange are complements, as are yellow and violet. These "opposites" do not make for close harmony or gentle combinations. Complements bring out the intensity and brilliance of each other. Thus, *complementary color schemes* are usually strong, demanding, and vibrant. Complementary colors will vibrate against each other (creating kinetic patterns) when placed very close together. They will make "motion" where there actually is none.

Complementary schemes are fine in bright, youth-oriented areas, where the creation of a shocking or attention-getting palette is desired. They can be fun, dynamic, exciting, and sometimes, irritating. However, it is possible to minimize or even eliminate some of the dynamic or irritating qualities of the complementary scheme.

This can be accomplished by reducing the *intensity* of the colors being used. Intensity refers to the purity and strength of the color. The addition of white or black will reduce the intensity, as will the addition of some of the complementary color (e.g., adding a little red to green). A pink and apple-green color combination may be basically complementary, but it is easier to live with than a pure, full-strength red and a fully saturated green!

Contrast

Colors are often selected for the amount of *contrast* they provide. For example: two light colors adjacent to each other provide little contrast; a light color next to a medium one provides some contrast; whereas, a light color next to a dark one creates bold contrasts. That is why one rarely, if ever, finds a garment, fabric, etc., designed with black and navy blue. This is an extreme example of minimal contrast.

Monochromatic Colors

If you start with one color and develop the full range of that color, from the palest off-white tint to the deepest, darkest shade, you will have a *monochromatic* (one color) *color scheme*. Baby-blue and sky-blue, through the intermediate blues, up to a navy or midnight blue, is a monochromatic scheme. This can be restful, easy

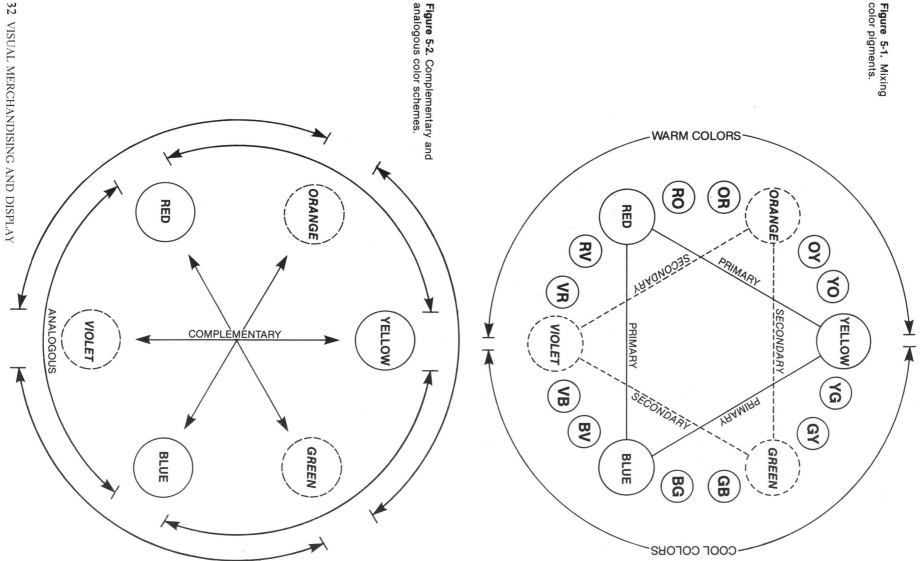

Figure 5-1. Mixing
color pigments.

Figure 5-2. Complementary and
analogous color schemes.

to accept, and provide a controlled setting for merchandise. It generally "sits back" and takes it easy.

Neutral Colors

"No-color" color schemes have much to offer the displayperson or store planner, but they must be used carefully. An all-white scheme, for example, can be young, exciting, sparkling, and ultra-chic, or a perfect foil for brightly colored merchandise. However, all white may also come off as absolutely sterile and bland, draining the color right out of the merchandise.

Beige-brown earth tones have been used a great deal by store designers in the last few years and they remain popular, people-pleasing and merchandise-complementing. The blending of the casual, but warm, off-whites and beiges with wood tones (from bleached oak to deepest ebony), plus an accent of glazed or unglazed terra cotta and some rusty browns, have a strong following. Generally, this kind of color scheme is easy to live with; it enhances the merchandise, but hardly ever overwhelms. It probably appeals to the rural instincts hidden inside each urban dweller.

From the past, and continuing strong into the future, comes the gray color scheme. When elegance, the chic, and ultra-new is desired, it can be found with gray—gray by its aloof, cool self or made even more icy with accents of lucite and chrome. Gray is a foil for bright colors; it tones them down. It is a relief for the whites; it makes white appear whiter. Gray is a buffer for black, relieving the gloom of this noncolor. Neutral gray has long been popular as a setting for silver, furs, and expensive giftware, but it is now reaching into designer areas and even bridal displays.

Black and white may be neutral individually, and most colors will coexist with them, but when used together, they demand and get attention.

Figure 5-3. White merchandise against a white background with a classic column capital, also white, is accented by metallic gold accessories and the terra-cotta floor. It all adds up to a bright, clean, young yet sophisticated, "trendy" display. The clear lighting intensifies the white-white look. *Bloomingdale's, New York.*

USING COLOR TO PROMOTE COLOR

The displayperson can usually control the color against which merchandise is shown. The background color is important because it can either add to or detract from the color of the merchandise presented. A white dress shown against a white background can be very effective—or a total disaster! Against a stark white background, a dress that is not a pure white, but a soft, lovely ivory color can look dingy and yellow. If, however, the background were a deep gray or very dark green, the sharp contrast would make the ivory dress appear whiter.

White against white is usually smart, sophisticated, and subtle. White against black is dramatic, sharp, and striking. The price and type of merchandise, the store's image, and the department or area in a store will determine which background is best for the white dress.

The white against white will be more dramatic and striking if a red light flooded the white background and left the dress "white," but softly outlined in pink, from the light reflected off the background. The white dress against the black background will seem more elegant if the background is softened with a blue or violet light to ease the sharp contrast between foreground and background. With colored panels or draperies to use behind and around merchandise, and assorted colored lights to "paint" those panels, the displayperson can create the best of all possible settings for the merchandise. The use and effect of colored light will be fully discussed in Chapter 6.

In many ways, the accessories shown with the merchandise can also affect the color. Imagine the white dress with a navy-blue belt, shoes, and handbag, and a red and blue scarf. The white will appear crisp and sparkling by contrast to the navy. Now, suppose that same dress were completely accessorized in toast-beige. The white is softened and warmed by its proximity to the beige. Popularly priced merchandise, however, will often rely on sharper and more contrasting accessories and displays. They help make the garment stand out and look like more for the money.

Visualize a bright red dress with emerald-green trimmings. The red appears redder and more intense because the complementary green intensifies the red. The same red with shocking-pink accessories will seem more red-orange because the "hot pink" of the accessories is bluer by comparison.

Understanding the effect of color on color will enable the displayperson to select the proper settings and accessories for the merchandise and the store's fashion image.

COLOR: A RECAP

1. The warm colors are red, yellow, orange, rust, and peach.
2. The cool colors are blue, green, violet, and blue-green.
3. The neutral colors are white, black, gray, and brown.
4. The primary or basic colors are red, yellow, and blue.
5. The secondary colors are orange, green, and violet. They are obtained by mixing two of the primaries.
6. A tertiary color is an "in-between" color obtained by mixing a primary with a secondary color.
7. Intensity is the purity, strength, and brilliance of a color.
8. A tint, or pastel, is a color with white added.
9. A shade is a color with black added.
10. A monochromatic color scheme is one that includes a range of tints and shades of a single color.
11. An analogous color scheme consists of colors that are adjacent to each other on the color wheel.
12. A complementary color scheme consists of colors that are opposite each other on the color wheel.
13. A neutral color scheme is a "no-color" color scheme of white, blacks, grays, or browns.

TEXTURE

Another very important aspect of color is the texture of material. The texture—the surface treatment or "feel"—can affect the color of the merchandise. Smooth and shiny surfaces reflect light and, therefore, always appear lighter. Satin, chrome, highly lacquered or enameled surfaces, waxed woods, etc., will all pick up and reflect more light than objects that are flat and lusterless. Rough, nubby, and deep-piled surfaces will absorb and hold light and, therefore, appear darker. Velvet, sandpaper, deep carpets, untreated and natural woods or tree barks—these will all appear darker. Smooth or shiny reflective finishes around merchandise will add more light to the presentation. The background will reflect more light back onto the product being shown.

Textures are also suggestive. They can suggest familiar symbols by which the displayperson attempts to explain the merchandise in terms of surrounding materials. Soft silks and satins suggest femininity and sensuousness. Velvet is deep and rich, dark and mysterious, subtle, elegant, and expensive. Rough textures, such as burlap, coarse linens, nubby wools, and tweeds, are masculine, "outdoorsy," rugged, natural, earthy, and wholesome. Gravel, sand, stones, brick, and ground-up cork suggest the great open spaces: sportswear, beachwear, camping, and the country.

In creating a setting for a bridal gown, for example, the textures utilized should suggest and, at the same time, enhance the softness and loveliness of the gown. A complementary texture to a satin and lace gown might even be rough wood planking. The gown would seem even more delicate, fragile, and feminine by comparison to the rough, burly quality of the wood. But what would this do to the bride-to-be and her illusions of romance? In this case, the background should be more of the same: The gown could be

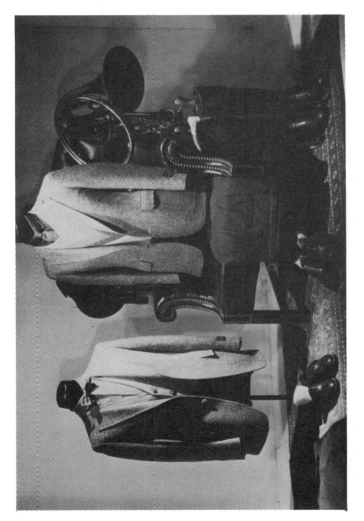

Figure 5-4. A masculine look is achieved by a mix of textures: woods, woolens, tweeds, rich leathers, the warm glow of the old brass horn, and the nail heads decorating the period chair. It is all so "tailored" and "British." *Macy's, New York.*

enveloped with other soft fabrics and gentle textures—wisps of tulle and net, ribbons and lace. Anything that suggests a fairy-tale setting and a "happily ever after" ending should be used with the bridal gown.

The use of opposite textures, however, can work very effectively in promoting other types of merchandise, especially when humor, scale, or shock are the attention-getting devices to bring the shopper over to the display. Imagine a pair of natural leather, outdoor hiking boots, nail-studded and roughly sewn, sitting on a lace-edged, red satin pillow with a sheer, silky fabric draped behind. The copy might read: "It will be love at first sight." The contrast may be silly and out of place, but it is intriguing, unexpected, and attention-getting. Or visualize a woman's nightgown—all pink and lace, soft and sheer—hanging from a peg on a wall of rough, split logs. The juxtaposing of two very different textures, the very feminine against the very masculine, makes the feminine seem more feminine and the masculine even more so. With a copy line like "Why rough it when you can go in style?"—the displayperson could explain the combination and maybe bring a smile to the viewer's face.

In an ensemble, there should be a relationship of textures, a flow and continuity rather than startling change, unless the merchandise is meant to startle and call for attention. A fine, wool challis tie, rather than a shiny silk one, is the choice for a tweed jacket, just as an oxford cloth shirt is more appropriate to the texture of nubby wools than is a fine broadcloth. Similarly, coarsely textured suits are more compatible with grained leather rather than patent-leather shoes.

Textures have to be balanced in a display arrangement. Rough textures usually seem heavier or suggest more "weight" in a composition or display. A roughly textured cube, for example, appears to take up more space and volume in the display area than a smoothly lacquered cube of the same size and color. Therefore, a displayperson may balance a small, coarsely textured element with a larger smooth or shiny one. A textured floor "sits" better than a smooth or shiny one, while a smooth ceiling "floats" better than a roughly textured one.

Some materials are especially popular for use in displays because they are texturally neutral (neither very smooth nor very rough) and because they are available in a wide range of colors. Felt, jersey, duvetine, and suede cloth have neutral textures and can be used with soft or rugged merchandise. Seamless paper is another favorite with displaypersons because it, too, lacks texture. These materials will be discussed more fully in Chapter 17, "Setting Up a Display Shop."

6 Light and Lighting

THE COLOR OF LIGHT

Color—as color—means little unless it is considered in relation to the type of light in which the color is seen. It is light that makes things visible. All colors depend on light. There is natural daylight and artificial light, which can be incandescent, fluorescent, or high-intensity discharge lighting (HID).

It is not quite that simple, however. These three broad classifications of artificial light are further subdivided. There are many different types of fluorescent lamp tubes available, ranging from a warm white deluxe which attempts to create an "incandescent" effect, to the cool, bluish, "daylight" quality usually associated with fluorescents. HID lamps are being improved daily and now even approach the warm end of the colored light scale. Incandescent lamps (i.e., bulbs) are warm and glowing, but filters or gels over them can change the color and quality of the light. Let us, therefore, consider the color of light, the effect of light on pigment color, and how light can affect the merchandise and the area that surrounds the merchandise.

Visible light is actually composed of the whole spectrum of colors from violet to red. Imagine a beam of light passing through a glass prism or reflecting in a pool of water or oil, and you will see that spectrum broken up into a rainbow of colors: from the violets, through the blues and greens, to the yellows, oranges, and finally red. All light is caused by waves of radiant energy which vary in length. The shortest wavelength of the visible spectrum is violet light; then comes blue light, green light, etc.; and at the other end of the spectrum, with the longest wavelengths, is red light. All these wavelengths—the entire spectrum—combine to form visible, or white, light, the light we see.

Ultraviolet light, X-rays, and gamma rays have shorter wavelengths than we can see. Infrared and radio waves are too long for us to perceive. Therefore, for the purpose of understanding light and color in display and store planning, this discussion will be limited to the colors that appear in the visible spectrum. We will find that some light sources reflect the shorter wavelengths and emit cooler or bluer light, while others have a warmer light and favor the longer wavelengths.

In order to comprehend the relationship between color and light and why an object is perceived by an observer as a particular color, it is important to understand that light is capable of being reflected and absorbed. The color of an object is seen as a result of the object's selective absorption of light rays. Thus, if an object is pure blue, for example, this means that it absorbs all the wavelengths of light except those of blue light, which are reflected back to the observer. The same occurs with other pure colors, but with a different wavelength being reflected.

For those colors that are not pure (i.e., containing a blend of colors), then two or more colors are being transmitted back to the observer. For example, an object seen as turquoise is reflecting blue and green colors while absorbing the others.

If the object is pure white, the full visible spectrum of light is being reflected back in approximately equal quantities. If it is pure black, then all colors in the spectrum are being absorbed by the object.

Light bounces from one surface to another, and in this movement it is capable of throwing off new colors. For example: A wall or panel is painted pink. A wedgewood-blue carpet is installed. If warm, incandescent lights are used, the carpet may turn slightly lavender from the warm pink reflection cast off by the walls. The incandescent light may also play up any reds that are in the warm blue carpet. (A warm blue has some purple in it, i.e., red and blue. Incandescent light reflects most in the red end of the spectrum.) If a daylight fluorescent light were switched on instead, the blue of the carpet might seem more sparkling and cool, and the walls would take on the lavender tone. The overall light will affect the color of the walls, the floor and the ceiling, and bouncing around as it does, most of all it can affect the color of the merchandise.

GENERAL, OR PRIMARY, LIGHTING

General, or primary, lighting is the all-over level of illumination in an area. It is usually the light that fills the selling floor from overhead lighting fixtures, but without including accent lights, wall washers, and display highlighting lamps. (These are forms of secondary lighting.) Also, it does not include "glamour" or decorative lighting: the sconces, counter or table lamps, indirect lighting, and so on.

Fluorescent Lighting

Some retail operations are illuminated by rows of fluorescent fixtures which span the length or width of the store. The fluorescent fixture is usually the least expensive and most efficient fixture to use from the point of initial cost, cost of energy, and length of lamp-life. Although it is often the popular choice for the contractor to install and the retailer to maintain, it is not always the best choice for many categories of merchandise. Fluorescents can produce a flat, even, and stultifying blanket of light which offers few shadows and provides little depth or textural interest. There are degrees of "warmth" and "coolness" available in fluorescent lamps, from the rosy quality of "warm white deluxe" to the blue of "cool white deluxe"—with many gradations in between. Westinghouse's "Ultralume" (prime color) is complementary to skintones and merchandise.

The merchandise—or the general type of merchandise to be tested under the lighting—should be tested under the various types of light bulbs. No one type or color will enhance everything, but the one that is generally most flattering should be chosen. Some merchandise, like diamonds, silver, kitchen supplies, and maybe even furs, may look scintillating in the cool, brittle light of "cool" fluorescents, but customers and salespeople may appear drained, haggard, and generally washed out in that same lighting. A sparkling white diamond on black velvet may seem all fire and ice, but it would be hard to sell if the finger onto which a ring is slipped, or the neck that a necklace caresses, looks waxy or marred by blemishes. Therefore, a soft, glowing incandescent lamp, placed near a mirror, will enhance the customer's skin tones as she looks at herself bejeweled. Even if the diamond itself, at that moment, is not super-blue-white gorgeous, the customer's appearance while wearing the jewelry is at its best. That's salesmanship! That's display!

Fluorescent fixtures and lighting can be shielded, filtered, or softened with grids, baffles, or diffusing panels—and all to the good. A baffle is any device used to direct, divert, or disseminate light. It can be a louver over a light, an egg-crate grid, or even an angled panel that redirects the stream of light. Fluorescent lamps can also be used in showcases or hidden beneath shelves to add the required warmth or coolness that the particular merchandise warrants.

In any area, a ceiling may be regarded as another wall, or the sixth side of a cube, with the walls comprising four sides, and the floor the fifth. As much as it might be desirable to use different colors of fluorescents in different areas, to do so would break the ceiling pattern and call attention to the changes of color overhead. It is advisable to test and then select a proper mix of perhaps two different color tubes that can be used in the same fixture and provide the best overall colored light for the store. A grid or diffuser will hide the fact that in a single fixture, daylight and warm white tubes are being used in tandem.

Incandescent Lighting

More and more stores are combining incandescent lights with fluorescent lights to create their primary lighting. The incandescents are used for warmth, for emphasis, for highlighting, as well as on the merchandise that thrives under them. The fluorescents may light up an aisle, wash a wall, or indicate a change of merchandise or department, but the incandescents do the selling.

In small stores and in special areas or closed-off

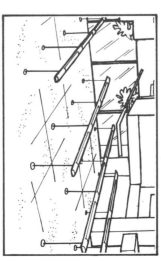

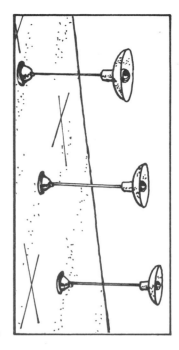

Figure 6-1, *above left.* Rows of fluorescent lighting fixtures.

Figure 6-2, *above right.* Cool fluorescent light is effective in silver and jewelry areas. The baffle arrangement over the lamps softens the effect and adds a decorative quality to the ceiling design. Other fluorescents are used around the perimeter of this cosmetics and fine jewelry department: Cool slimline tubes light up the counters, while warm incandescent lamps are placed next to the mirrors on the counters where the customer will see herself. *Rich's, Union City, Georgia.*

Figure 6-3, *left.* A high-hat lighting fixture directs the beam of light down onto an area without much spread of light.

Figure 6-4, *below.* Drop-lights.

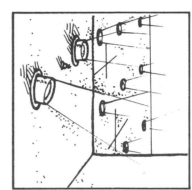

departments, incandescent light bulbs can be used as the only kind of lighting in the general, overall scheme. However, incandescents are more expensive to install and use. They do not burn as efficiently or as long as fluorescent tubes. They also give off more heat, which can increase the air-conditioning load, and thus use more energy. Some stores feel the increased costs are worth it because of the effect incandescent light produces.

Incandescent *spotlights* are high voltage lights and are called *PAR bulbs*. They can be used as a primary light source, but are usually used as secondary lighting. (See the "Secondary Lighting" section below.) Although these lamps cost more to purchase, they do have a longer lamp life. A PAR bulb can burn for 3,000 hours or longer.

An alternative to the PAR bulb is the *R or reflector bulb*, which is lower in wattage (about 150 watts) and made of clear glass with a metallic reflector surface mounted behind the bulb. Although it costs less to purchase than the PAR bulb, the reflector bulb does not burn as long.

Floodlights are also incandescent bulbs, but they usually have frosted glass envelopes, or enclosures, and are less concentrated, having a wider beam spread than spotlights.

Incandescent bulbs can be set into recessed high-hat fixtures in the ceiling, clustered in chandeliers, or hung as droplights. They can be mounted into housings that ride back and forth on ceiling tracks, and can be directed or focused on merchandise or displays. Bare bulbs, silver-bottomed bulbs, 5-inch globe-like

Figure 6-5, above. An HID lamp which provides illumination at reduced energy consumption by means of an electric current passing through any of several assorted gases. The most common types: mercury vapor lamp, metal halide lamp, sodium vapor lamp.

Figure 6-6, right. The high-hat lights are visible across the top of the photograph. The black track-light installation is used to spotlight the displayed merchandise on the wall, above the shelves, as well as the merchandise on the shelves. *Lord & Taylor, Chicago.*

bulbs, or tiny, round complexion bulbs can be decoratively lined up, clustered, or "polka-dotted" on the ceiling to please the eye, add charm to the design scheme, and "stroke" the merchandise.

High-Intensity Discharge Lighting (HID)

The HID lamp, which is very energy efficient, is becoming a strong contender in the field of general, overall store lighting, in some cases nudging out the fluorescents with their long and readily apparent fixtures. The HID's are relatively small in size (compared to the fluorescents) and will, like the incandescents, provide shadows and highlights.

The mercury-type HID may be too green, the metal halide type may appear too blue, and the sodium type is quite yellow, but new developments are producing warmer and more flattering types of light. General Electric's Multi-Vapor II is an improved metal halide-type lamp that produces a light similar to a standard cool-white fluorescent which is satisfactory in some areas. It is still cooler and bluer than an incandescent lamp, however. Westinghouse has a high-pressure sodium lamp (HPS), Ceramalux 4, which works well at the warm end of the color wheel, but it is still yellower than an incandescent lamp.

Incandescent spotlighting can be used to accent and highlight with HID overall lighting, but may require colored filters (like a pale, "daylite" filter) to go with a Multi-Vapor II arrangement so that the different types of light do not jar each other. The Ceramalux 4 provides a warm ambience and mixes well with warm white deluxe fluorescents or with regular incandescents. However, since HID lamps do provide so much light, they are best used in areas where the ceiling is at least 15 feet high; otherwise, they will create an excessively bright and sharply lit selling floor.

SECONDARY LIGHTING

Flat, shadowless, overall lighting can create a lethargic and boring selling floor. Glare or overly bright, strong light can be irritating and a detriment to selling. Shadows and highlights are necessary; they can delight, intrigue, and pique the imagination. Sparkle and shimmer can stimulate and titillate. A selling floor and especially a display need changes from light to dark, from highlights to shadows. They need flash and sparkle and should make the viewer's eye travel over the area. Secondary lighting should accomplish all of this.

Secondary lighting devices can be "candle-lit" chandeliers, wall sconces which suggest warmth and elegance with only a minimum of actual light, lights on a track which move to supply extra light where it is needed, and hidden lights which wash a wall with light or color and beckon the customer into the department for a closer look. Secondary lighting can also diffuse a ledge area with a glow or an aura of light. It can be a spotlight on a display or the light in a case or under a counter.

Incandescent bulbs—from tiny bee and twinkle lights, to small candle-like or complexion bulbs, and on up to full-sized globe, pear, or reflector-type bulbs—are

Figure 6-7. The cool, primary light in this gift area is provided by the large, decorative fluorescent fixtures set into the dropped ceiling. Swivel spotlight fixtures are partially embedded in the ceiling and can be directed to highlight and warm the cool silver merchandise. Fluorescents are also used as a secondary lighting source in the fascia strips over the merchandise displayed along the perimeter wall. The lighting, here, is a careful and effective mixture of warm and cool lighting, enhancing the silver color of the merchandise and the elegance of the department. *Hutzler's, Baltimore.*

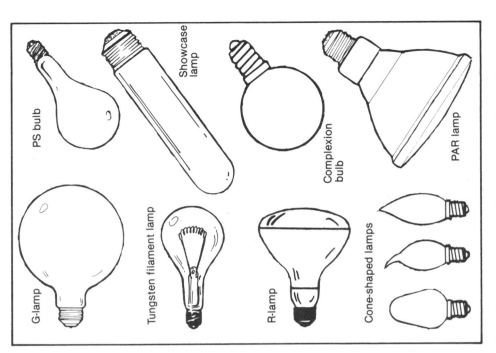

Figure 6-8. Incandescent bulbs come in a variety of shapes and sizes. These are only a few (not depicted in scale).

most frequently used for secondary lighting. The long showcase or "sausage" lamp is an incandescent that somewhat resembles a mini-fluorescent tube in shape, but it gives off a warm light and does fit, almost invisibly, into display cases or under shelves.

When lamps are hidden behind valances or recessed under grids or baffles, and warmer colors are not needed, fluorescents may work effectively to provide secondary lighting. However, incandescent secondary lights will add highlights, provide shadows, mold and dimensionalize the merchandise, and flatter the customer's complexion.

COLORED LIGHTS AND FILTERS

Just as pigments can be mixed to produce new colors, colored lights can be mixed to create new and different color effects. The primary colors of light are red, green and blue.

White light can be produced by mixing the three primary colors. Red and blue light together will produce a magenta or a purplish red. Blue and green will combine to form cyan or cyan-blue, which is actually a bright blue-green. Red and green create a yellowish or amber light. Thus, the secondary colors of light are magenta, cyan, and amber.

The use of colored glass or plastic filters over a source of white light will change the color of the light by adding or subtracting various colors from the white light. Magenta and amber filters, used on the same filter lens and with incandescent light passing through them, will produce a red light. The magenta (red and blue) will absorb the green light present in the amber light (red and green). The amber, in turn, will absorb the blue out of the magenta, leaving only the red light which is common to both. Thus, by filtering out or blocking certain colored light (or wavelengths of color), a different light can be produced.

The displayperson should be especially concerned with the mixing of colored light on solid, pigmented surfaces. This is usually accomplished with colored filters and gels. A red filter placed over a white light on a white or light neutral surface will turn that surface red. The red filter absorbs all the blue and green light waves present in the white light that is going through the red filter; only the red wavelengths will pass through to the painted surface. A blue filter will absorb the red and green wavelengths, producing a blue light on the white painted area.

The color chart in Figure 6-11 shows the effect of the primary and secondary colors of light on the primary and secondary pigment colors. There are, however, many colored glass filters and plastic gelatins on the market, as well as shades and tints of these colors, which subtly can add to the intensity of a color or gently neutralize some of its intensity.

There are all sorts of pinks and "blush" tones available to warm up skin tones or suggest a sunset. There are ambers that go down to pale straw and strained sunlight. A "daylite" filter is a clear, light blue which will fill an area with the suggestion of a spring day or will chill shredded styrofoam with icy blue shadows. The green gels go from the pastel yellow-

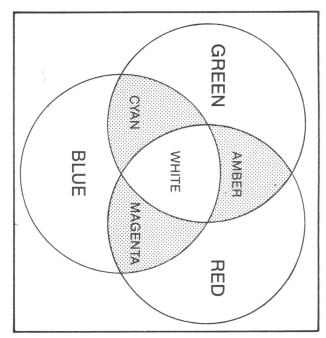

Figure 6-9. Mixing colored light.

greens to the deep atmospheric blue-greens, or cyans.

In most cases, lighter tints are usually used on displays to enrich the color presentation without appreciably changing the actual color. Strong, deep colors are used to create atmosphere—the dramatic side or back lighting, the mood lighting of a window or ledge display, for example. Deeper colored lights are mainly reserved for modeling and shaping the merchandise by adding color to the shadows and folds as well as by reflecting color from one surface to another.

A word of advice for the displayperson on the use of light on skin tones—both that of mannequins and customers: Green light should be avoided. It plays havoc with the color of cheeks and lips and with blond and red hair as well as enhancing every skin blemish. Cyan is even worse, although it may work for Halloween or an "out-of-this-world" presentation. Pinks and rose tints are usually most becoming to most skin tones, from the palest white to the darkest browns, and enhance the warm colors in merchandise.

Figure 6-11, *opposite.* This chart shows the effect of colored lights on primary and secondary colored pigments. For example, a green colored light on a red fabric or on a red painted surface will turn the red into a "muddy" brown, while a red light on a green surface will make the green appear dark gray.

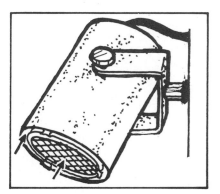

Figure 6-10. The arrows indicate a colored glass filter placed in front of a spotlight housed in a metal fixture.

SHADOWS

Shadows have color. Even if a display has a neutral gray or white background, there will be a definite color in the shadow created by the merchandise in front of it. The merchandise does prevent the light from hitting the back wall, but it contributes something to the darkness it causes. It is called a *simultaneous contrast.*

A red garment shown before an absolutely neutral background will produce,' to the viewer's perception, a

Figure 6-11.

| | Primary Colored Pigments | | | Secondary Colored Pigments | | |
	RED	BLUE	YELLOW	GREEN	ORANGE	VIOLET
RED	Brilliant Red	Brown-Purple	Almost White	Dark Gray	Pale Orange	Rich Wine
BLUE	Violet	Bright Blue	Green	Turquoise	Gray-Brown	Blue-Violet
GREEN	Brown	Turquoise	Yellow-Green	Bright Green	Old Gold	Dark Gray-Green
AMBER	Orange-Red	Dark Gray	Pale Yellow	Gray-Green	Bright Orange	Brown
CYAN	Gray-Brown	Blue-Green	Light Green	Blue-Green	Brown	Deep Cold Blue
MAGENTA	Lake Or Cerise	Ultramarine Blue	Orange	Blue-Violet	Bright Red-Orange	Red-Violet

Primary Colored Lights (RED, BLUE, GREEN) / *Secondary Colored Lights* (AMBER, CYAN, MAGENTA)

greenish tone in that gray shadow. The shadow will appear to have a touch of the complement of the color in front. The slightly greenish cast will cause the red to seem redder and brighter—as complementary colors do. If the displayperson does not want to increase the brilliance of the red merchandise, he or she can light the background using a pink, amber, blue, or violet filter, or any of several other colors. The color-lit background will soften the red by making it appear more pastel (with the pink filter), more red-orange (with the amber), more violet (with the blue), or more magenta-red (with the violet).

SUGGESTIONS FOR USING LIGHT EFFECTIVELY

1. Avoid bright, white lights directly on a mannequin's face, elbows, or shoes. Save the brightest lights for the merchandise, and avoid anything that will detract from the merchandise.

2. Use colored light to create the right setting for the merchandise. Save it for props and backgrounds. If colored light is used on a garment to intensify the color, stay with the pastel filters: pale pinks for the reds and red-violets, pale straw for the yellows and oranges, daylight blue for the cool colors, and nile green for the greens.

3. It is more effective to light across a display rather than directly down on it. This can create unpleasant and unattractive shadows. The upper left light can be directed over to the lower right side of the display; the upper right light is then directed over to the lower left. This creates a cross-over of light, a more even, more diffused light, and nullifies areas in the display space that are too bright or too dark.

4. The lighting in a window display should be checked at night. Many imperfections, such as wrinkles, are more apparent under the artificial light when the softening influence of daylight does not enter the window. Colored lights will also look different when there is no other source of light with which to contend. What may have seemed perfect during the daylight hours, at night may appear harsh or garish. It is also advisable to check that the lights are not "flooding over" into the street—into the eyes of passersby and the road traffic.

5. There is nothing particularly attractive about electric wires unless they are meant to be part of the decorative scheme. Find ways to "lose" them—hide and disguise them.

6. Display lights are expensive to use. They use up energy. It is wise to set up a timer device which will automatically turn off all lights sometime during the night after the street traffic has diminished and the store lighting no longer serves any purpose of display or image.

LIGHTING: A RECAP

1. General or primary lighting is the overall ceiling light of a selling area. It does not include the accent or decorative lighting.

2. Secondary lighting is the accent and decora-

tive lighting: chandeliers; sconces; wall washers; indirect lighting; spotlights; and lights under shelves, in cases, and in counters.

3. Fluorescent lighting is efficient and relatively inexpensive to install and maintain. The tubes are available in a wide range of "white" light, from cool bluish to warm white deluxe which has more of a peach tone. Smaller tubes can be used in showcases, under shelves, and behind baffles as wall washers.

4. Incandescent bulbs produce warmer and more flattering light than the fluorescents, but emit more heat. The lamps do not burn as long or as efficiently as the fluorescents. They are available in a wide range of sizes, shapes, and wattages. The lamps can be decorative as well as useful. The incandescent spotlight is a display "must."

5. The HID lamp is an efficient and relatively inexpensive light source which is being color improved for use inside the store.

6. Different light sources can be used on the same selling floor. It is possible to highlight and accent a fluorescent primary lighting scheme with incandescent secondary lighting.

7. White light is composed of a rainbow of colors of different wavelengths, from violet to red.

8. The primary colors of light are red, blue, and green.

9. The secondary colors of light are magenta, cyan, and amber.

10. A colored filter produces a particular color of light by filtering out or absorbing all the other colors in the white light except the color of the filter or gel.

Figure 6-12. This chart shows the effect of different lamps on painted surfaces of various colors. A similar change takes place on similarly colored merchandise displayed under these various lamps.

Paint Color	Approximate Reflectance Factor	Incandescent Filament	Warm White Fluorescent	White Fluorescent	Standard Cool White Fluorescent	Daylight Fluorescent	Warm White Deluxe Fluorescent	Cool White Deluxe Fluorescent
Cherry Red	.13	Brilliant Orange-Red	Pale Orange-Red	Pale Orange-Red	Yellowish Red	Light Red	Orange Red	Good Match
Orchid	.44	Light Pink	Pale Purplish Pink	Gray-Pink	Light Pink	Light Pink	Pale Pink	Light Pink
Plum	.04	Deep Orange-Red	Dull Reddish Brown	Dark Brown	Light Reddish Brown	Deep Bluish Purple	Reddish Brown	Darker Brown
Chestnut Brown	.19	Medium Yellowish Brown	Light Yellowish Brown	Gray-Brown	Light Brownish Gray	Light Gray	Dark Brown	Good Match
Peach	.58	Pinkish Yellow	Light Yellowish Pink	Light Yellowish Pink	Very Light Pink	Fair Match (Lighter)	Light Orange	Good Match (Yellower)
Orange	.44	Bright Orange	Light Orange-Yellow	Pale Yellow	Light Yellow	Gray-Yellow	Yellowish Orange	Good Match
Canary Yellow	.44	Orange-Yellow	Fair Match (Sharper)	Greenish Yellow	Light Yellow	Fair Match	Good Match	Good Match (Brighter)
Light Yellow	.58	Vivid Orange-Yellow	Medium Yellow	Medium Yellow	Light Bright Yellow	Light Greenish Yellow	Deep Yellow	Bright Yellow
Light Blue	.46	Light Yellowish Green	Pale Grayish Blue	Weak Greenish Blue	Blue-Gray	Fair Match (Lighter)	Grayish Blue	Grayish Blue
Medium Blue	.23	Blue-Green	Light Gray-Blue	Purplish Blue	Light Gray-Blue	Fair Match (Lighter)	Purple-Blue	Reddish Blue
Silver Gray	.97	Light Yellow-Gray	Light Yellowish Gray	Light Brownish Gray	Very Light Gray	Bluish Gray	Yellowish Gray	Light Gray

7 Line and Composition

LINE

Line is direction. It is a major part of composition (see the following page) and, after color, most important in creating a response to the merchandise in a display. Lines can be vertical, horizontal, curved or arced, and diagonal. The way in which these lines are utilized and combined, determines the effectiveness of the merchandise presentation. Each line suggests something else, and like letters combined to form words, lines are arranged to make selling "pictures."

Vertical Lines

What is more inspiring than the soaring spires of a Gothic cathedral? Is there anything more classic or elegant than a tall, fluted Ionic column? How about the power and majesty of a stand of cypress trees? Proud people stand tall and erect. What do the spire, the column, the cypress, and the proud person have in common? They are all straight and vertical. They emphasize and exemplify the vertical line. When a display is mainly a vertical one, filled with straight elements that seem to join floor and ceiling, the viewer will get the message: strength, height, pride, majesty, dignity.

When the vertical elements are not only tall but also thin, an impression of elegance and refinement is conveyed. For example: A mannequin stands erect, arms at her sides or only slightly bent, head uplifted and shoulders back. She will not look "military," but it is more likely that she will add stature and "class" to the garment she is modeling. Fur coats, evening gowns, bridalwear, and well-tailored suits are shown to advantage on a vertical figure. The long, straight, falling line of a garment can be enhanced by the "dignified" mannequin which, in turn, will add verticality to the entire display. A straight line is also direct and forceful, or rigid and precise.

Horizontal Lines

Long, low, wide, spreading lines—the bands that run across a window or over a hang unit—suggest an easy-going, restful quality. All is peace and calm in a horizontal presentation. A reclining mannequin, relaxed and at ease, is perfectly compatible with robes, lounge-wear, or nightwear. The horizon sets the world to rest; lazy ripples and gentle waves are horizontal. As the line stretches out and makes objects look wider, it also tends to make objects look shorter. A pattern of horizontal lines will cut the vertical effect and reduce the "uptight" or dignified feel of a design or setting. A

balancing of the horizontal with the vertical can create an easy, restful, but elegant setting.

Curved Lines

The curved line personifies grace, charm, and femininity. It is soft and enveloping. The curved line or arc can ease the tension that might be produced by too many verticals. It is the circle and the sphere—the sun and the moon; also, the heart, billowing waves, rolling hills, fluffy clouds, the swirl of a seashell, a spiral, an opening rose. Curved lines can also be used for a spotlight or target against which an object is shown, or a spiral that leads the eye from object to object.

Diagonal Lines

The diagonal line is a line of action; it is forceful, strong, and dynamic. The diagonal is a bolt of lightning, a firecracker going off, a thrown javelin, rain streaming down, a shove or a push, a seesaw or a sliding pond, an arrow, or a pointing finger leading the eye right down to where the action is. The active sportswear mannequin, for example, is often all angles: arms akimbo, knees bent, head thrust back, and shoulders shrugging. That mannequin is a study in diagonals. It is possible to suggest movement and excitement in a static and predominantly vertical or horizontal presentation by adding some forceful diagonals.

COMPOSITION

Composition may be defined as the organization or grouping of different parts or elements in order to achieve a unified whole. In display and visual merchandising, composition is the arrangement of lines, forms, shapes, and colors into a pleasing whole which directs the viewer's eye to the various bits and pieces of the setting and relays a particular message. The quality of the composition will depend on the elements used and where and how they are used.

Balance

A well-designed display should be balanced. This involves the creation of an easy-to-accept relationship between the parts of the composition. If a design were cut in half by an imaginary line drawn through its center, and one half were an exact replica or mirror image of the other side, that would be a classic example of *symmetrical* or *formal balance.* In reality, however, the objects on each side of the imaginary line are usually of similar weight and prominence, not an actual mirror image. For example: If in one side of a display, a

Figure 7-1, *above.* The long, straight, fluted columns stress the vertical line in this presentation. The carefully dressed, standing mannequin is essentially vertical from its head down to its crossed-over leg. The diagonal line of the seated, more casually dressed figure, as well as the crossed-over leg of the standing mannequin, add some movement and dynamism to this overwhelmingly vertical display. *Barney's, New York.*

Figure 7-2, *opposite top.* The long horizontal line of the couch and the flowing horizontal line of the merchandise suggest a luxurious, soft, and gentle kind of merchandise presentation. A painting of the actual display, hung low on the back wall, only adds greater emphasis to the long horizontal design.

Figure 7-3, *opposite left.* The torn sheets of the horizontal seamless paper suddenly becomes softer and more feminine because of the wave-like curves of the rounded edges. The rough-textured dress appears more graceful and delicate thanks to the deckle-edged paper. The arc in the drape of the shawl reinforces the curvilinear line. *Gimbel's, New York.*

Figure 7-4, *opposite right.* The wide stride of the semirealistic mannequin and the echoing diagonal of the reclining beach chair set the otherwise static, horizontal display into motion. There is force, direction, and a sense of movement in an elegant, high-fashion display. *Bergdorf Goodman, New York.*

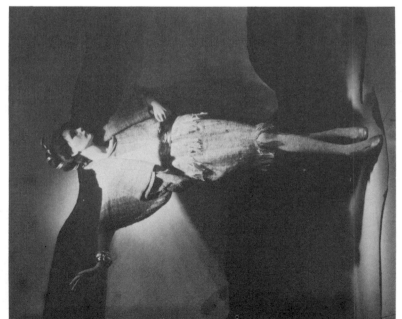

Figure 7-5. The tall vertical element in the middle divides the window into two perfectly balanced and symmetrical halves. However, the clever displayperson has used care and imagination in balancing the sides with dissimilar merchandise. Notice how the two plates in the left foreground have been counterbalanced with a "heavier" dish and a copy card on the right side. Gump's, San Francisco.

mannequin is sitting on a chair, while on the other side a similar mannequin is sitting on a comparable chair, both halves of the composition would be considered the same, equal in weight and importance. This is formal balance and, although staid and traditional, can be very effective where expensive or quality merchandise is being presented.

Asymmetrical balance is more informal and often more interesting. Although the two sides appear to be of equal weight, they are not replicas of each other. The individual units comprising the display may differ, but they achieve a dynamic balance of weight and size at each side of the imaginary central line. For example: There might be two mannequins on one side balanced by a mannequin standing next to a draped table. If, on the table, there is a vase filled with flowers and foliage extending to about the same height as the mannequin's head, then visually, the table with the vase and flowers will be equal in weight and shape to the second mannequin on the other side.

Sometimes, the creative and experienced designer can do marvelous things by balancing color with form. A strong or hot color may appear heavier than a pastel or cool color, so a mannequin in a vivid red dress might be balanced with an armoire painted antique white. This asymmetrical or informal balance is more casual, more interesting, and certainly more exciting.

At times, a display presentation can be completely lacking in any sense of balance and still be very good. This is done for a reason. To create an effect, a lack of balance may be used as an element of surprise: to catch the viewer looking into an "empty" window and won-

dering where the display went. Or the displayperson may be catering to a particular traffic flow. He or she may find that most shoppers travel north to south on the store's side of the street. It can make for a better presentation if the merchandise is shown in the southern half of the window—angled to face and attract the shopper walking from north to south. The empty or near empty, less weighty, northern part of the window gets less attention and, therefore, little, if any, merchandising.

Dominance

In every composition, it is advisable that some element be dominant. There should be some unit or object which by its color, its size, or its position in the composition attracts the eye first and possibly directs the viewer to other parts of the composition.

In most displays, the dominant element is the merchandise, often with a big assist from a mannequin that is wearing it. In the "one-item" display, the single unit should dominate—should be the eye-catcher and the eye-filler, and the rest of the design or composition should exist in order to make this one item seem more beautiful and more special. However, some stores with very special images will play games with their viewers. Knowing how very "special" they and their merchandise are, the store designer will casually drop an exquisite single item into a beautifully conceived composition, leaving it up to the shopper to find it. But this can be successfully done only where the store and the displayperson know what they are selling—and to

Figure 7-6. This display is an excellent example of an assymetrical composition. It appears to be a haphazard series of wooden piles, set in sand, with turtles moving about and shoes casually set about on the risers of assorted sizes. However, if the viewer examines the display more closely, studying the number and placement of objects on each side of an imaginary center line running vertically through the display, he or she will appreciate how carefully the total "weights" of the many separate pieces have been balanced on either side of the line despite the overall casual appearance. *Nordstrom, Seattle.*

Figure 7-7, *above.* New York City had a transit strike and it rained for days. The "wet" and weary, raincoat-and-galoshes dressed figure would never have made it without her varied assortment of light and convenient bags. The mannequin in the yellow raincoat dominates the display and gets the viewer's attention. The rest follows. *Bloomingdale's, New York.*

Figure 7-8, *above right.* The dark canvas chair in an even darker window, with only the white wooden parts to define it, plus the sharp spotlight on the glass starfish (the merchandise) and the stenciled copy on the chair back, make this a very successful window. The very small piece of very fine merchandise in the very large window seems to "grow" in stature by means of the setting, the lighting, the composition—and the idea behind the display. This display plays with the idea of a "star," as in a "movie star" (the director's chair) and the nautical starfish (the yacht chair). A "one-of-a-kind" display. *Gump's, San Francisco.*

whom—and can afford the luxury of these little "games."

A mannequin can be dominant in a display by virtue of its size or the color it is wearing. A small object, like a diamond brooch, can be made dominant in a composition by sharply contrasting it with its background, without any distracting props nearby, and with a strong light on the piece. An object may also be made dominant by the arrangement of lines and shapes, the weights of the various elements of the composition, and gradations of color and light. By using these various techniques, the viewer's eye is directed to the main object or the featured item of the display.

Contrast

Contrast is the comparison of elements in order to show a sharp difference between them. It consists of a juxtaposition of different forms, lines, or colors in a composition in order to intensify each element's properties. For example: It is a white gown displayed against a midnight background; a diamond bracelet on a black velvet pad; a pair of red shoes on a green grass mat.

A difference in texture or an incongruity in the objects themselves can also heighten the contrast: a lustrous satin blouse lying on a rough tree bark or a power saw nestling on a fluffy angel-hair cloud. The outrageous difference in the feel and texture between the item or merchandise and its environment will attract attention and maybe even promote the softness, ruggedness, or smoothness of that item. The effective use of contrast makes it possible for the "feel" or

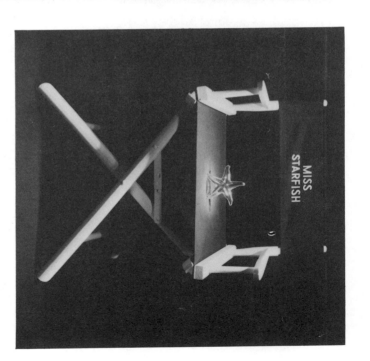

MISS
STARFISH

"touch" of an item to be more apparent to the eye without actually touching or stroking the object.

Proportion

Contrast can also consist of a difference in proportion—the relationship of the size, scale, or "weight" of elements and between each element and the entire composition. A pair of baby shoes, for example, will appear more delicate and cherishable when placed next to a gigantic teddy bear. A 4-foot tennis racket will bring attention to mere human-sized tennis shoes. The displayperson must be careful to consider not only the size of the merchandise and props, but the size of the display area as well.

Experience has taught us to take the size of certain objects for granted. We know, for example, that a mannequin is life-size. Yet, the mannequin, in proportion to a greatly oversized table and chair, would appear to shrink from its actual size. Our mind knows the mannequin is still life-size, but our eyes are not so convinced.

Certain proportions or relationships in a composition or display, especially for common objects, are easily accepted by the viewer's eye: A ring will fit a mannequin's hand; a hat will sit on a mannequin's head. Put the same feathered hat into a straw "nest" that is 3 feet in diameter with "eggs" the size of footballs—the hat now appears to be small and fragile. The "nest" is out of proportion; it is overscaled.

Proportion and contrast are important elements of good composition. Drastically changing the proportions between items, and dramatic contrasts of color and texture can work wonders in attracting attention to a display and in helping to promote an idea or a look. These attention-getting techniques will be discussed in greater detail in Chapter 18.

Figure 7-9. The oversized and portentous pen signs the name of Calvin Klein, the designer, with a flourish that cannot be ignored. The subtlety of the white-on-white of the mannequin against the background gets a dynamic thrust into attention from the black pen diagonally moving across the composition, dramatically underlining the designer's contribution to the merchandise being presented. Dramatic lighting also helps draw the viewer's attention to both the oversized prop and the merchandise. (The huge pen was made by the store's visual merchandising personnel from mailing tubes covered with flint paper and mylar.) *Filene's, Boston.*

Rhythm

A good display composition should have a rhythm, a self-contained movement from element to element, from background to foreground, from side to side. The rhythm should lead the viewer's eye from the dominant object to the subordinate object (or objects), from the major presentation of an ensemble down to the arrangement of accessories or alternate parts of the outfit.

This flow, for example, can be created by the manner in which a mannequin is posed. Her hand may be resting on a chair back which happens to have a coat draped from it; a scarf, which is casually tossed over the coat, is trailing onto the floor over to an arrangement of shoes, bags, another scarf, a flower, some toiletries. The eye had been led first to the mannequin (dominant in size, color and "weight"), down to the chair, and then

Figure 7-10. The mannequin on the far left looks at the mannequin next to it. Its body pose and arm stress the action towards the right. The arm of the center mannequin leads the viewer down to the seated figure, whose arm, in turn, directs the customer to look at the toiletries in the foreground. The Polo logo on the right side of the display area leads the viewer back into the body of the display and balances out the weight on the left. *Filene's, Boston.*

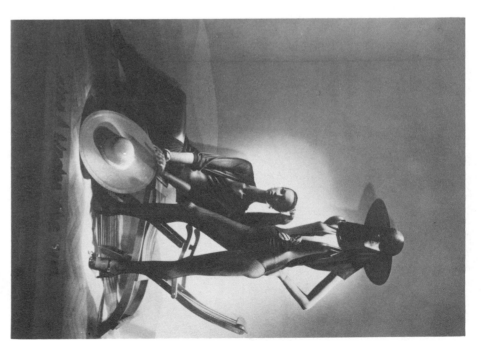

Figure 7-11. The bright spot on the face of the mannequin on the right, otherwise hidden under a black hat and scarf, leads to a highlight on its bent arm, which in turn directs us back to the left and the face of the seated mannequin. The next highlight appears on the hands and lap of the seated mannequin, and the viewer's attention is led to the burst of color and light on the red hat—and the message on the floor directly in front of it. Basically, this is a triangular arrangement: the floor is one "leg," the standing figure is the perpendicular "leg," and the "hypotenuse" starts at the back hat on top and follows the diagonal of the seated mannequin's pose. *Saks Fifth Avenue, New York.*

Figure 7-12. The perfume bottles, by themselves, are too small and insignificant to carry even a shadow box of the size shown. The overscaled, plaster cast noses (used in life-drawing classes), repeated over and over again, catch the viewer's eye. They can then follow the nose to the scents which are well arranged on a series of cubic risers. The copy card reads: "For him to smell." This was one of a series of cosmetics displays which also included molds of eyes (for eye makeup) and mouths (for lipsticks). *Woodward's, Vancouver, British Columbia, Canada.*

to the cluster on the ground. That downward sweep may be subtly reinforced by a background design of lines or shapes, and by the use of color and lighting, which also lead the eye in the same direction.

The eye will naturally go around in a circular route if the objects are arranged to lead that way—like a snail's shell swirling inward to a central point. The eye will follow a triangular trail or a pyramidal pattern that leads from a flat, weighted base to an apex, or point. A successful rhythm or flow is a gentle one; one that guides the viewer in easy movements from one stop to another along the way. In some cases, like "sales" or "hard-sell" promotions—where more dynamism is demanded—a jumpy and jarring presentation will be more effective.

Repetition

Repetition of a color, a line, a shape, or a form can add to the success of a display composition. By repeating or reiterating an idea or a motif, that concept becomes more emphatic, more important, and thus, more dominant. In this way, even a small object can be made to stand out in a large display area—because the eye has been "trained" to look for it. Try to visualize a dark floor with an appliqué of red footprints "walking" across it. At the very end—in a pool of light—is a pair of red shoes. The pattern or repetition of the red footprints will carry the viewer's eye forward to the single pair of shoes, which now dominates the composition and the viewer's eye—and mind.

8 Mannequins and Dimensional Forms

SELECTING A MANNEQUIN

The selection of a mannequin is probably one of the most important professional decisions a displayperson is called upon to make. There are so many mannequins available: various sizes and age groupings, facial and ethnic types, makeup and hairstyles, poses and attitudes. In addition to the many "images" to select from, there is also the serious consideration of construction and cost.

A mannequin may be a store's most valuable asset: It is a "silent salesperson," speaking the clearest fashion message. A mannequin will stand tirelessly for hours and days, in the same place, in the same position or attitude, always smiling, fresh, and pleasant. A mannequin does not gain or lose pounds or inches; it does not get colds or headaches, it does not ask for time off or for cost-of-living increases. However, it does require "love" and attention. Mannequins should be carefully handled—not manhandled. They are usually constructed to take a certain amount of wear and tear, but they can chip, crack, and be disfigured.

A mannequin should be given "time off"—a rest period out of the customer's view—but this is more for the customer's sake than the mannequin's benefit. Too much familiarity with a particular mannequin's makeup, hairstyle, and pose, can cut down on its efficiency in "selling" a new and different outfit. A change of hairstyle (a different wig) may help, or an alternate pose, accomplished by a change of arms, may do it. When selecting and purchasing a realistic mannequin, it might be economical and good display planning to invest in some "alternate" accessories. It will give the mannequin a longer and more versatile life.

TYPES OF MANNEQUINS
Realistic Mannequins

The realistic mannequin of the past looked like a famous model or a classically beautiful movie star. Today's realistic mannequin, more often than not, looks like the face *outside* the display window, the one looking in.

More and more mannequins are becoming more natural, more true to life, more animated, and more identifiable as the people who shop the stores. The mannequin may be young, wholesome and homebred, or it can appear worldly, sophisticated, and right out of the champagne-and-caviar circuit. Its nose may have a slight bump, with its eyes too close, lower lip too fleshy, teeth a bit bucked, but who is perfect? Whatever the mannequin is, it will be well made up, proportioned to wear a particular size, and well-positioned to show off a certain group or style of merchandise.

The realistic female mannequin can be a chubby preteen, a blossoming teenager with freckles and pigtails, a junior at college, or a junior who is petite, or even a mature petite. It can be a svelte size 7, an exquisite 8, or a fuller 14½. Mannequins depicting the fuller woman are being seen more and more frequently. A greater number of manufacturers are sculpting and making "bigger" mannequins that are attractive and proportioned.

The same realistic female mannequin that appeals to the bright, sparkling young woman on her way up, can be equally appealing to the comfortable, successful woman who has "made it." All it takes is a change of makeup and a different wig style. In some areas of the United States, particularly in the West, the mannequins have a tan and an outdoorsy glow because the customers in these areas revel in a "sunshine" way of life. In other areas, where life primarily is indoors under artificial light, complexions may be softer, paler, and more delicate. If a store's customers want the latest in fashion, a mannequin's makeup, no matter what the skin color, should be in keeping with the current "look" as mandated by such fashion "bibles" as *Vogue* and *Harper's Bazaar*. The subtler, more delicate application of color to the mannequin's cheeks and eyes can provide the right look for a store that caters to customers who buy traditional styles. (Many stores send mannequins to specialists to have the makeup updated or changed.) Thus, makeup and wig styles can target in on a specific type of customer.

The mannequin's pose can also help suggest the type and class of merchandise being presented. The erect mannequin with only a slight bend to an arm or a subtle weight shift to a hip is ideal for showing formal clothes, fur coats, coats and suits, or elegant lingerie. Tailored clothes are best shown on an "unanimated" mannequin. The vertical line promotes the unbroken flow of the garment—the sweep of a gown—and as discussed in Chapter 7, it does suggest elegance and refinement.

When action clothes are shown, they look even sportier when the mannequin is all angles and diagonals: arms akimbo, head thrown back, hip thrust out, legs spread or seemingly in motion. The diagonals suggest the dynamics of movement and add to the excitement of the merchandise presentation. Bent arms and legs, however, are difficult to dress and may cut the line of the garment, causing creases in the pants and sleeves. If the fabric of the garment is heavy or bulky, the resulting wrinkles at the bent joints may resemble a "washboard" of bunched-up fabric without any regard to the flow or design of the garment.

Using seated mannequins makes for a change of pace. They add variety and interest to an arrangement of two or three mannequins. Where the display areas have ceilings too low to allow the use of a standing mannequin, sitting, kneeling or bending mannequins can work effectively to show separates, casualwear, lingerie, and active sportswear.

There are also horizontal mannequins available (lying down flat on the back or stretched out on one hip). These should be used only for special merchandise: nightwear, lingerie, swimwear, and some sportswear. Though the relaxed and easy horizontal line can enhance the presentation of sleepwear, it does not necessarily show the merchandise to its best advantage.

Since mannequins are rather expensive and usually limited to just two or three years of being "in fashion," smaller retail operations generally limit their purchases to two or three mannequins. It is suggested that where the budget for mannequins is limited, the displayperson should not select mannequins in which the makeup is too highly stylized or the pose too extreme. The best choice would be figures that are standing in a natural and relaxed attitude with just enough bend to the arm and leg to suggest an at-ease stance. While it might not be the most effective for every kind of garment, this type of mannequin can still be used to show a full range of merchandise—from the most formal to the very informal.

Many mannequin manufacturers sculpt figures that will relate or interact with other mannequins of the same collection. Two or three mannequins can be used together in a natural and realistic arrangement or grouping. The displayperson can show related merchandise, alternate colors, and/or different accessory setups in one display area, by showing a cluster of mannequins wearing variations of the same costume or examples of coordinates, pleasantly involved with each other. Some groupings are designed to include both males and females interacting with each other. By using alternate arms which are available for the same mannequin, it is possible to create different positions, and by adding, subtracting, or replacing one of the mannequins in a group, it is possible to form a whole new tableau or scene-from-life.

Types of Realistic Mannequins—Most female mannequins manufactured today are a *misses* or *missy* size: a size 8 which can also wear a 10 (sometimes even a 7 or 9), but whose body proportions are for a "perfect" 8. Depending on the manufacturer and pose, this mannequin can stand anywhere from 5 feet, 8 inches tall to almost 6 feet tall. The measurements are approximately a 34 bust, 23 to 24 waist, and 34 hips; and the shoe size will vary from 6½ to 7B, on up to 8 and 8½B. (These measurements vary with the manufacturer.)

At one time, the displayperson would spend hours and reams of tissue paper in padding and puffing a dress, or pinning away loads of excess fabric in the back

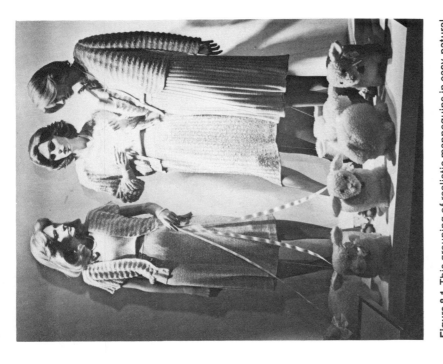

Figure 8-1. This grouping of realistic mannequins in easy, natural poses can show a wide range of garments. These three were designed to "work" together—to create a situation where three figures can interact. Notice the natural-looking wigs. *Lord & Taylor, New York.*

because the mannequin did not really "wear" its clothes. Today's mannequin will usually carry off the costume with style and flourish and little or no pinning. Some garments may still require a little "filling out" to emphasize the fullness of a skirt, the roundness of a sleeve, or to encourage a limp fabric to make a crisper statement.

The *junior mannequin* is a size 7 with all the proportions to match (32-22-32). Bust, waist and hip measurements may vary slightly, depending on the manufacturer. The figure averages about 5 feet, 7 inches to 5 feet, 9 inches in height and is a bit shorter in the waist than the missy mannequin. Many juniors are positioned and made up as young and active figures, but with the proper pose, makeup, and wig, this figure can be representative of a young executive or sophisticate.

Junior petite is the smaller woman's mannequin (about 5 feet, 5 inches tall), short-waisted, and wears size 5 or 7, with clothes proportioned for the smaller woman. Again, wigs and makeup can make all the difference; this figure can be a cute and perky high-school cheerleader, or mature enough to be the mother of the bride.

Smaller in all proportions, the *petite mannequin* has a 32-inch bust, 21 to 22-inch waist, and 32-inch hips. It is only about 5 feet to 5 feet, 4½ inches tall. This figure wears a size 4 or 6. The shoe size is about 6 to 6½B.

The *full-figured mannequin* is the size 14½ woman with bigger bust, waist and hip measurements, about 5 feet, 9 inches to 5 feet, 11 inches tall. This figure is larger, but well-proportioned in a fuller way. This mannequin represents the woman who wears the half sizes.

The *preteen mannequin* is designed to wear the young girl's dress, sizes 8 to 10, which is proportioned for the ten to twelve-year-old. The sculpting suggests the beginnings of a woman's body, but the figure is still relatively flat, uncurved, and childlike.

The *male mannequin* is about 6 feet tall and wears a size 39 or 40 jacket and size 32 trousers (with an inseam measurement of 31½ inches). The chest measurement is about 39 to 40 inches, and the shoe size is anywhere from 9 to 10. Without clothing, many male forms seem "skinny" and not virile enough for shorts, swimsuits, and active sportswear. However, active-sports figures are appearing on the market which, in addition to their animated poses, have better muscular definition.

Some manufacturers also produce a *young man mannequin* which wears "preppie" sizes, i.e., size 16, 18, or 20.

Child mannequins range from tiny tots to the preteens and teens in a variety of facial and ethnic

Figure 8-2. These full-figured mannequins are used at the entrance to a department that carries garments for the "larger" woman. They are raised up on platforms and stand before a T-wall. This is a much more effective way of identifying a merchandise area than using a sign that some might consider offensive. *Joske's, Dallas.*

types, degrees of realism, and natural or stylized poses and makeup. The various types include "the kid next door"—freckle-faced, eyeglasses barely poised on a snub nose, and maybe even braces capping the teeth—to a porcelainized, Victorian-like doll with no sculptured features, but an artfully painted face and hairstyle. Depending on the child's size and the target market (are you appealing to the young mother, the sports-conscious father, affectionate grandmother), the choices are many.

Mannequin Accessories—Most of the realistic mannequins manufactured today come with removable wigs. It is usual to purchase several wigs for a mannequin, especially if the displayperson or retailer is buying several mannequins from the same group. The different wigs add some variety to the presentation and change the mannequin's appearance.

The displayperson or retailer should select hairstyles as well as makeup that are compatible with what their current customers are wearing and with the way they see themselves. A new wig or having an old wig recut or restyled can sometimes "save" a mannequin.

Fashions change, and what may be "in" one year may become dated the next. A mannequin with perfectly acceptable proportions and anatomical details may become obsolete because the hairstyle is no longer in fashion.

There are two major types of wigs used for mannequins: *hard wigs* and *soft wigs*. A hard wig is a highly lacquered and very artificial-looking wig in which all the "hair" is set firmly and rigidly in place and then lacquered or plasticized—never to be restyled. At one time, this type of wig was virtually the only kind used. The hard wig usually features coarser "hair," less subtle colors, more elaborate and decorative styles, and is generally better suited to the semirealistic or highly stylized mannequin.

Soft wigs emulate the softness of natural hair and usually can be combed and brushed. Some synthetic hair fibers can be reset with hot rollers. The texture is more natural; the wig looks and feels more like real hair. Most realistic wigs have a skull cap for a base and hairs are woven into it. Some of the better and more natural wigs have the hairs at the forehead—the ones that form the hairline—set in by hand in a slightly irregular pattern to simulate a natural hairline. The hairs are then feathered and blended back, giving the hairline an indistinct rather than a sharp, artificial look.

Some manufacturers provide an alternative to eyes subtly painted directly on the mannequin. They produce mannequins that have very natural-looking glass eyes set into open eye sockets. These eyes can be focused so that the figure can be made to "look" in any direction, including up or down. When used in groupings, they can actually "look" at each other.

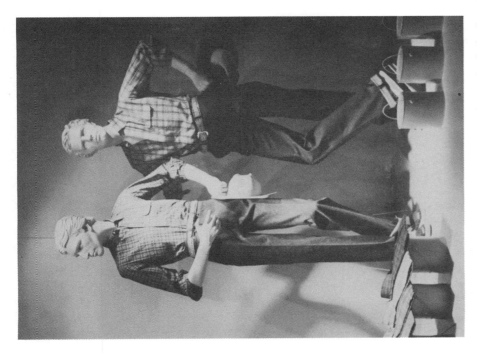

Figure 8-3. These semirealistic male mannequins are realistically sculptured, hair and all, and are completely devoid of makeup or even a natural skin color. They are finished in white and are adaptable to many kinds and styles of merchandise. *Macy's, New York.*

Semirealistic Mannequins

Semirealistic mannequins are proportioned and sculpted like realistic mannequins, but with makeup that is neither natural nor realistic, but more decorative or stylized. It may also possess a completely realistic face with sculptured features, but without any makeup at all. The entire figure may be all white or all black, or a color to match a particular department or area. The "hair" may be part of the sculpture—not changeable, replaceable, or restylable. Although the viewer knows the mannequin simulates a real "type," the lack of makeup definition keeps it from being categorized as a realistic mannequin.

Some displaypersons find the semirealistic male mannequin preferable to the realistic one. They feel that makeup and removable wig on the realistic male mannequin make him appear unmasculine in comparison to the all-white, bronze, or terra-cotta semirealistic, semiabstract, or abstract male mannequin.

Semiabstract Mannequins

The semiabstract mannequin is even more stylized and decorative and less natural or recognizable as a "real" type or person than the realistic or semirealistic mannequin. The features may be painted on or merely suggested, such as a bump for a nose or a hint of pursed lips. The semiabstract mannequin will often have a hairstyle painted onto its otherwise smooth, egg-like head. This type of mannequin is doll-like and decorative, and more popular-priced than elegant in appeal.

Abstract Mannequins

The abstract mannequin represents the ultimate in style and decoration. The arms and legs may be overly long or slender. It is more concerned with creating an overall effect than in reproducing natural lines and proportions. Rarely is there an attempt made by the sculptor to indicate features or specific details: fingernails, elbows, musculature, etc. The abstract figure is frequently finished in white or black, or sprayed in a color to match an interior design scheme or a specific color promotion. Some manufacturers will supply abstracts in chrome, copper, gold, metallic, or pearlized finishes.

The abstract mannequin is a quite sophisticated and versatile figure. Depending on the pose, it can wear a wide range of clothing: fur coats, gowns, lingerie, or sportswear. In small retail operations, where the display budget and the number of mannequins available are limited, the abstract mannequin may prove to be especially satisfactory. There are no wigs to take care of or change; the "shoes" are often sculpted right

ALTERNATIVES TO MANNEQUINS

Three-Quarter Forms

A *form* is a three-dimensional representation of a part

Soft Sculptured Figures

The soft sculptured figure is a European favorite that is making inroads into the United States display scene.

Headless Mannequins

The headless mannequin has a full-size, realistic or semiabstract body with arms and legs, but no head. The pose is often a natural one—a body swing, for example—and it may stand, sit, or recline; but, since it is headless, it offers no face, no personality, and no "image."

A headless mannequin will work in windows where height is a problem. A regular mannequin may appear overly compressed by a ceiling that is too low. Where the ledge is high and the fascia or ceiling comes down low, the headless mannequin may solve the problem of how to show, on a form, a complete outfit with curves and dimension. Since there is no head, makeup, or wig, this type of form is considerably cheaper than a realistic mannequin.

onto the figure. Because it has no ethnic qualities and is so nebulous and indefinite, the abstract mannequin can be whatever the visual merchandiser cares to make of it with color, accessories, or the surrounding trim. The abstract mannequin can wear the clothes of the future or of the historic past and look more comfortable in these fashions than a realistic figure will. It crosses color and ethnic lines and knows no age limits.

of the human anatomy, such as the torso, the bust, or the area from shoulder to waist or from hips to ankles. The three-quarter form has a body extending to the knees or just below the knees, and can have an adjustable rod (located beneath the form or in the butt) and a weighted base. It usually has a head. (A headless three-quarter form that comes just to the knees is commonly called a *torso form*.) The legs are usually parted. It may or may not have arms. (The *dress form* is an armless version of the three-quarter torso.) The lack of detailing means that this neutral, three-dimensional body form does not make a "statement."

The three-quarter form can wear a wide variety of clothes. There may be a degree of swing and movement to the torso. The form can be raised or lowered on the rod to accommodate it to the height of the area in which it is being used and to the merchandise it is required to wear. The torso can be lowered almost to the cut-off knees in order to model swimsuits, shorts, a teddy, or a slip, or it can be raised way up to show off a long gown, a robe, a full-length skirt, or even trousers.

These forms are not as expensive as mannequins, but do very little to promote a fashion image. In experiments conducted on the selling floor, it has been found that the partial form or torso is more effective than a hanger or draper, but less effective than a mannequin.

Figure 8-4. These semiabstract mannequins are more stylized and slightly more elongated than realistic or semirealistic mannequins. Here, they are effectively used to show coordinated beachwear. The ball-bouncing seals are not only attention-getters, but the balls repeat the colors of the swimsuits. *Macy's, New York.*

Figure 8-5. This eye-catching arrangement of soft, knit pieces of fabric stretched across this open-back window provides not only a background, but also a foreground for these abstract mannequins in fashionable attire. *Georges Rech, New York.*

They are life-size dolls—male, female, and all ages of children—and are available covered in black, dark brown, or off-white, jersey-like fabric with little or no facial details. The skeleton is a bendable wire armature that can be shaped and positioned. The armature is imbedded in a soft, spongy, foam filler that holds its shape inside the jersey "skin."

The figures are abstract, nonrealistic, and if well-handled, they completely disappear in the display setting. They hold and give shape to the merchandise, but the dark body becomes invisible when seen against a dark background. The lighting will pick up the merchandise, but will disregard the body wearing it. The floppy figure needs to be positioned properly in order to look real; it has to be propped, pinned, and secured in place, or wired in order to stand. The soft sculpture may require extra padding or primping.

Some U.S. manufacturers have come up with funny, frolicsome, white canvas "dolls" that add a light-hearted, eccentric quality to the display. These figures are not as costly as regular mannequins. They are novelties and can be very effective in active sportswear, sporting goods, maybe swimwear, or in any display that reaches for a humorous approach. Soft-sculptured children's figures are especially popular and adaptable. (See Figure 3-7 for an example of soft sculptured figures.)

Articulated Artist's Figures

These life-sized figures are based on the small wooden miniatures used by artists and designers to get correct anatomical proportions and poses for figure drawing when a live model is not available. Movable joints can be swiveled or turned into new positions. They are usually made of wood or white plastic.

The abstractness of the full-sized figure lends itself to decorative and undressed applications as well as fully dressed and accessorized setups. These figures can be made to stand, and can interact with other abstract, articulated forms. They can wear only accessories (belts, ties, scarves, hats) and still not look undressed. The figures—male or female—have no age, no personality, no ethnic quality, and can be anything to anybody. In addition, they are fun to work with—in windows, on ledges, in the interior.

Dressmaker Forms

This limbless, headless, but very human torso is usually set on a wire "bird cage" and supported by an ornate, cast-iron base with casters. The padded body, usually covered in canvas or linen, has long been associated with custom-made clothes, with couturiers, fashion designers, and fine tailoring. (They are also known as

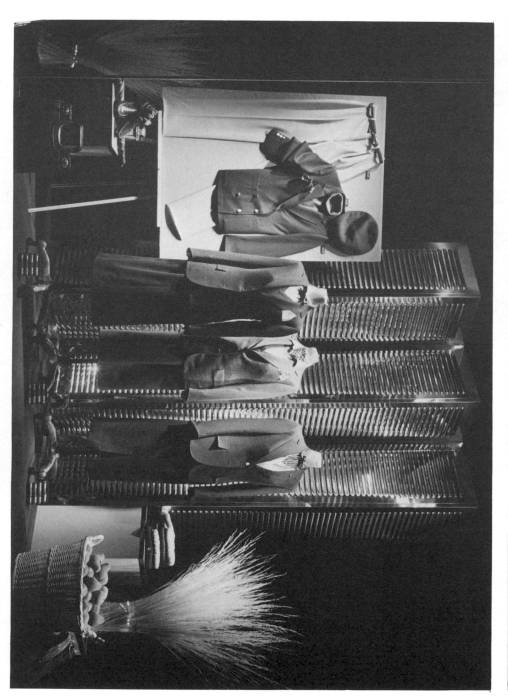

Figure 8-10. This vertical window features three tailored suits on old-fashioned dressmaker forms with cast iron bases. The "pinup" board on an artist's easel, on the left, adds a casual touch to an otherwise classic or traditional setting. *Nordstrom, Seattle.*

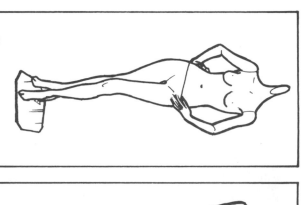

Figure 8-6. A headless mannequin.

Figure 8-7. A three-quarter form.

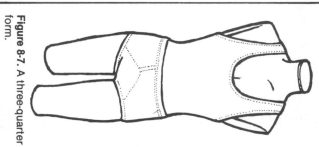

Figure 8-8. An articulated artist's figure.

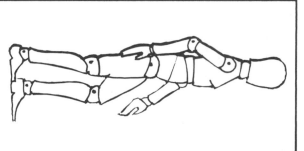

Figure 8-9. A dressmaker form.

model forms.) Not only will this form give shape to the merchandise, it gives a sense of class and value, of fashion and style.

A dressmaker form can be recovered in more elegant fabrics (jersey, velvet, or moiré) and in colors that go with the interior design of a department or shop. Fabrics, notions, and accessories can be pinned and draped on these forms. A whole ensemble can be arranged on a dressmaker form—even shoes can be hooked into the basket below—and scarves can be twisted around it or a hat can be perched on the finial that crowns the neck. Dressmaker forms will work in windows (especially where height may be a problem) or on platforms and ledges. It is a worthwhile investment where there is a tight budget, and trimming time is a problem.

The European display market now has millinery heads that match the coverings on dressmaker forms. A millinery head set on top of the cutoff neck creates a "whole" look.

Cutout Figures

The cutout figure is trendy, high style, and avant-garde—young, fun, and sassy. True to human proportions, this figure is a silhouette cut out of wood or heavy board. Clothes are pinned or draped over them for a frontal or elevated view of the merchandise. Since the figures are flat cutouts and virtually two-dimensional, they provide very little form to the merchandise. The garments can be made to sag on the figure, or the displayperson can stuff and fill the garments with pads and tissue in order to provide greater form and roundness.

Some stores use cutout forms that are almost cubistic—reminiscent of Picasso—in order to dehumanize the forms even further. Other stores, however, when using cutout techniques, have attempted to make these forms appear more "real." Life-sized photographs of males and females—full frontal views—are applied to wooden silhouettes about 3 or 4 inches thick. The arms may be removable to facilitate dressing this type of "mannequin." The end effect is sophisticated and trendy, with a sense of style and a semblance of reality. This is a boutique look rather than a department store approach.

Inflatables

Inflatables are life-sized "balloons" that simulate parts of the human anatomy. The most popular inflatable resembles the lower half of the body (waist, hips, and legs) and is used to show jeans and pants.

These forms will work for some merchandise and for certain types of stores. They show, impersonally,

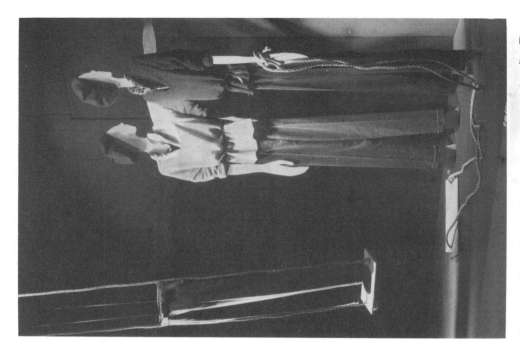

Figure 8-11. These flat, wooden cutouts wear casual outfits. They enhance the elements of youth and fun in this display, yet remain neutral enough to keep the emphasis on the merchandise. The rope tied to the wrist of the figure on the right leads to the swing on the floor and then up to the swing on the left, on which is a paper-stuffed pair of pants free of any forms. *Lane Bryant, New York.*

clothes with dimension and form. The inflatables are stiff and rigid; they usually lack grace and beauty of body line, but they are inexpensive and can be used in multiple groupings for garments that do not have to project a high-fashion look.

Other Forms

Most of the following forms are made of vinyl and are vacuum-formed, or, in some cases, made of rubber mâché and cast in a mold.

BLOUSE FORM: See *bust form.*

BODY TRUNK: A male form that starts at the diaphragm (above the waistline) and continues to just below the knees. Shorter forms, however, will be cut at mid-thigh. It is used to show shorts, underwear, swim-wear, etc. Also called a *trunk form.*

BRA FORM: A headless, armless form that ends just below a defined bustline, with or without shoulders. The forms are usually scaled to wear a size 34B. Junior bra forms are proportioned to a 32A bust.

BUST FORM: An armless, headless form that ends just below the waistline. It has a defined bust and is used to show ladies' blouses and sweaters. Also called a *blouse form* or *sweater form.*

COAT FORM: A headless, usually armless male form that starts at the neck and ends around the hips. Used to present suits, jackets, and sweaters. Arm pads or bendable rod arms may be used with this form. It also comes with an adjustable rod and base. Also called a *suit form.* (See Chapter 9 on "Rigging a Suit Form.")

LEG FORM: *See stocking form.*

PANTS FORM: A male or female form that goes from the waistline down to, and including, the feet. Men's forms will usually wear size-30 trousers with a 32-inch inseam. Female pants forms are designed to wear a size 8. If the legs are crossed, one leg will be removable to facilitate dressing the form. It is often provided with a foot spike that will hold the form in a standing position. Also called a *slacks form.*

PANTY FORM: A waist-to-knees form for showing panties, girdles, or bikini bottoms. These forms are about 2-feet tall and are usually used for counter and ledge displays.

PANTYHOSE FORM: A lightweight, female form that extends from waist to toes. The toe can be set into a toe bracket permitting the form to stand in an upright position. It may also be inverted to rest on its waist with the legs up. The same form can also display stretch tights and slacks.

SHELL FORM: A half-round, lightweight, partial torso form similar to a bra, blouse, or sweater form. The front is fully sculpted, but the back is "scooped out."

SHIRT FORM: The male version of the bust, or blouse, form. See *bust form.*

SLACKS FORM: *See pants form.*

STOCKING FORM: A form in the shape of legs used for merchandising hosiery. They have hollow tops into which the top of the hose can be inserted. The forms are available in assorted lengths depending on the merchandise to be displayed, such as thigh-high, knee-high, or calf-high. Also called *leg form.*

SUIT FORM: *See coat form.*

SWEATER FORM: *See bust form.*

TRUNK FORM: *See body trunk.*

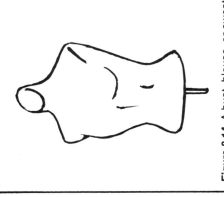

Figure 8-14. A bust, blouse, or sweater form.

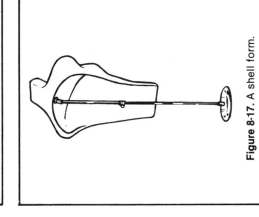

Figure 8-17. A shell form.

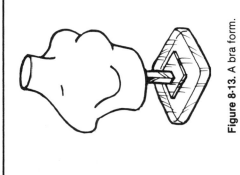

Figure 8-13. A bra form.

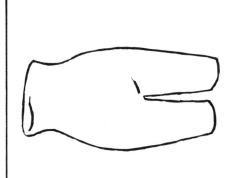

Figure 8-16. A panty form.

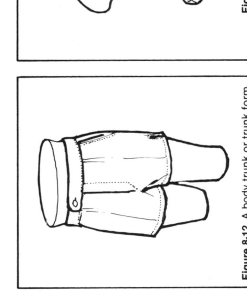

Figure 8-12. A body trunk or trunk form.

Figure 8-15. A pants form or slacks form.

9 Presenting Merchandise on a Three-Dimensional Form

DRESSING A MANNEQUIN

In order to dress a mannequin, it must first be taken apart and then carefully reassembled as the various items of merchandise are put on the figure. After "dressing" a mannequin for some time, the displayperson will develop his or her own technique for handling the mannequin and assembling the parts. For the beginner, the following steps will serve as a convenient way to start.

If a mannequin has a removable wig, it should be carefully taken off the head and set aside so that it will not be crushed while garments are being pulled over the figure's head. If the mannequin has a nonremovable wig, or if the displayperson does not choose to remove it, a plastic bag, slipped over the head before the dressing starts, will help protect the wig.

The head and neck are part of the bust or torso, and this upper half is usually removable at the waist or hips from the legs below. To remove the top from the bottom, one simply holds the torso securely, gently rotates it to the right, and then lifts it up. The fitting that connects the parts consists of a peg extending up from the lower half, and another element, similar to a keyhole, buried in the base of the upper half.

If the hands are removable, hold the arm securely with one hand and rotate the mannequin's wrist to the right in order to disconnect the hand from the arm. The hand has a peg or extension that locks into the keyhole slot in the base of the arm. To avoid confusion when reassembling, it is important that the dresser keep track from which side the various parts came (e.g., right hand replaced on right arm).

The arms are hooked into keyhole slots in the shoulders of the mannequins. Holding the torso securely, move the arm a bit to free it from the socket where it is hooked in, then raise the arm up and out from the socket.

If the mannequin is to wear shorts, pants, or pantyhose, one leg will probably need to be removed. The legs are hooked into the torso, and are removed from it in the same manner as the arms.

The assorted parts should now be lying before the dresser, on a clean, soft floor cloth or drop cloth. Of course, the dresser's hands should also be clean. Even though most mannequins do have washable finishes, they should be handled very carefully. Some displaypersons use soft paper or clean cloths during the dismantling and the reassembling of the mannequin.

The lower half of the mannequin is usually dressed first. The pantyhose or hosiery (of the proper shade to go with the outfit) is put on first. Invert the lower half of the form and remove one leg. With this lower half in the inverted position, pull the hose and/or

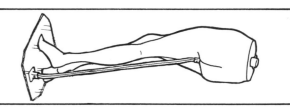

Figure 9-1. A butt rod.

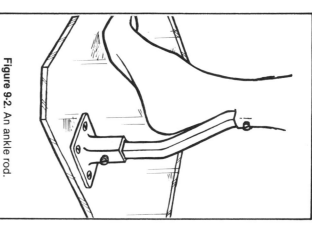

Figure 9-2. An ankle rod.

trouser leg over the leg still attached to the torso. Insert the "free" leg into the other leg of the hose or trousers. Secure the detached leg and pull the hose and trousers up to the waist.

If the mannequin has a butt-rod fitting (an attachment on the buttocks into which the floor rod is inserted so that the mannequin can stand), an opening has to be provided in the crotch or the backseam of the pantyhose (or trousers or shorts) to permit the butt rod to slide into the fitting. (If the shorts have wide legs, it might be possible to have the rod go up through the garment leg into the fitting without opening the seam.)

Many new mannequins, particularly those designed primarily to wear pants or active sportswear, are equipped with ankle-rod fittings. In this case, the fitting for the supporting rod is inserted into a piece of hardware attached to the back of the mannequin's leg—above the ankle. Another alternative is for the displayperson to wire or nail the mannequin to the ledge or into the window, and thus do away with the need for any supporting rods.

A skirt, if the mannequin will be wearing one, is put on next. If the outfit includes a top that will be tucked into the waistband, the skirt opening is not closed at this time.

The mannequin is now ready for shoes. When a mannequin is purchased, the manufacturer will supply information concerning the appropriate shoe size and heel height. If the store does not carry shoes in stock, the displayperson or management could try to make arrangements with a local shoe store to have them supply the right type and color of shoes—in the right

size—to go with the costume being presented. Often, this sort of arrangement can be accomplished in exchange for a credit in the window which states: "Shoes courtesy of…" If such an arrangement is not possible, the display department should invest in purchasing several pairs of basic shoes in basic colors—but in the current season's style—to use on the mannequins. A mannequin's feet are no longer bound in ribbons, and it is not proper for an elegantly dressed and accessorized mannequin to appear in public without shoes.

With the shoes securely on, the dressed lower portion of the mannequin can be set into the butt or ankle rod which is attached to a floor plate. If the mannequin will eventually be wired in place, lean the dressed lower half against a soft, clean, nonabrasive surface, until the upper portion of the mannequin is ready.

To attach the top half to the bottom, place the two parts together so that the projecting peg, on the top of the lower part, fits into the keyhole slot at the base of the upper torso. Turn the torso gently to lock it in place. The two parts will now make a smooth, even line.

If a sweater or over-the-head blouse or top is to be displayed, pull it on, and then proceed to slide the detached arms up through the sleeves. Fit the peg on the end of the arm into the keyhole slot at the shoulder. Do not force it. Be sure to insert the right arm into the right slot and the left arm into the left slot.

If the garment is a button-up-the-front (or back) type, put it on over the shoulders. Next, fit the "action arm" (the one with the most bend or twist) in through the proper sleeve and then into its slot. Follow with the other arm. Lock the second arm into place and then proceed to button up the garment. If a tie or neck scarf is used, this could be the time to put it on the mannequin.

If the ensemble includes a jacket, cardigan, or coat over the sweater or shirt, the outer garments should be slipped on over the shirt or sweater before the arms are inserted into the sleeves and locked into the shoulder joints. In this case, it is simpler to slip the sleeves through each other and then introduce the arm through the armhole opening with the wrist end down. The arm is then ready to fit into the shoulder slot. When the arms are positioned and the shirt cuffs are buttoned down or turned back, the hands are then joined to the slot in the wrist and turned into place. The cuff is then pulled down. (If a bangle bracelet is part of the accessory setup, it is slipped on before the hand is set in place.)

Smooth down the front of the blouse, shirt, or jacket, and gently tuck any excess fabric around to the sides (preferably under the arms, since the back may also be viewed). If the costume requires it, pull the skirt or slacks up over the bottom of the shirt, close the top of the skirt or pants, and smooth down the seams. If a scarf or ascot is to be worn under the shirt, blouse, or sweater, it should be put on before the shirt is buttoned—and it should be smoothed down to avoid any unsightly lumps.

Any beads, necklaces, chains, or over-the-head jewelry are added before the mannequin's wig is set back in place. The other accessories (handbags, gloves, pins or brooches, sunglasses, ribbons, etc.) can be added after the wig is replaced.

A mannequin that is to wear a dress, gown, or all-in-one garment may have the garment dropped over its shoulders after the pantyhose is on and the mannequin is standing erect. Other garments, such as skirts, will be easier to put on by "stepping" the mannequin into them, and pulling them up from the bottom, before the removable leg has been secured. This would depend on the top opening of the garment.

Some costumes will require a slip or a petticoat to fill out the dress properly. Others may require some padding or puffing with tissue paper or soft pads.

A mannequin that is dressed in one area and then transported to the display space or window, should not be moved with the butt or ankle rod attached to the mannequin and the floor base. After the mannequin is located where it will be set up, the supporting rod should be set into the proper attachment on the mannequin and then on the floor or platform. The mannequin, up to this point, is treated just like one that will be wired or nailed into place.

RIGGING A SUIT FORM

The man's suit form is traditionally a gray jersey-covered torso made of papier-mâché. It is headless, legless, and often armless. The unit is supported by a rod that is attached to a base. The neck is a straight cut, sometimes capped with a neck-plate of chrome, brass, or covered with fabric. Some coat or suit forms are equipped with ball-jointed arms that can be bent into realistic positions. More often than not, the trimmer who dresses, or "rigs," a suit form will have to rely on padded sleeve inserts to give substance to the loose, limp, hanging jacket sleeves.

As a form of economy, some displaypersons or retail store owners use plastic dickeys (false shirtfronts with color and tie definition molded in) to fill the jacket opening. From the point of view of merchandising and display, it would seem to be a false economy. If the store does sell shirts and ties, this would be an excellent place to show these wares. Shirts and ties are "accessories" to a man's costume, just as blouses and scarves are to a woman's ensemble. The showing of a complete outfit can lead to extra sales. Many men will buy a shirt and tie to coordinate with a selected suit.

If an actual shirt is used, it is put on over the bare suit form. The collar button is left open until the tie is placed under the shirt collar; the collar is then closed. The tie should be tied neatly and securely, and "dimpled" to sit perfectly in the inverted "V" of the collar and to hang straight down over the shirtfront. Many trimmers still prefer the very neat and symmetrical Windsor knot; others use more casual or more fashionable ways of knotting a tie.

Some classic trimmers or riggers tuck the sleeves back, out of sight, while they carefully pin, in the back, all the extra shirt fabric in two equal folds or pleats. This will create a smooth, wrinkle-free shirtfront. If a vest is to be shown, it is now put on the form and then buttoned. Some trimmers allow the shirt sleeve to go through the sleeve jacket and then extend about ½-inch below the cuff of the jacket.

A jacket will hang below the usual hipline of the suit form. In order to make the jacket lie just right and not flap in the open space below the elevated form, the rigger will sometimes cut out cardboard shields to pin onto the "hips" of the form. These will conform to the line of the bottom of the jacket. The jacket is now placed over the well-smoothed-out shirt and the cardboard cutouts.

If arm pads, or sleeve pads, are used, they are pinned to the inside of the jacket—at the shoulder—and then brought down through the sleeve. If the cuff of the shirt sleeve is seen below the jacket cuff, the shirt sleeve will be behind the padding. The sleeve pad can then be pinned to the form for a smooth, close-fitting line with the suit form. Some trimmers prefer a more casual or relaxed kind of rigging. They will not pin the sleeve or sleeve pad to the form. Instead, they may prefer to fold the sleeve, bend it, or suggest some form of animation. Shaped rolls or wads of tissue can also be used in place of sleeve pads.

Once the jacket is centered and set perfectly and squarely on the form, the dresser will often anchor the jacket in place by means of some pins placed in back, under the collar, and in front, under the lapels. If the suit has been properly pressed and/or steamed, and is wrinkle-free, the trimmer should not have too much trouble smoothing down the jacket fabric so that it will mold itself to the shape of the form beneath it. This might require an assist from a hand-held steamer. Pins may be used along the way to hold the jacket in place, but they should be hidden and employed only when necessary.

If pants are to be displayed with the jacket, they can be pinned underneath the form and then draped over the surface on which the suit form has been placed. They can then be rolled, cascaded, rippled, or

Figure 9-3. This more relaxed and casual type of rigging is in tune with the lightweight suits and the promotional concept featured in this display. The sleeves are "animated" to fit into the "pockets," and the trousers are laid down flat in front. The "sweet birds of success," flying about in the lower right, are cut out of the financial pages of the *New York Times* and the *Wall Street Journal*. The copy card reads: "Yves St. Laurent Blue Chips." *Gimbels, New York.*

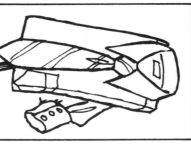

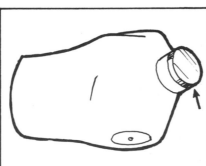

Figure 9-4, *left.* This shirt and tie are pinned and shaped for display over a shirt board.

Figure 9-5, *right.* This shirt form is capped with a neckblock (indicated by the arrow).

just sharply folded over the table, riser, or ledge, or allowed to stop just above the floor.

Instead of cutting off the excess fabric of the trouser legs or sewing an invisible hem—or anything else that would permanently shorten the legs—the displayperson could turn the excess fabric back inside the trouser leg, simulating a finished pants leg. This is called a "quick" cuff. The proper pair of shoes, set below, could meet the turned back cuff; or a store may reverse the pants and have the waistline end up at the bottom, using that opportunity to show a belt worked through the belt loops. Depending on the space, the store's stock, and the availability of alternate accessories, the trimmer can do many things, in many ways, with the space below and around the form.

Displaying a shirt without a jacket presents other problems. Some displaypersons will opt for a shirt board (a flat board about 10 inches by 14 inches), onto which the shirt can be folded with only the shirtfront and perhaps a folded-over sleeve cuff visible. The board can then be pinned onto a wall or panel. An easel, slightly angled and set behind the shirt, makes it possible to show the shirt on the floor, counter, ledge, or inside a showcase.

When a shirt form is used, the shirt is carefully pressed to get out all the fold-lines before it is placed on the form. If a tie is to be included, it is slipped under the collar, and the shirt is then buttoned. The first pin is inserted (into the form), at the top button, to keep the shirt in place. The shirtfront is then pulled taut and another pin is placed near the bottom button. The shirt is then smoothed out over and around the shoulders.

Two more pins are inserted in the back yoke of the shirt to keep it from sliding. The excess fabric is gathered around in the back and arranged into two symmetrical folds or pleats which are then pinned. The pins should be as invisible as possible and worked from underneath. The shirttail and any excess hanging from the bottom of the shirt is then folded up, and in small, neat, tight pleats, pinned to the underside of the form. Longsleeved shirts can either have the sleeves pinned at the cuff, close to the body of the form, or treated more casually with pleats, ripples, or even "postured" to give some semblance of reality.

FORMS AND CUSTOMER ATTITUDE

The more sophisticated and expensive the merchandise, and the more educated and selective the customer, the more abstract and nonrealistic the mannequin and the merchandise presentation can be. The displayperson may not have to define the shape or fit of the garment, but instead may have to spend more time showing the fabric, the details, and the accessories.

The more popular or moderately priced the merchandise, the more realistic and literal the merchandise display must be. The customers of the popularly priced store want to see it all—all the variations and combinations. They will not necessarily be impressed with clever "tricks" of folding, pinning, or placing clothes on the floor, on panels, or on flat cutouts. They want to see the form, the fit, what goes where, and who is wearing it.

Whichever mannequin, form, or dimensional device is used, its selection must be determined by what it will do for the merchandise and how it will affect the customer's attitude towards the merchandise and the store that is selling the goods. It always comes back to the store's image.

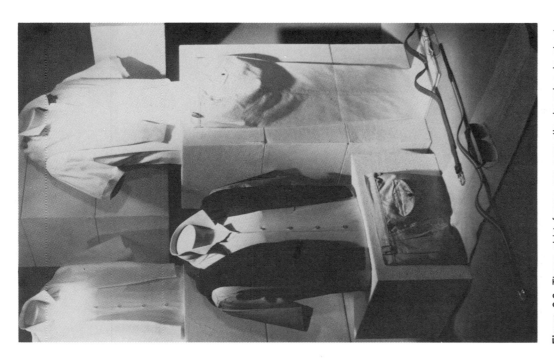

Figure 9-6. These shirt forms are casually dressing in short-sleeved sports shirts. Although the shirts have been pinned to effect a sleek, front-on view, the collars are raised for a jaunty attitude and the sweaters are draped over the shoulders in an easy-going manner. White blocks, simulating cinder block, are risers for the shirt forms as well as providing a "wall" to pin the pants on display. The composition of the dressed shirt forms, pinned pants, snaking belts, and accessories (including sunglasses) is pleasant, coordinated, yet casual. *Gimbels, New York.*

10 European Display Techniques

INTRODUCTION

Attitudes and concepts in merchandise display not only vary from country to country—they can and do vary from city to city and from store to store. There is no one right "answer." In this book, the author has tried to indicate some techniques, some "truths," some tried and tested methods and approaches. However, there is no one way that will do all and be all for every store and for every type of merchandise.

Many small stores, especially in France, Italy, Germany, and England, show their merchandise—just their merchandise—without any great effort to establish their customers' image. Their own image is established and reiterated in the merchandise they show, how much they show, and how that merchandise is shown. They usually set out their wares in simple-to-see and easy-to-relate-to arrangements. They present garments, accessories, and alternatives all together. They do not make decisions for the shopper. They do not say, "This is what you should wear!" Rather, they seem to be saying, "These garments can be worn in a variety of ways and in many different combinations. You, with your own good sense of style and what is right for you, will put together the parts that please and suit you."

Many shoppers in the United States are intimidated by the vast number of choices available to

them—the many, many possible ways to go, the quick-changing swings of fads and fashions. On the other hand, Europeans and boutique clientele, all over the world, seem to make their own decisions. Each purchase appears to be an "investment" and part of an on-going wardrobe rather than an individual "outfit."

In many cities in Europe, the "promenade" is a way of life—and a way of shopping. Stores will close on Saturday, after lunch, and sometimes remain closed until Monday at noon. The store's windows, however, will remain "open" much of the time. The lights will stay on until midnight; the merchandise, even expensive furs and silver, will remain on view through the long weekend. At night and through the weekend afternoons, it is a thing to do: to "do" the windows on the main boulevard. This activity almost seems choreographed. First, the pedestrian strolls up one side of the street; each window is examined, scrutinized, and digested—and the prices noted. The return stroll is on the other side of the street, following the same procedure. Along the way, there may be a stop for some coffee with time out to watch all the other strollers. Since the stores are all closed, no attempt is made at that time to get the strollers inside. Rather, it is a less promotional, more leisurely approach to presenting one's wares—a display truly intended to "show" the merchandise in the best possible presentation.

It is important to understand this type of shopping

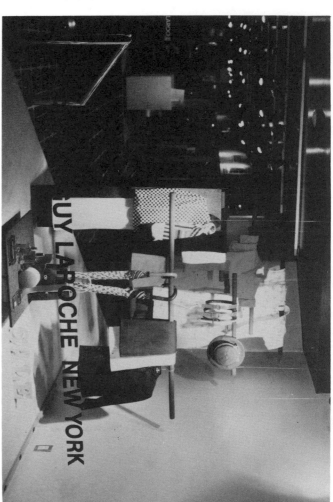

because there is a trend at present toward creating shopping streets without vehicular traffic in many urban renewal areas. These urban malls are used for sitting, strolling, and shopping. Even in bustling New York, some streets are closed to traffic at certain times of the year just to allow pedestrians to stroll the shopping streets and sidewalks more freely and leisurely. This slowdown of the tempo on Main Street is giving downtown a new look and can affect the type of displays being created.

Many shopping centers and malls, as they are designed today in the United States, do not encourage strolling. When the stores are open, they consist of large, gaping openings, ready to swallow in the passerby with little or no window presentation at all. When they are closed for the night, the view is of assorted grids, grills, and metal meshes. Some malls, however, are designed with stores that have windows, store fronts, and actual entrances. In these malls, strolling is encouraged, even after closing. The promenade is enhanced by the cafes, restaurants, and theaters that continue operating through the evenings and weekends.

With this brief introduction, it should be easier to understand these small shop or boutique-type display techniques, which are here labeled "European."

EUROPEAN TRIMMING TECHNIQUES

Although some European stores and boutiques do use mannequins (often abstract or soft-sculptured), there are some other methods of merchandise presentation in which the garment is almost completely on its own, with perhaps a little assist from a few straight pins, some tissue paper, and loving hands. Of course, these techniques—lay-down, pinup, and flying—are now practiced in American stores as well.

Lay-down Techniques

The art of lay-down is all in the folding, the pleating, and the placement of garment next to garment and of accessories next to the featured garments. It requires all the basics of good composition: color, line, texture, balance, and the ability to direct the viewer's eye from object to object in a smooth and harmonious manner. Lay-down can be used in windows, on ledges, in cases, pinned onto boards, and against walls or columns.

For a window lay-down presentation, the merchandise is arranged on the floor of the window. Often, a step or two, a platform, or a riser is added for interest or to separate groupings.

The following is an example of a typical lay-down presentation. A jacket, with a blouse or shirt folded inside, may be artfully stretched out on the top of a platform with maybe one sleeve akimbo and the cuff tucked into the jacket pocket. The skirt (or pants) could then start from under the jacket and flow down off the platform onto the floor of the window where the skirt could swirl out to its fullest, or could be rippled, or be finely pleated. The skirt (or pants) might then be crossed or banded with a selection of belts which could lead the shopper's eye over to a pair of shoes backed up with a handbag or two and several pair of well-arranged gloves. To the other side of

Figure 10-1. This lay-down type of presentation in a vertical plane also serves as an excellent "semiscreen" for an open-back window. A variety of merchandise with many alternate recommendations is presented, and the customer can pick and choose whatever pleases her. *Guy LaRoche, New York.*

the skirt (or pants) there could be an assortment, fanned out or in echelon, of other tops and scarves or neckties which would also complement the outfit being shown. There might also be some suggestions of appropriate costume jewelry, flowers, or toiletries. In a typically European display, there might also be a draper or costumer (see Chapter 11, "Fixtures") in the window—on the platform, behind the layered jacket, with a coat, hat, scarf, and maybe a pointing, rolled-up umbrella leading to the arrangement below.

This type of merchandise presentation does not suggest "image," as we usually think of it. With this type of display, it is assumed that the customer knows what is wanted and liked, and that he or she will be able to select and put together an outfit from the various alternatives suggested.

In most effective lay-down displays, a color theme is promoted and various alternate choices may be offered to tie in with a general scheme. If two or three different color "stories" are to be promoted in a single display window—or with a single basic outfit—each story could be effectively separated from the others by placing each on a different level or platform and by allowing the basic or neutral color to carry through from group to group. The major color promoted on the uppermost level could become the accent at the center level, and the color "lead" from the middle becomes the accessory color at the lowest level. Let us translate this into an actual example: A navy suit is trimmed with red on level one. On level two, a gray outfit is highlighted with the navy from level one. On level three, the red dress is trimmed with the gray from two.

Lay-down requires that the merchandise be pressed or steamed and in perfect condition—just as the merchandise should be for any presentation. Here, however, the trimmer cannot "fake it" by hoping the mannequin or form underneath will smooth out the wrinkles, or by pushing the creases aside. In this form of display, the garments are usually brought up very close to the viewer, allowing a close perusal. The buttonholes, the stitching, the matching of plaids and patterns, the meeting of the collar, the dimple in the tie—they are all up front.

The nature of the garment fabric should be "explained" by the type of lay-down used. If the fabric is soft and flowing, it should be allowed to spread out gracefully, to float or drape. If it is hard, crisp, and tailored, the lines should be sharp and precise.

Another form of lay-down is the draping of garments over furniture, on tables, or "sitting" on chairs. With this method, the body of a dress (or jacket), for example, is pinned or draped over a chair back. The sleeves are placed on the chair's arm rests or they are posed on the "lap" of the garment. The skirt (or pants) starts on the chair seat and hangs over the edge.

Hosiery or pantyhose can be used to fill in the gap between the skirt and the shoes that are sitting on the floor, looking natural and at ease. A hat can sit on top of the chair back, a scarf and/or jewelry can be shown at the neckline, and a bag can be hooked from the arm of the chair. Or, in a men's wear display, a shirt may sit against the chair back wearing a properly knotted tie. An auxiliary accessory grouping can be arranged on the floor, near the shoes. This arrangement is young and trendy and can work for separates as well as dresses—for men as well as women. Lingerie could be shown draped over a chaise lounge, or sunwear out on a beach chair. The possibilities are endless and the results should be amusing.

Pinup Techniques

Pinup techniques make use of a panel, wall, or some vertical surface onto which a garment can be pinned, shaped, and dimensionalized. A form or mannequin is not used; pads, tissue, and straight pins are. The garment is pinned onto the panel and then the tissue is crumpled and added to fill out the garment where form is needed: the bust, the shoulders, possibly in a sleeve or at the hips. Accessories are pinned on at appropriate locations; shoes are included on the floor in front of the "dressed" panel.

Humor and wit can help with this type of presentation. Since it is obvious that there is no "body," the more animated and "realistic" the position of the pinned-up garment, the better. Sleeves can be slipped into pockets or waistbands. They may be folded to hold flowers, a bag, or just wave "bye-bye." Gloves can be pinned inside the sleeves for "hands," and rolled-up tissue, slipped inside each finger, can give form and action to the glove. A shoulder bag might be slung over the shoulder. A hat might be pinned, brim down and crown out, to simulate a missing head. Pantyhose can be used to suggest legs—especially if the toes end up inside the shoes on the floor and if the shoes are properly positioned—not just set there. When the outfit includes trousers or pants, the legs can be crossed, bent, dipped, or spread for action poses. The excess fabric of the trouser leg can be tucked inside boots or shoes, or rolled in undulating waves like a French croissant, or pinned down on the floor next to the appropriate shoes. The important thing to remember here is the condition of the merchandise to be pinned. Nothing short of perfection should do! It is possible for a garment to lose an unwanted crease in a pinup technique, but do not depend on it.

Sometimes an outfit can be pinned up in an abstract geometric arrangement similar to the paintings of Piet Mondrian. It is comparable to a lay-down presentation except that it is pinned to a board and shown

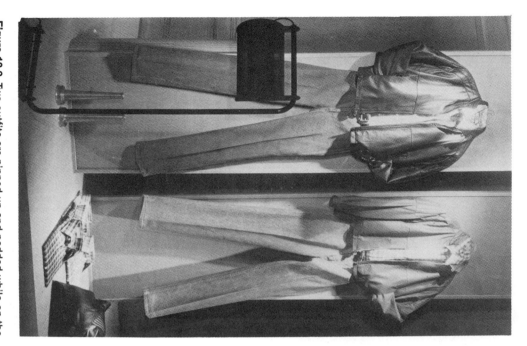

Figure 10-2. Two outfits are pinned up and padded while on the floor is a lay-down of some other costume variations. The light fixture on the left adds interest as well as a bright light on the displayed merchandise. *Saks Fifth Avenue, New York.*

vertically rather than horizontally. This type of pinup presentation is especially effective when shown on an easel with something soft, like a coat and scarf, draped off the side and leading down to an auxiliary lay-down arrangement.

Another simple, semi-pinup arrangement uses a traditional hat stand or coatrack. The garments are draped off the hooks on top, but padded, rounded out, and pinned in order to provide some feeling of depth, form, and detail. If the shoulder and front of a jacket are important, the padding should emphasize these features and the garment should be positioned on the rack to show these parts prominently. The skirt (or pants) could be pinned into the jacket so that the complete outfit is "hung" on the rack. It would also be fitting for a coat, scarf, hat, and umbrella to be hooked onto the stand, to complete the outfit.

Ideally, the use of pinup or lay-down techniques should alternate with mannequin presentations for a change of pace, for a different look, to surprise and amuse the customer, and to suggest that something new is happening. Using only pinup or lay-down methods can be as dull as using the same mannequins or forms over and over again. Either of these two techniques could be used in conjunction with a mannequin or a dressmaker form. Variety and change are the essence of fashion and fashion presentation.

⭑ **Flying Techniques**

Flying is a display technique whereby the merchandise is pulled, stretched, and manipulated by means of almost-invisible fishing line or very fine piano wire. The wire is attached to the hem, sleeve, shoulder, etc., of the garment and then pulled back and secured by pinning or nailing it into the ceiling, floor, a side wall, or back wall. This stretching pulls the garment into abstract shapes with little resemblance to the way it would look in actual use. Flying basically provides an angular and crisp presentation which could be very effective for active sportswear, separates, and fun and trendy merchandise, but which could be a detriment to soft, flowing garments when the fabric is pulled taut.

In this type of display, the merchandise "flies" and floats in the open window space. One garment often visually overlaps or flies in front of another garment. The viewer sees a pattern of bits and pieces, but not quite a whole garment or an outfit. Flying is not recommended if the merchandise to be presented is an outfit made up of parts and accessories. It works better where a line of merchandise is shown: all sweaters, all slips, all skirts. It can be effective if the main feature of the merchandise is pattern or color—not shape or form. A window of flying towels or pillows and/or pillowcases—scarves, caftans, or T-shirts—could be a change-of-pace display that works when done well.

Figure 10-3. In this clever and effective combination of flying and pinup merchandise presentation for active sportswear, there is lots of free action, humor, and accessorizing. In this abstract display, the forms and mannequins may be missing, but the merchandise is scoring points. *Macy's, New York.*

11 Fixtures

A store without fixtures is a store that is not finished! It is not ready to accept, hold, stock, and show merchandise. It is not equipped to transact sales, take money and make change, and wrap the purchase. There would be nothing in the store to tell you what is being offered, what the selection is, and what alternatives and/or accessories are available. Simply, a fixtureless store is one that is not equipped to function. (Mannequins, figures, and forms are also fixtures of a kind—a very important kind. Thus, they have rated separate chapters. Please refer to Chapters 8 and 9.)

WINDOW FIXTURES

A display window without fixtures is merely a box with walls—one of which happens to be all glass. The merchandise placed in a fixtureless window probably will have to be laid out on the window floor, all at the same level, all in the same line—unless the displayperson knows about flying techniques. (See Chapter 10.) Even when pinning, draping, and shaping a garment, a fixture has to be present to hold the merchandise. Fixtures are not necessarily only frames, stands, easels, rods extending up from weighted bases, hangers, and racks made of chrome, wood, or lucite. Fixtures can be many things—things that were never originally con-

ceived to raise up, hold, show, and contain a selection of merchandise.

Fixturing can be compared to interior designing. It is the selection of the "furniture" for the selling area of an establishment. It is this selection of the right "accessories," and details that creates the personality or the image of that selling space. A sofa, which might dominate a living room, might be compared to the larger stocking racks, gondolas, or perimeter wall hang-rods. Just as a sofa ordinarily will seat the most guests and disappear under the load, so will these larger fixtures carry the most stock and become invisible under and behind the merchandise they carry. T-stands, counter fixtures, and specialty units are the "individual chairs," and they show a smaller and more select group of merchandise. The featured displays; the displayers; the drapers, costumers, and valets; the merchandise pinned on the fascia—these are the "pictures on the wall" and the "accessories" that add charm, life, excitement, and personality to an environment.

There are certain "basic" fixtures used in window display, including stands; platforms and elevations; costumers, drapers, and valets; easels; and pipe racks. It must be remembered, however, that these fixtures may also be used in the interior of the store, on ledges or on the selling floor.

These basic fixtures can be metal or plastic fabrica-

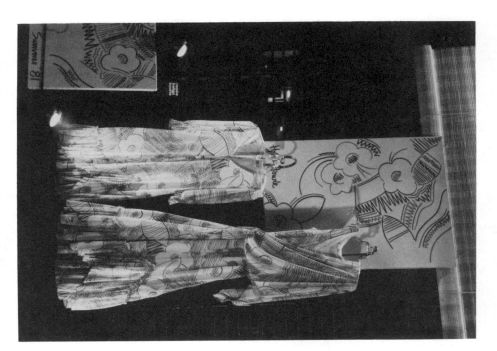

Figure 11-1. Two drapers are used to show the two gowns made of a special fabric. An enlarged drawing of the fabric print becomes a background in this open-back window and also provides the design for the poster shown in the lower left of the window. The height of the drapers is adjusted to show "the long and the short" of the same dress design. *Helga Howie, New York.*

tions specifically designed to hold or elevate a pair of shoes, a shirt, or a skirt; or they can be props or decorative elements which can work effectively as drapers or costumers. These fixtures elevate merchandise; they hold up and/or give body or form to the merchandise.

Stands

The stand is a very widely used, basic fixture. It comes with an assortment of tops that may be slipped interchangeably into an adjustable rod set into a weighted base. The base sits securely on the floor (or on a platform, elevation, counter, or ledge) and the rod may be adjusted to the desired height for presenting the merchandise.

The top element can be a straight rod, like the top stroke of a "T," and can hold an assortment of scarves, ties, towels, or any soft, drapable merchandise. The *hanger top* consists of a gentle curve (like the arc of a coat or dress hanger), and serves to show a dress, sweater, jacket, and so on. This fixture is also called a *draper*. Another kind of hanger top ends with two reverse curves (like a handle-bar moustache). It serves to display lingerie and other sleeveless garments that hang from straps and do not have sleeves or shoulders to keep the garment from slipping off a regular hanger top. There are also special attachments for hosiery, shirts, shoes, millinery, etc.

Stands are usually used in a variety or assortment window as a means of building up—from the glass line to the back of the display window—a variety of merchandise. The smaller items are set low and up front. As they get larger, the merchandise gets higher and set farther back. A truly elegant and beautifully designed base can provide a stand that will enhance, hold up, and provide a drape-away point for a lovely piece of lingerie in a one-item or a related merchandise window presentation. (See Chapter 14 for a discussion of "Types of Display.")

Platforms and Elevations

Platforms and elevations are buildups used to provide interest and to help separate merchandise in mass displays. They can be cubes, cylinders, or saddles of any size or shape. Elevations can be tables and chairs and other pieces of furniture so long as they can be used to raise up a mannequin, a form, a stand, or an arrangement of merchandise. An elevation can also be a platform that covers a large portion of a display floor.

Platforms or elevations are used to separate mannequins in a window or on a traffic aisle inside a store, so that each figure can be seen in its own "space," at its own level. The use of elevations is also discussed in Chapter 14 under "Buildups."

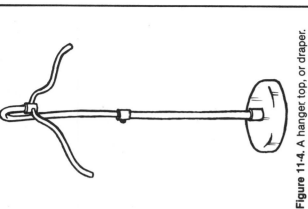

Figure 11-4. A hanger top, or draper.

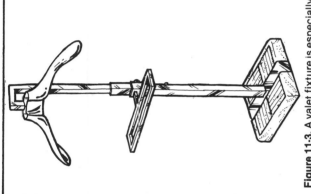

Figure 11-3. A valet fixture is especially useful for men's wear.

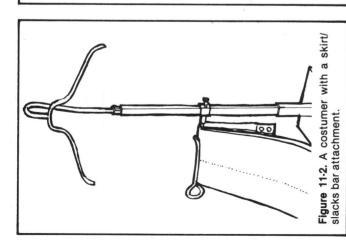

Figure 11-2. A costumer with a skirt/slacks bar attachment.

Costumers, Valets, and Drapers

Costumers, valets, and drapers are important fixtures that show coordinated or complete costumes on a single stand.

The costumer is a free-standing fixturing unit used on a floor, ledge, or counter, depending on its size. It has a hanger set onto the top of an adjustable upright, which is set into a weighted base. The unit usually has a skirt bar which makes it possible to display a pair of pants or a skirt under a blouse or jacket.

The valet, very similar to the costumer, has a heavier and wider hanger along with a slacks bar, which makes this fixture especially useful for men's wear. As in most fixtures designed today, the hanger and the slacks or skirt bar attachment is adjustable, riding up or down on the vertical rod. Sometimes, it includes a shoe platform raised off the floor, but still attached to the same vertical rod on which all the other pieces are assembled. When using either fixture, a scarf, jewelry, a handbag, a tie, and maybe even a hat can be draped over the various parts of the collected costume. In a specialty store, a boutique, a one-item-type window, or even a related merchandise presentation in a limited space, the costumer and valet are excellent and reliable fixtures.

The draper is also a hanger on a stand, adjustable in height, but without a skirt or slacks bar. It is usually smaller than the costumer and the valet; a compact unit meant to be used on a counter or on a buildup. It may be produced with a bendable armature that allows the sleeves of the garment to be positioned after the jacket, blouse, or sweater is hung or buttoned over the top hanger. Coordinating skirts or slacks can be laid out at the base of the draper.

Easels

An easel is an adjustable folding frame or tripod. Small easels may be used in a display or in a store window to hold a price card or message. Larger ones are designed specifically to hold a shirt and tie at an angle. A very large artist's easel is also used; a fully accessorized outfit, pinned up on a board can be placed on this size easel, as is done with an artist's painting in progress. (See Figure 8-10.) A coat, bag, and/or scarf can be draped from the top of the easel.

In some "arty" type operation, this very recognizable unit will do wonderfully well at suggesting the unique and aesthetic design value of the merchandise. In the one-item display, the single garment is shown as a "masterpiece"—"one-of-a-kind." In a related merchandise display, an ensemble is gathered together and presented as a total composition. The outfit may be labeled "The Designer's Touch," "The Choice Collection," "Composition in Blue" (or in "Red," "Gray," etc.).

Easels also serve effectively off of aisles, as a lead-in to a department or special shop. They can be companions to mannequins on ledges, on T-wall platforms, or on islands to show alternate choices or other accessories. The smaller easels serve as supports; they present merchandise in a perpendicular plane and keep small items, like handbags, books, prepackaged goods, and such, upright or at a slight incline for better viewing.

Figure 11-5. Here, the easel becomes the major prop in the display and also provides the novel idea of presenting the mannequins as three-dimensional "fashion sketches" by setting them against oversized canvases. This total presentation ties in with the "art" quality card which reads "Lingerie as Art." *Bloomingdale's, New York.*

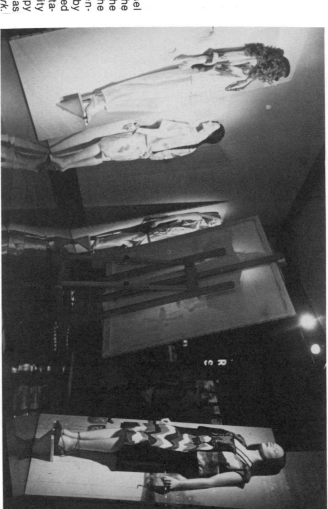

Pipe Racks

A pipe rack is a utilitarian fixture, with wheels, made of round tubing and resembling an inverted "U." It may have a flat wooden base to which the wheels are attached.

Sometimes, for special attention or to promote a clearance sale or to suggest a great diversity of merchandise (in a line-of-goods window, for example), a pipe rack or a simple A-frame rack will be used in a window. It really does not "show off" the merchandise. It is another recognizable symbol for workshops, studios, ateliers, and other places where clothes are made and hung on the rack, ready to go. It is also used as a vehicle to move clothes from one place to another. The pipe rack can suggest clothes in the process of being made or clothes being delivered. It also has a negative connotation, suggesting "cheap," "discount," or "mass production." If the store is saying, "We are getting rid of everything—everything goes," the pipe rack in the window will imply the drastic price reductions and the movement out of the store. This is really an example of using a fixture as a "prop" rather than simply as a showing or holding device.

COUNTER FIXTURES

Counters are important areas within the store in need of fixturing. They are points of purchase, where sales are actually made. It is here that the customer can be convinced—have his or her mind changed or miss the point entirely. The counter is the selling field where the "give and take" between salesperson and customer can be improved and the sale expedited by the use of good and sufficient counter fixtures.

The counter fixture is small; the base is balanced or weighted to keep the fixture from toppling when fully stocked. Ideally, a fixture is no more than 24-inches tall and rarely goes over 36 inches when adjusted to its greatest height. A taller one would be an insurmountable barrier to the give and take between customer and salesperson.

One of the major problems in retailing today is theft. The counter fixture puts the merchandise right out on top of the counter and invites the potential customer to touch it, try it, and eventually purchase it. However, fully dressed counter fixtures that extend much higher than the salesperson's eye level are invitations to shoplifters to take without being seen. The size of the counter fixture is crucially important.

Assorted Counter Fixtures

The counter fixture is a displayer as well as a holder of merchandise. There are a great many fixtures available today that are designed to show and hold specific merchandise, although a displayperson could make one fixture "do" for another. Assorted fixture tops are made to hold certain items or accessories in a way that will show them off to their best advantage and keep them from slipping off, or in the case of "pilfer-proof" units, keep them from "walking off." Figures 11-7

Figure 11-6. A pipe rack is a theatrical prop and, here, it also carries a whole collection of multicolored and multistyled tops and bottoms. The amusing faces are attached over the pinned and padded outfits which are hung from the pipe racks. The only mannequin used (fourth from left) makes a break with the repetition of the display pattern. *Ohrbach's, New York.*

Figure 11-7, *left.* A tie displayer.

Figure 11-8, *center.* A costumer with a hanger set on the top of an adjustable upright.

Figure 11-9, *right.* A flex-arm displayer. The hanger continues down into flexible cable "arms" which can be bent into animated positions.

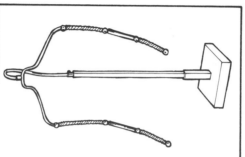
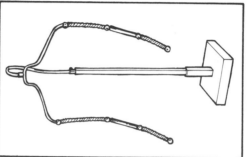
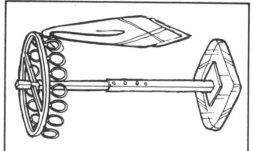

Figure 11-10, *left.* A hook stand, a counter unit that can hold bagged or carded merchandise, chains, etc.

Figure 11-11, *center.* A rope displayer, a counter unit designed to show necklaces, chains, etc.

Figure 11-12, *right.* A circular, spinning, scarf wheel.

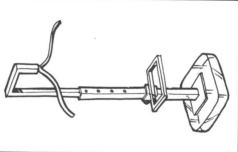
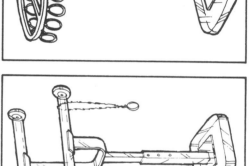
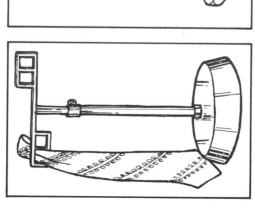
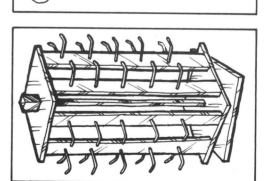

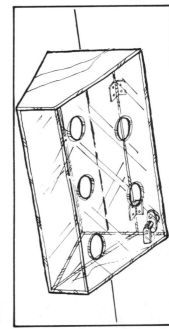
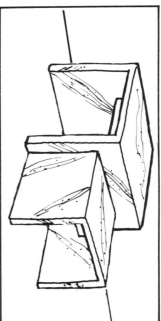

through 11-13 are some of the usual counter fixtures required to furnish counters in various departments adequately.

There are other "furnishings" required and used on counters. In cosmetic and jewelry areas, a *mirror* is a must. A customer may try something on and want to see how it looks. A hand mirror can and probably will disappear. A mirror on a nearby wall or column might do, but it means the customer must leave the sphere of influence and the watchful eye of the salesperson. A weighted mirror, with an adjustable or tiltable frame is needed. A *lamp* will usually be close by. The lamp, with a peachy, incandescent light emanating from it, adds warmth necessary to the sale of cosmetics, perfumes, and sometimes, jewelry. The lamp also supplies a high point to an otherwise horizontal look, and a highlight to the general, overall lighting around the counter.

Trays or bins may be useful adjuncts to counter selling. *Risers, saddles,* or small *elevations* will add interest to a display of small items (such as toiletries and cosmetics). More and more often, a bowl of fresh *flowers* or a thriving *plant* is becoming a counter "fixture." It enhances the merchandise, it relaxes the customer, adds to the ambience, and affects the eventual sale.

"Pilfer-Proof" Fixtures

In pilfer-proof fixturing, the basic concept is to lock in the merchandise. The customer can see it, but cannot freely touch it. For example, perfume testers are placed on counters, and the customer is invited to spray herself with any of the featured perfumes. Large, "dummy" bottles of perfume, filled with colored water, may be placed on the counter, next to the tester, but the actual perfume for sale is kept below—inside the counter.

Better jewelry and handbags are now being locked in fixtures that require a salesperson with a key to open and to take the item out of the fixture for the customer's closer examination. Merchandise in pilfer-proof fixtures should not look as though it has been locked up with chains and padlocks. The security measures should be artfully camouflaged and discrete.

LEDGE FIXTURES

Ledge fixtures are larger and more imposing than counter fixtures. Some are placed where the customer cannot reach or touch. A costumer or a valet, mentioned earlier as window fixtures, will show a completely accessorized outfit on a ledge, as will a torso, three-quarter and even, possibly, a dressmaker form. These fixtures require a space at least 5-feet high.

Figure 11-13, *top.* A security case, or a pilfer-proof case.
Figure 11-14, *bottom.* Risers and saddles are buildups, groupings of geometric shapes and forms to create multilevels for the display of small associated merchandise, such as cosmetics, toiletries, small leather goods, and shoes.

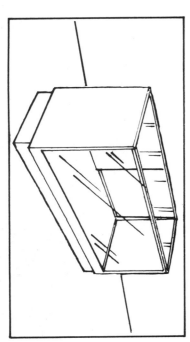

Figure 11-15, *top.* Ledge fixtures are being used here to display merchandise above a bin unit.
Figure 11-16, *bottom.* A typical showcase with glass top and front.

Some ledge fixtures are set at or above eye level and are not necessarily barriers or screens. When the displayperson feels a particular ledge unit can become a safety shield for pilferers, he or she should trim the unit, leaving look-through areas in the merchandise arrangement or, alternatively, should select a lower unit. The same fixture used to top the ledge will also be found on top of the upholstered or laminated cubes and platforms that are interspersed on the selling floor. If the unit is set on or adjacent to an aisle, it should be high enough to be seen through or over the traffic, but not so high as to block the merchandise presentation inside the department or shop.

Units that show and hold merchandise on counters, platforms, or ledges within reach of the customer require constant care and attention. The merchandise will be handled and manhandled—and a softly draped scarf over an outfit on a draper will be fingered and moved about. This type of display is an open invitation to touch, and the displayperson or the salespersons in the area must be responsible for the upkeep of the merchandise on view. More and more stores now have a visual merchandise program set up to help their sales staffs understand how important it is for all merchandise to be set up at its visual best. The displayperson's job does not end with setting up the display. It requires follow-up attention and "repairing" of displays that are within touching distance. Some stores are enclosing their displays within glass or plastic cases in order to prevent the need for some of that upkeep.

FLOOR AND FREE-STANDING FIXTURES

Floor and free-standing fixtures are units designed to hold and show merchandise out on the floor—where the traffic is. The following major types of fixtures are discussed below: the counter or showcase, round rack, T-stand, quad rack or four-way face-out, as well as other types of floor fixtures.

Counters or Showcases

The counter or showcase is out on the floor and stands on its own, but is not traditionally part of what is called "floor fixturing." These pieces of furniture, for showing, holding, and selling merchandise, combine the storage capacities of a cabinet, the selling surface of a table, and the display potentials of a shadow box. The unit may be made entirely of glass, with everything under the selling surface on view. It can be all wood, laminated, or combined with metal and look like a closed cabinet.

Until the end of the 1960's, the counter or showcase was all but rooted into the floor of the selling area; large, immovable units that were set out to stay. With stores in need of greater mobility, flexibility, and the ability to rearrange their layout as merchandise changed, the counters become lighter looking and, in some instances, almost table-like. The feeling of "floating" furniture has taken over on many of the main floors of department and specialty stores. To reinforce the light, airy look, some units have indirect lights located below the counters in order to light the floor beneath.

Round Racks

More traditionally a floor fixture than the counter, and probably the "granddaddy" of commonly used fixtures, is the round rack. This unit usually consists of a circular hang-rod, 3 feet in diameter, raised anywhere from 45 inches to over 6 feet off the ground. It is set on an adjustable upright that it securely attached to a wide, weighted base, which is stable and holds the floor, even when fully weighed down with merchandise.

The round rack, when fully stocked, carries almost 115 inches of shoulder-out merchandise in an area less than 5 feet by 5 feet. This is, at the same time, the big advantage as well as the big disadvantage. It is good to be able to show a great deal of merchandise in a small area of selling space, but all with shoulders out? This disadvantage of not being able to see more than the sleeve of a garment can be remedied by setting a draper on top of the round rack, as a superstructure, and displaying fully one of the garments from the collection sandwiched in below. (See Figure 11-18.)

For some classifications of merchandise, the round rack may be ordered with two or even three tiers of hang-rods: children's wear, bras and panties, bikini swimsuits, prepackaged goods, etc. Merchandise should not be indiscriminantly loaded onto the round rack just because it is a mass unit. It should be carefully arranged by color and style. (The dressing and stocking of fixtures is discussed in the next chapter.)

T-stands

At the other end of floor fixturing from the round rack is the T-stand. It is a specialty unit—a highlighter or accent piece. It is small, light, carries a minimal amount of merchandise, and makes "big" fashion statements. Originally, the T-stand was simply an upright rod attached to a heavy base with a cross bar (like the top of a "T") on top of which about a dozen garments could be hung. These "lightweights" were set out on the selling floor to show what was new and what was being featured. They were, and still are, used along an aisle to

Figure 11-17, *left.* A round rack.

Figure 11-18, *center.* The super-structure on top of this round rack is used to display one of the garments stocked below.

Figure 11-19, *right.* A T-stand with one straight arm and one waterfall.

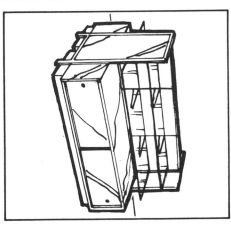

Figure 11-20, *left.* A quad rack, or four-way face-out.

Figure 11-21, *right.* A typical gondola, with adjustable shelves and storage space below.

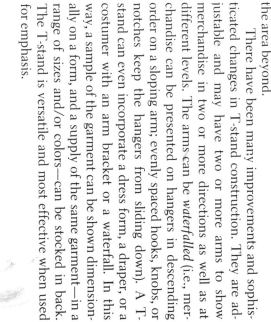
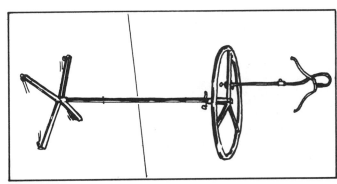
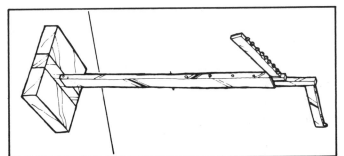
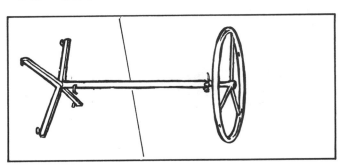
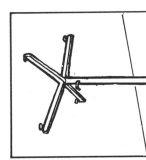

explain what kind of merchandise is being housed in the area beyond.

There have been many improvements and sophisticated changes in T-stand construction. They are adjustable and may have two or more arms to show merchandise in two or more directions as well as at different levels. The arms can be *waterfalled* (i.e., merchandise can be presented on hangers in descending order on a sloping arm; evenly spaced hooks, knobs, or notches keep the hangers from sliding down). A T-stand can even incorporate a dress form, a draper, or a costumer with an arm bracket or a waterfall. In this way, a sample of the garment can be shown dimensionally on a form, and a supply of the same garment—in a range of sizes and/or colors—can be stocked in back. The T-stand is versatile and most effective when used for emphasis.

Quad Racks or Four-Way Face-Outs

This unit stands somewhere between the T-stand and the round rack, in use and in size, on the selling floor. Basically, it is a four-armed fixture with each arm extending out from a central core. Most often, each arm is turned out at right angles from the center or upright; in a floor plan, this configuration will look like a pinwheel or a swastika. The idea behind this design is that, from certain angles or approaches, the customer sees a "shoulder-out" arrangement of the collected merchandise, but when coming at the unit straight on, the facing arm will present a "face-out" or "front-forward" view. The potential customer will be able to

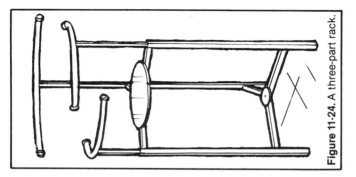

Figure 11-24. A three-part rack.

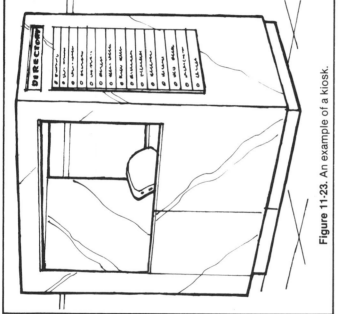

Figure 11-23. An example of a kiosk.

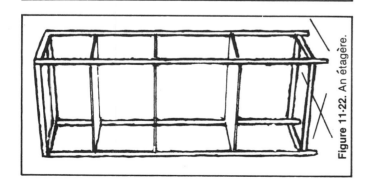

Figure 11-22. An étagère.

see the front of the first garment on that particular arm. The arms that extend out in the four directions are often individually adjustable, up and down, so that the merchandise can be seen at four different levels. Some manufacturers are making quad racks in which some or all of the arms are waterfalled. The viewer sees not only the entire front of the first garment, but can see the upper part of the following garments in ascending order.

Because the quad-rack unit is designed with four separate views, it is ideal for showing separates or coordinate fashions. On one fixture, it is possible to show skirts, pants, jackets, and blouses that go together. The pants should be hung from the highest arm to accommodate the extra hang space necessary, and the blouses (or vests or sweaters) will probably be hung on the lowest level. The four arms can also be used to tell coordinated color stories. This will be discussed in the next chapter.

Other Floor Fixtures

A *gondola* is a long, flat-bottomed merchandiser, usually with straight, upright sides. This fixture is most commonly designed with adjustable shelves combined with a table surface and storage cabinet or drawer space below. Since it has a central dividing panel (perpendicular to and equidistant from the end uprights), the gondola is two-sided. The unit is frequently used in groups on the selling floor and oriented perpendicular to the traffic aisles. The ends of the gondolas can be turned into valuable display areas. Gondolas are

often found in linen, housewares, china and glass departments, etc., because the shelves are particularly adaptable to stackable and prepackaged merchandise.

A French term for a displayer shelf unit, an *étagère* is an open, multishelf, displayer fixture, most often used to show china, glass, home furnishings accessories, and small gifts.

A *kiosk* is a self-standing booth or structure on the selling floor which may accommodate a salesperson as well as merchandise. It can be used as a miniboutique, an outpost, or for an enclosed information or special-events desk.

An *outpost* is a free-standing, self-contained selling unit that contains a stock of a given type of merchandise, along with display and signing relevant to that merchandise. The outpost features merchandise not ordinarily sold in the department in which it is set up (e.g., a cosmetics outpost in a junior department; handbags in a shoe department).

A *three-part rack* is a round rack comprised of three separate but equal arcs. Usually, the height of each arc is individually adjustable. It is more effective for showing separates, coordinates, or assorted colors and styles of a particular item.

A *C-rack* is basically one-half of a round rack. (It is also called a *semicircular rack* or a *half-circle rack*.) It consists of an arc-shaped base with a similarly arc-shaped hang-rod above it. The two arcs are connected by two adjustable uprights. A pair of C-racks can be combined to form a two-part round rack. If each arc of the two-part round rack is set at a different height, it is possible to get greater variety in the merchandise presentation. Two C-racks, placed end to opposing end, make an S-rack, which also has a greater potential for variety of merchandise presentation. The C-rack can be used for dresses, coats, suits, and coordinates.

A *vitrine* is a glass-enclosed, shelved cabinet or showcase. It often has glass shelves and partitions. A vitrine is usually a decorative piece, sometimes made to look antique. Like the étagère, it is used to display small, "precious" items or accessories.

A *spiral costumer* is a corkscrewing or descending waterfall extended out from a central upright or post. The merchandise is visible from all around (360 degrees), but the presentation is essentially "shoulders out," with an occasional glimpse of the front of some of the merchandise.

SELECTING A FIXTURE

In selecting a fixture to use on the selling floor, there are certain criteria or expectations the displayperson may have with regard to making that selection. The criteria include appearance, construction, end use, upkeep, and finishes.

Appearance

How does the fixture look on the floor? Does it go with the architecture and interior design of the area—the "look," the period—with the other fixtures and furniture already selected or in use? If the interior of the shop attempts to be "quaint and charming" (Early American, for example), a shiny, slick, chrome fixture would be shockingly out of place and out of character. A weathered wood unit or some other natural or "antique" type piece would be more fitting, more in keeping with the established image. The new fixture would also have to be in scale and in proportion to the area.

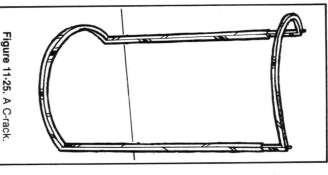

Figure 11-25. A C-rack.

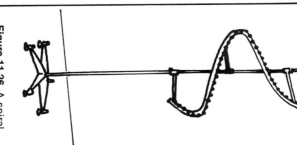

Figure 11-26. A spiral costumer.

Construction

Is the unit flexible? Is it adjustable? Can the arms that hold the display or stocked merchandise be raised or lowered as hemlines and fashions dictate? Can the fixture be adapted for use with different types of merchandise if the shop is a seasonal one and sells anything from swimsuits to full-length stormcoats—and everything in between? Are the parts or elements of the fixture rearrangeable and adaptable? It is not absolutely necessary that one fixture do everything, but in a small shop with a limited fixture budget, the more versatile the fixture, the better.

End Use

Ask yourself the following questions to determine if the fixture meets the intended end use: Does the unit make full use of the valuable area of the selling floor that the fixture will occupy? Does it hold as much merchandise and show it in the most desirable manner? Can the unit be adjusted to double or triple hang, if the merchandise is small (e.g., children's wear) or short merchandise is small (e.g., shorts, miniskirts, etc.), or can the hang levels be varied for variety and interest? Is there a way of displaying in all the unused "air space" above the unit, an area that can be seen from many parts of the shop but often goes unused? Is the unit still low enough and open enough to discourage pilferage?

What is the display value of the fixture? Does it have maximum merchandise exposure? Is there some "front-out" viewing of the collected stock? Can the featured garment be dressed and accessorized? Does the fixture lend itself to creating color and style excitement? Does it allow for the coordination and combination of merchandise? Does it "show and sell"?

Is the unit a self-selector, one that the customer can "shop" by himself or herself and still find what is being looked for? Is it self-explanatory? Can the merchandise be removed and replaced on the fixture without too much difficulty for the customer? Does the fixture contain and hold the merchandise—safely and securely—with few ill effects to the merchandise, or does it create "as is" merchandise by increasing wear and tear?

Upkeep

Is the fixture serviceable, dependable, reliable, and safe? Will it stand and not topple when loaded with merchandise or used as a swing by a customer's child? Does it require constant care, repair, polishing, and housekeeping? Are the parts replaceable and easy to get? How good, how reliable, how dependable is the manufacturer/supplier? Will they stand behind their product with some sort of warranty?

Finishes

What the fixture is constructed of and how it is finished will not only affect its "floor life," but its appearance on the floor.

Chrome is currently the most popular finish for fixtures used for counters, floors, and walls. It is made by electroplating chromium onto another metal. Stronger and often superior fixtures have a base of steel with an electrolytic deposit of chromium on it. Fixtures can also be made of brass or nickel and then given the bright, silvery, chrome finish. *Polished chrome* and *mirror chrome* are only two of the standard names for this shiny finish. The more care given to the preparation of the welded steel, nickel, or brass—the polishing and cleaning of the raw metal framework—the better the chrome finish will be.

Generally, chrome fixtures can be moderate in cost and are usually quite durable. A good finish is uniform, smooth, unblemished, and without the pinkish or coppery discolorations that may occur in welded corners. Chrome-plating does not require an outer lacquer coating to prevent discoloration or tarnishing from oxidation as other finishes may require. A chrome finish will resist scratching and scarring from normal use, such as stacking and moving metal hangers along chrome hang-rods. It is a popular look in department store fixturing.

A variety of finishes in chrome is available. They are referred to as antique, rubbed, satin, and brushed finishes. The surface to be chrome-plated is first treated with an abrasive material to roughen it. This, in turn, will tend to dull the shine on the final chrome-plated surface, but will still maintain the silvery quality. These duller and more satiny looks can be quite elegant and are considered more "masculine" than the usual high shine. With the addition of some color rubs, the resulting toned-down and deeper silvery-gray surfaces are referred to as either a stainless-steel finish or a pewter finish.

Nickel-plated surfaces are similar in appearance to chrome-plated surfaces, but that is about as far as it goes. It is not as durable or efficient a finish; it will oxidize and discolor after some period of exposure to

the air. Nickel does require a coat of lacquer to seal the finish and protect it from air and moisture. As with most metals treated with a coating of lacquer, it will eventually scratch and scar—the air will get through — and there will be discoloration. Nickel-plating is not frequently used for better fixtures. The nickel finish may have a yellowish cast when compared to the cool, silvery-blue color of chrome.

Brass fixture finishes are second in popularity to chrome, but this finish does need extra preparation and care. The bright, golden gleam of a brass finish can be applied over steel or nickel, or even on soft brass itself. Brass metal, not the finish, is rarely used to make large floor fixtures, though it is used in counter fixture construction. The metal is too soft and too easily scarred, dented, or bent. When a brass-look is desired, a sturdy and dependable steel, is usually brass-plated.

Brass finishes are subject to oxidation and air discoloration, just as brass metal is. Lacquer must be applied to seal it. Harder, more scratch-resistant lacquer finishes are "bake-dried" in ovens rather than dried in the air as with most other coatings. The brass finish is only as durable as the lacquer coating on it; once the protective coating is nicked or scratched, it no longer protects the finish. Air gets through and tarnishing begins. Dark brown lines and spots develop where the lacquer was rubbed away by the erosive movement of hangers, metal clips, and such. Some manufacturers produce brass-finished fixtures that feature chrome hang rods or metal arms where there is constant rubbing and friction. The fixture "glows" because most of it is in brass, but the "working" parts are protected in chrome.

Brass is also available in satin finishes; soft, low-luster finishes which can be very smart, elegant, and particularly attractive in wood-filled men's departments. Deep walnut and mahogany tones are enhanced by rubbed, antiqued, darker brass finishes. Creamy whites and very light neutral tones look even more refined with the soft gleam of satin-finished brass—very feminine and very expensive looking.

Copper and *bronze* finishes also need special care, special handling, and special lighting on the selling floor, if they are to resemble copper or brass closely. A copper finish tends to be a pink or rusty-gold color; the bronze is often brown and dark with just a mere metallic glint. On the selling floor, bronze may go black and lifeless, and copper may become dull. These finishes must also be protected with a baked-on coat of lacquer if they are to resist discoloration. The oxidation, however, would not be as obvious because of their darker and duller finishes.

Both finishes are usually "special order," i.e., they must be ordered. They are more expensive to fabricate and no way as foolproof as chrome-plating. The color of the copper and bronze may vary from plating run to plating run, and thus a group of bronze counter fixtures could go from light to dark brown over the series of plating runs it would take to complete the whole order. These two finishes, in the right areas, with the right lighting, and on or near the right colors, can be very different and fashionable. A copper finish goes well with natural, light woods and could create an earthy, traditional, provincial, or masculine setting.

Painted finishes include baked enamel, lacquered, and epoxy paint finishes. All of these methods are used to create fixtures with color. The metal or wood that is to be colored has to be cleaned, sealed, primed, and prepared before being given the particular color coating, and allowed to dry in specially heat-maintained ovens or kilns.

More and more colored units are appearing in children's, junior, and active sportswear shops and/or departments. They are also becoming increasingly popular in hardware, gourmet, and kitchen supply areas. For many years, painted fixtures were white, black, or metallic gold, but today there is no limit to the range of colors available. The use of colored fixtures adds to the ambience of a shop or area, cuts down on the sharp and sometimes shrill quality of chrome, and creates a "unique" or very fashion-oriented statement. How and where one uses color on fixtures will depend largely on the type of merchandise involved. Most painted finishes will eventually scar, scratch, or scrape off. Enamel painting is the cheapest and least durable finish, but even enamel can be made more efficient if it is applied electrostatically.

12 Dressing Fixtures

Stores and even departments in the same store may vary in format and image, but there are certain methods that are generally followed for dressing fixtures with the merchandise they are to hold and display. Some stores will display their merchandise by size, and in that size arrangement will show a variety of styles, patterns, and colors. Other stores or departments will show by color or by pattern and style. In the latter situations, it is simpler to get a good, sharp merchandise presentation as well as a pleasant, overall ambience in the selling space. It is not quite as simple when the merchandise is varied and multicolored, multipatterned, long and short, and in between.

T-STANDS

The T-stand is an aisle-facer. It is a feature presentation unit that should be trimmed lightly and emphasize a look, a color, or a special style. It is even more effective if it is located near a mannequin where the garment is shown dimensionally. If there are spacers on the arms, only one hanger per hook should be used, and all the hangers should be the same. (See Figure 11-19.)

Whether the T-stand has a simple, straight arm at the top or an angled waterfall, the garment that faces out toward the approaching shopper should be dressed; this lead garment should be completely trimmed. If the T-stand is showing navy suits and the skirt is clipped onto the jacket hanger, a coordinating blouse should be shown under the jacket of the first suit. There could be a scarf tied on, a piece of costume jewelry, and maybe even a shoulder bag. The first garment can almost be treated as if it were a costumer, and a special hanger might be used on the lead garment to allow more of the skirt (or pants) to show below the jacket. Some T-stands are fashioned with a draper or dress form as part of the unit.

If this navy suit is also available in gray and red, then all three colors might be shown on the single T-stand—the lead garment making the most effective statement for the design as well as the area. The red garment might have the most attention-getting color, but if navy is the color being presented in this area, the front outfit should be navy, followed by the gray, with the red garment bringing up the rear. If a descending waterfall arm is used on the T-stand, the lower garments should be navy, followed by gray, and ending with the red on top. The navy garment would get the full front-dressed treatment.

If blouses or sportswear—all of the same design, but in assorted colors—were to be shown on a T-stand with a waterfall, the usual technique would be to follow the rainbow and go from the neutral off-whites to cream and ivory; to beige-tan and brown into the warm colors—yellow, gold, orange, peach, rust, pink, red, cerise, lavender, and violet; and then into the cool colors, ending up with blues, greens, grays, and black.

Now, that is a lot of color for a little T-stand to hold; so limit the amount of merchandise and the colors on each T-stand, but follow the basic scheme. Again, if the area is featuring a lot of red, the lead garment should be red; then go on to the red-violets; into the violets, blues, greens; then yellow, orange, and so forth. It is a logical use of the rainbow—adapted to the promotion. Following the spectrum works! People think of and see colors in that pattern and, as mentioned in Chapter 5, the analogous color scheme is an easy one to live with; neighboring colors coexist and lend each other character and color.

A final reminder: Merchandise on T-stands should be changed frequently. There should always be a new "show."

STOCK-HOLDERS

Stock-holders are "bread-and-butter" fixtures, the "workhorses" that actually hold the selling stock. They may display—and they should display—but primarily they are "stockers." Two examples are the quad rack and the round rack.

Almost all stock-holders are used in the following manner: Merchandise is hung from left to right—the way most people read or scan—from the lightest colors to the deepest, from the warmest to the coolest, from the smallest sizes to the largest. Color is the big "come-on," the single most important attention-getter. When a variety of styles are shown, the assorted styles are grouped by color. If there are six styles of blouses available in red, then style A, in red, will be hung from the smallest to the largest size available; followed by style B (also in red), sized from smallest to largest; and so on until all six styles are shown in red. The procedure will begin anew with the next color available that follows red: a red-violet, a lavender, a purple, or whatever. Remember, this is not a rule! This is a technique that does work in stores involved with mass-merchandising and with a popular appeal. It works where there is a great deal of merchandise to get out on the selling floor and a minimum of sales help to fetch, carry, and answer questions.

Quad Racks

The quad rack or four-way face-out fixture is usually placed just past the T-stand, in the front of the selling area. Though the quad rack is a "mass merchandiser" —when and where the merchandise and stock permit—it is used to show coordinates or special promotional merchandise. The design of the quad rack allows four frontal views of the displayed garments. From whatever angle the customer approaches, one arm should basically be facing in that direction. (See Figure 11-20.)

The main idea of showing coordinates on the single fixture, with each arm holding another component of the outfit, is that from this single fixture a customer can put together a complete ensemble of three or four parts. All the parts that are displayed "go together," are grouped by color and by size, and unless a particular piece is not available on the rack in the customer's size, the customer can make his or her selection and bring it to the cash/wrap desk without any sales assistance. Again, the lead garment—a jacket, for example—could be "dressed" with all the component parts of the outfit.

A draper set in the middle of the quad rack, and elevated over the stocked arms could also effectively display the "total look." The use of some elevated points in a merchandise presentation is good, when they attract attention and help lead the viewer from area to area. However, a landscape of "peaks" with hardly a "valley" in view can be quite demanding—and deadly—as a selling ambience. The use of too many high points means nothing is really highlighted. It can also cause an obstructed view of the back of the selling space.

Round Racks

Round racks are the real, no-nonsense, all-shoulder-out, mass-merchandising fixtures. (See Figure 11-17.) When the quantity of stock decreases, the merchandise can be consolidated and some of these fixtures can be removed from the central area. It is better to have fewer fully stocked fixtures than many partially filled ones. Psychologically, when the fixtures are sparsely stocked, it looks as though what remains are "leftovers" and, therefore, less desirable or saleable.

Although round racks may be used for sale merchandise or clearance items as much as possible, the following setup is probably best for the customer's convenience and comprehension and for the general look of the area. When a single "rounder" carries assorted coordinates, they can be presented in the following order: pants, being the longest, are first; followed by skirts. Next come long-sleeve jackets, then short-sleeve jackets, and vests. Sweaters, solid-colored blouses and printed blouses finish the round rack and, thus, bring the viewer and the merchandise full circle. It goes from long to short, from solid to print, and from the smallest size to the largest. If a single classification of merchandise is being shown, color again is uppermost: warm to cool to neutral. The strongest, most attention-getting, or most saleable color faces the front of the area or the store.

When color-coordinated groupings are arranged on the round rack, they go, within the single color, from the viewer's left to right: tops, jackets, vests, and bottoms (skirts, slacks). This is followed by another color grouping in the same order. Between the two color groupings, print blouses, which can be used with either of the color coordinates, may be shown. For example: a red color-coordinated group followed by blouses printed in red, white and blue on a red ground, may be followed by a coordinated group of gray merchandise. This, in turn, may be followed by more printed blouses; this time, gray, white and blue printed on a red ground. Either of the groups of blouses will work with the red ensemble or the gray one. This arrangement informs the customer that an extra gray skirt with the red-coordinated group will greatly increase the outfit's use and versatility. The trimmed rack is doing what a salesperson would ordinarily do: It is making suggestions and assisting the customer in putting together the right colors and parts.

Some round racks, called *three-part racks*, are made up of three equal arcs or segments. (See Figure 11-24.) The height of each arc may be individually adjustable. They can conveniently show three separate groups of color coordinates on a single unit. It can also show pants on one level (the highest), jackets on another, and shirts or vests on the third arc. Each arc should be treated by color—light to dark, warm to cool to neutral—and by size—small to large in each color. The treatment all depends on the type of merchandise, the amount of stock, and the kind of department.

Where the merchandise that is to be presented is small or short, it is possible to use a two- or three-tier rounder. If two levels of shorts are being shown, for example, the color range should still go from left to right, with the shorts grouped by color and by size within each color. But—and this is an emphatic "but"—the smaller sizes of a color should be hung on the top tier and the larger sizes of the same color should be hung directly below, on the bottom tier. This is called *vertical presentation.* Should the merchandise consist of color-coordinated bras and panties, for example, the mauve bras would be on top and the matching mauve panties would be placed directly below—always from small size to large within a given color.

Sale merchandise is usually located between the aisle and the perimeter or back wall of a selling area. Advertised sale or promotional merchandise should be prominently located and properly signed for quick identification. Clearance merchandise is usually set

further back in the area and signed. When the merchandise for clearance or sale consists of odd pieces and broken size lots, it might be better merchandising to arrange the offerings by size rather than color. However, if color groupings can also be done, do it; it looks so much better.

THE BACK WALL

There is a psychology in the presentation and build up of stock in an area, in a shop or in a department. The lowest fixtures are up front; the next area, or midsection, is next in fixture height; and the back wall is the highest merchandising area.

The basic idea is to make the back wall visible from the aisle or the front of the shop or area. The stocking of the back wall should not be minimized or disregarded. Store planners will wash the back walls with light for added emphasis. They will use light under the fascia for attention and attraction, even spotlighting some of the superwall (the area over the stocked merchandise).

The back wall is best used for coordinates with tops over bottoms, or to create an impact for the classification of the merchandise contained within this area. The walls, whether they be used for hanging, shelving, binning, or combinations of all these, are also treated in the light to dark, small to large, left to right manner of merchandising. Because the lowest hangrods, shelves, or bins will not be visible from up front, a vertical presentation is used. Ordinarily, the lower part of the back wall is all but hidden by fixtures, sales help, and customers collected in front of it. The merchandise that is to be hung on the two levels of the vertical presentation will be shown red over red, yellow over yellow, and so on; the larger sizes on the bottom, smaller sizes on top; blouses on top, skirts and trousers on the bottom.

Ideally, the back wall should be broken into coordinated groupings or color patterns to stimulate the customer, please the viewer's eye, and alleviate the curse of uniformity and boredom from seeing an endless row of sweaters or jackets hung at the same level or binned without a break.

By using slotted standards set into the wall and the wide variety of brackets available to secure into the slotted uprights, the visual merchandiser can raise or lower hang-rods, occasionally setting in a waterfall or face-out rod to break up the all-shoulder look; or set up a display on a shelf or pinned directly onto the wall in order to explain the merchandise around and below the display. Even row after row of binning on the perimeter wall can be broken up by devoting one of the bins to a dimensional presentation of some of the merchandise

Figure 12-1. The perimeter wall of a boys' department area. The two areas, at the far left and right, show double-hung, shoulder-right, shoulder-out merchandise. The center area is a combination of face-out merchandise and a water-fall, with pants, below, hung on a rod; it also has set-in slotted standards. The shelved compartments, to the immediate left and right of the center area, have a wide assortment of sweaters and shirts in a variety of sizes and coordinating colors; suit forms and horse-head props are found in the "above reach" area. The entire wall is lit by lighting set into the over-hanging fascia, above. *Bloomingdale's, King of Prussia, Pennsylvania.*

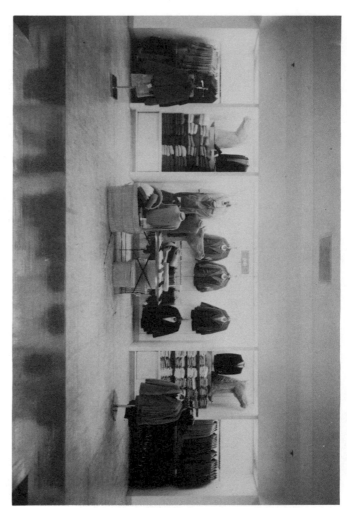

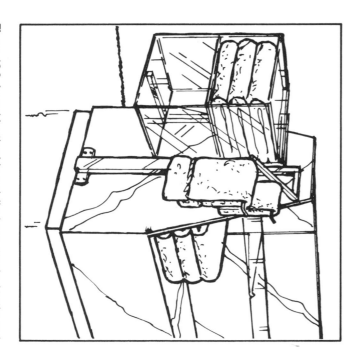

Figure 12-2. A combination bin and displayer attached to the end of a gondola. This end unit may show the featured color and/or pattern as well as a group of related items.

that is neatly folded or bagged around it.

Sometimes, merchandise will be presented on the wall at a level that is too high to be reached comfortably by the customer. This top level may be reserved for the display of color-coordinated accessories that go with the merchandise below, or it could be used for reserve stock. These visual focal points, or displays, on the heavily stocked back wall are absolutely necessary to stress the "new" and the "special" contained within and below.

GONDOLAS

Where there are gondolas on the selling floor and they are shelved or binned (see Figure 11-21), it is advisable to carry through the same aforementioned "color-size" procedure. A gondola, carrying a complete color and size range of women's knee-high socks, for example, could show a rainbow of the colors across the unit, while at the same time, each color would be vertically presented according to size. The vertical line up of a single color presented in a horizontal rainbow of color is effective. It is easy to look at, and more important, it is easy to shop.

Since the merchandise that is usually stocked on the gondola is either folded or bagged, display is desirable. A draper set on top of the gondola can be used, or a displayer specifically designed for the type of merchandise (e.g., a towel displayer, a linens displayer, a bust form for sweaters or blouses, etc.).

The displayperson can also set up an end table, a

Figure 12-3. This bargain square, an "instant" seasonal muffler shop, was created by the arrangement of tables, fixtures, and counters in a relatively small area of this department store's selling floor. The fixturing includes a ladder effect extending up and over the counter. It meets the perimeter wall, extending down to form slatted bins which are used, along with the rungs of the ladder, to display a wide assortment of colored mufflers and caps. A promotional table, right off the aisle (in a contrasting floor covering), holds and displays more of the featured merchandise, further defining the promotional area. The "Muffle Up" sign helps identify the bargain square, as does a muffled up penguin on top of the ladder. *Jordan Marsh, Boston.*

bracket, or a fixture to cover the flat, unmerchandised end of the gondola. *End displays* are especially effective when the gondolas are set perpendicular to the aisle; this is what the customer sees as he or she approaches the area. The end display can be anything from the merchandise itself simply unbagged or opened up, fluffed out, draped, and shaped, all the way to a mini-environmental setting which shows towels, for example, with a bathroom sink and all sorts of decorative gotogethers displayed in a semirealistic scene: a draped shower curtain as a background, a wastepaper basket, a makeup mirror, and maybe, if space and material permit, a laundry hamper with more towels neatly tied and stacked on top. A softly draped towel will always "sell" better than a folded one, but it is the neatly folded one that the customer wants to take home.

AISLE TABLES

Aisle tables are promotional or feature tables set in an aisle for impact selling. They may be elegant—skirted, flounced, and covered with cloth, and maybe highlighted with an attention-getting lamp; they may even be beautifully arranged with a draper and platforms or risers to form a "wedding cake." Or, they may simply be *dump tables*, a term that sounds just about as awful as the end result may be. They can be arranged to form a *bargain square*, or an *economy square*, conveying the image of "come and get it," "what you see is what you get," "there isn't any more." The dump table may be piled with merchandise that looks as though it had gone through a wind tunnel, and then been jumbled and plopped down on the table. To the aesthete, this is a very inferior display, one that certainly does not add to the store's image. But is it really so bad?

Many people, and that includes people with money, love a bargain. There is adventure, excitement, and a sense of discovery in shopping in bazaars, flea markets, and garage sales. Occasionally—and only occasionally—a dump table can be an effective merchandising device, but it takes a good and talented visual merchandiser to make it fun, exciting, and an adventure in scavenging rather than a demeaning, ragpicking task.

If the concept is used as a "special sale" technique and then "displayed," it will work and can even enhance the store's image. Imagine a main aisle treated as a street fair with stands, push carts, and fold-up displayers adding to the "look" as well as holding the merchandise. How about converting an aisle into a Near Eastern bazaar with billowing and swagged tents, and the merchandise tumbling out onto Oriental-type rugs or falling out of tubs, vats, or overscaled straw baskets? It could be an import event with stenciled crates and shredded packing materials supplying the holding space and the proper ambience.

Stores that pride themselves on their "better" or more expensive images, should tuck away the out-and-out "clearance" or "as is" tables toward the rear of the department. In popular price and discount operations, however, they are expected—right out in the open—in the middle of things.

13 Systems Used for Store Planning and Display

In addition to the specific types of fixtures enumerated in Chapter 11, there is an increased use of "put-together and take-apart" bits and pieces that can be made into fixtures and merchandisers as needed. These are grouped under the generic heading of *Systems*.

A system can resemble a set of building blocks, a sophisticated tinker toy, a nursery school jungle gym, or a "Lincoln Log" construction, grown to lifesize or larger. It can be a collection of rods, tubes, panels, or vertical and horizontal elements that are assembled by means of assorted joints, joiners, and connectors. It can be clips or slotted joiners that secure plastic panels or sheets of glass, wood, or composition board. Systems are manufactured in steel, aluminum, wood, and various plastics. They can be fragile, weblike constructions that are all but invisible; or they can also be heavy-duty scaffolding able to rise two or three stories and sustain a heavy load.

What most good and practical systems have in common is the ability to be easily assembled, disassembled, reassembled, and rearranged in new and different ways, in new and different places. A good system is stable, versatile, adaptable, modular, and is designed with many accessories which enhance the unit aesthetically and functionally.

A system can be used to make a displayer, a fixture, and a stocking and selling merchandiser. It can be assembled to create a complete wall of hang-rods, bins, shelves, and maybe even dressing rooms. It may be designed to contain its own lighting and signing elements. With a system, the store planner/displayperson can start with the perimeter wall and erect a whole selling environment without once needing to nail or screw into the wall, bolt down into the floor, or suspend or reinforce from the ceiling. A system may supply the wall hanging or the on-floor stocking. It may serve as a feature unit, or be devised as counters, tables, and cash/wrap desks.

The most remarkable thing about using systems is the relative ease with which one can put them together and take them apart. It usually requires few tools; the ones most frequently used are a soft mallet (for pounding the finger joints into the tubes) and a regular or Phillips screwdriver. A few systems require an Allen or hex wrench. The displayperson has to study the system, get to know what parts are available, and determine what the unit can do. We will outline, below, some of the major categories of structural systems available today.

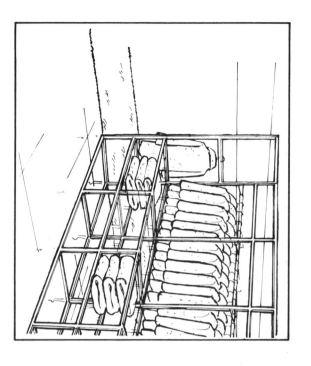

Figure 13-2. A modular system consists of same size, interchangeable units or elements that can be combined to make up a specified modular size; e.g., a 2-foot module made up of a single 2-foot unit or two 1-foot elements. Most important in a modular system is the strict adherence to the dimensions, the detailing of the connections and connectors, the availability of accessories, and the ability to rearrange parts visually and simply.

Figure 13-1. This pipe and fitting system creates an entire shop: wall fixtures with shelves, bins, or hang-rods; fitting rooms, free-standing floor fixtures, and counters. All parts are adjustable, adaptable, and rearrangeable; and even the built-in light canopies are movable. *Lubra System, Ferdinand Lusch GmbH, Bielefeld, West Germany.*

TYPES OF SYSTEMS

Hollow Tubes with "Finger" Fittings

It is possible to obtain metal or plastic systems consisting of precut or standard lengths of hollow rods or tubes, round or square, and joiners or connectors that look like fingers. These finger-extensions fit into the open end of the tube and thus effectively "plug up" that end. At the same time, another finger in the same connector joint will fit into another tube. A two-pronged or fingered joint can be used to form a right angle, or an "L." Four equal lengths of tube joined by four "L" joints will form a rectangle.

A "T" shaped connector will join three pieces of tube in one plane. This will form what is essentially one long line with one line bisecting it. Another type of "T" joint has two extensions at right angles to each other, and the third finger extends up or down. In effect, a corner can be turned with this joint, and a continuation made with an open tube above or below. A cube could be constructed by combining twelve tubes with eight of these right angle "T" joints.

An "X" joint brings together four lengths of pipe into a cross or "X" shape. Another four-pronged joiner forms a right angle and connects with rods above and below the angle. A five-fingered joint forms the "X" and has one finger open to connect above or below. A six-pronged joint forms the "X" and receives tubes or rods above and below the "X."

There are many variations on this type of system. Some use round tubes from 1/2-inch up to 2 or 3 inches

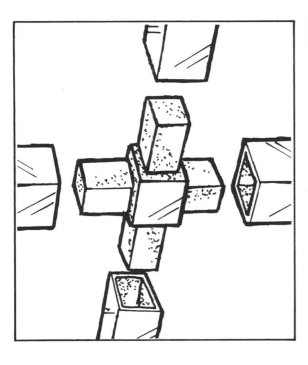

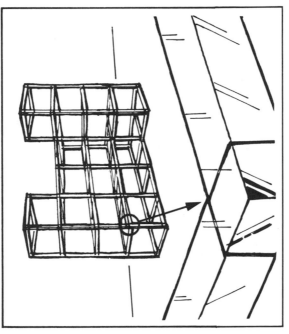

Figure 13-3, *top.* When the four hollow tubes slide over to join the four-fingered fitting, a cross or "X" is formed.

Figure 13-4, *bottom.* The system shown here uses square tubing of various lengths with finger projecting connectors of many configurations. It allows two to six tubes to connect at a single junction (indicated by the arrow).

in diameter. The sizes of the square tube systems are just as varied. The following are some of the better promoted and easily available "finger" systems: Kason's Rocker-Lok and Anchor-Lok, Abstracta, Unicube System, Metrex Display System, MEG "Moduline 11," and Kidde Merchandise Equipment Group.

Clamps

A vast collection of systems are available based on variations of a clamping device that holds or joins round rods or tubes. Often these clamps are hollowed-out spheres that come apart. They have shaped contours which will accommodate the proper size rod or tube. The rods are set into the proper "pocket" in the clamp and secured in place by means of setting a screw which closes the two or three parts of the come-apart clamp.

Other systems have clamps that are external units. Still other systems have viselike clamps that work with sheets of plastic, glass, wood, or composition board. These joiners function like hinges and connect the panels at various angles so they can stand as walls, screens, or dividers. Some systems are available with colored tubes, but their painted surfaces are easily scuffed or scratched.

Some clamp systems are: Opto Clamp System, Tris and Tris Block from Societa Italiana, Multi-Blok, Klem System, and Viava System from International Promotional Shops.

Extruded Uprights

This group of modular systems is based on vertical multifaceted and multislotted metal or plastic lengths into which horizontal elements, brackets, panels, or other structural elements are slipped and then secured. Some of these extruded metal (often aluminum) tubes are designed with four sides for assembling. Some have six sides, and others have as many as eight; with these, it is possible to form hexagonal or even octagonal structures. The store planner/displayperson is not limited to right angle turns only. Again, the more accessories, the greater the possibilities for variations.

Following are some of the extruded upright systems available: Allied Trend Systems, Cardinal Shopfitting System, Syma Structures, Technal of America Universal Aluminum System, Standex Structural Aluminum Design, Daymond Modular System, and System Standex.

Slotted Joiners

These are like Tinker Toys, only bigger, and are produced in an infinite variety of shapes, sizes, and materi-

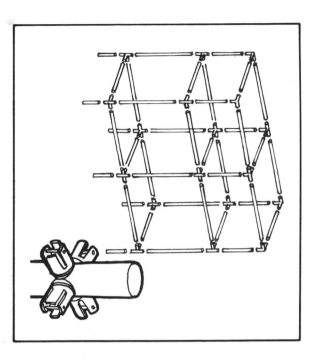

Figure 13-5, *above.* This system combines round metal tubes by means of fingered fittings, detailed in lower right.

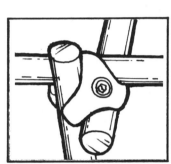

Figure 13-6, *right.* The Opto tube and clamp system.

als. Basically, they are either cubes or spheres that are precision-slotted or drilled with holes. Some systems are designed to accommodate sheets of glass, plastic, or composition board to form shelves, bins, or rectangular structures. Others work with rods and tubes to make skeletal frames.

There are many varieties available today because they are simple to use and even simpler to disassemble and store. Among the most commonly used are: Ultima, Glass Cubes (J.C. Moag Corp.), Stackable Q-Bits (Sutton Designs), Natural Wood System (Coastal Trader), Twist-Lock Connectors (Cal-Tuf Glass Corp.), Unistrut (Meroform), Clip Master System (Outwater Plastics Inc.), Deco-Project, Raum Technik Studio System, and Voluma Connector System.

Slotted Uprights

Slotted uprights are not quite a system in the same way as those mentioned above, but they are certainly simple, adaptable building devices for fixturing and store planning. Slotted uprights are usually steel or aluminum squared tubes that are precision slotted on one, two, three, or four faces. We have already mentioned, in Chapter 12, the convenience and myriad uses of slotted upright standards that are secured onto walls and partitions. These slotted uprights can be used with the finger joints to make self-standing units, or can be secured at the floor and at the ceiling, or spaced away from a wall or column by means of *outriggers* (horizontal members, attached to a wall or column, which serve to support and keep a horizontal or vertical element away from the bearing surface). The great variety of brackets and attachments that work with the slotted wall uprights will, in most cases, work on these square vertical poles.

Slotted upright standards are made by Garcy, Kason, Crown Metal, International Promotional Shops (Kissystem), and Ready Metal ("Z" Wall).

SELECTING A SYSTEM

There are other specialized systems on the market which cannot be put into one broad category or another. The displayperson would be wise to send for the manufacturer's literature, which not only states what the system will do, but will usually provide illustrations of the many components, attachments, and refinements. Some systems are produced in different diameters, assorted colors, and with accessories that might be available in some sizes, but not in others.

To use a system effectively, the displayperson or store planner must know what it will and will not do.

Figure 13-7. A reusable shop or exhibit system with which to construct complete enclosures and free-standing units by means of slotted joiners. The small disks (slotted joiners) that appear at the corners of the assembled pieces are used to create the lucite bins and the opaque bases and walls. The system also has the necessary accessories for closing and sliding doors, walls, shelves, rails, and bins. The lighting is built in with the system. *Equiplus, Aachen, West Germany.*

Figure 13-8. Slotted uprights come in a variety of widths, thicknesses, types, sizes, and slot spacings.

Since each system is somewhat different and has its advantages and disadvantages, more or fewer accessories, and different degrees of adaptability, the displayperson should consider the following aspects before selecting a system for a specific use.

Looks—How will it look in the designated space? Will it look right with the type of merchandise that will be shown? How does it go with the store's image? Will the system be too "spidery," too kiddiecute, too metallic, or too woody? Will the system appear overwhelming in the space it will fill? Will it blend with other fixtures or architectural elements already in the area? Will it scale properly with the architecture and the merchandise?

End Use—How long will this particular system be used in the specific area? If it is to be a semipermanent arrangement which may only require occasional, minor adjustments, but will, essentially, be installed until the "shop" is changed, the store planner or displayperson may wish to consider a system that locks or may be secured rather permanently.

Construction—How much weight will this assemblage have to sustain? Will it be carrying children's clothing, lingerie, separates, or will it be used for heavy outerwear and leather coats? Will the hang-rods and shelves be sturdy enough for the load intended, or will they sag or bow? Does the designer have to plan to use more uprights or shorter hang-rods to sustain the weight?

Upkeep—Will the materials used in the manufacturing of this system hold up in daily use over a prolonged period of time? If it is made of metal, will the finish stay bright and shiny, or will it require polishing or replating? If it has been painted or lacquered, will the painted surfaces be subjected to rubs, scars, strains, and stains? Can the surfaces be retouched? If the system is made of wood, is it hard and scuff-resistant? Can scratches, scars, and blemishes be easily removed in the store? If the shelves or bins are made of plastic or glass, will they break easily, discolor, sag, or bow? Will the edges be resistant to chipping? Will the exposed corners present a problem?

Adaptability——Is the system simple to assemble and reassemble? Is it too simple? Will unauthorized individuals undo what a displayperson has done? Are new washers or fillers needed every time a unit has to be put together? Does it require special bolts, screws, or nuts which can cause untold problems when a screw is missing? Are the replacement parts easy to get? Will the basic size and scale of this system work in most areas in a store, or is the system too specific? How safe is the unit? Will it stand without being reinforced into the floor, wall, or ceiling?

Price——Since price is such a variable, the selection must be based on the projected use and adaptability of the particular system.

CONCLUSION

It is only in the last few years that systems have been more commonly used by store planners and displaypersons in the United States. Since the early 1970's, environmental selling spaces and seasonal shops have become the responsibility of the merchandise presentation department. They are expected to come up with clever, charming, ambience-filled boutiques or "shops" in no time at all, often at a minimum cost. Displaypersons are beginning to recognize the great advantage of these collapsible systems which can be quickly converted from a bunch of rods, tubes, and connectors into a three-dimensional entity housing and showing merchandise—and even carrying its own decorative "skin," signing, and lights.

Systems are practical because they are so versatile. Study the systems that are available. Consider all the advantages and disadvantages. Select the most convenient, practical, and adaptable one—for the price—and remember, save the parts. A system will serve only as long as the bits, parts, and pieces are carefully taken care of. Keep track of all the elements, store them carefully, mark the cartons and boxes, and your system will be a worthwhile investment.

14 Types of Displays and Display Settings

TYPES OF DISPLAYS

The primary purposes of displays are to present and to promote. A display is at its best when it simply shows a color, an item, a collection, or just an idea. Types of displays include the following:

One-Item Display—A one-item display is just that—the showing and advancement of a single garment or any single item. It might be a gown designed by a top designer, a one-of-a-kind piece of ceramic or jewelry, or a new automobile.

Line-of-Goods Display—A line-of-goods display is one that shows only one type of merchandise (all blouses, all skirts, or all pots and pans), although they may be in a variety of designs or colors. A window display showing three or four mannequins wearing daytime dresses of assorted colors, styles, and prints would be an example of a line-of-goods display. However, for a more effective presentation, and for better comprehension and acceptance by the shopper, there should be some connection or relevance indicated as to why these three or four articles are being shown together. They could all be the same color, or designed by the same designer, or the same fabric or print, or they could all feature a common theme.

Related Merchandise Display—In a related merchandise presentation, separates, accessories, or other items which "go together" are displayed because

they are meant to be used together, because they are the same color, or because they share an idea or theme. It could be an "Import Window" where all the items are from the same country (from clothes to handicrafts, to kitchen utensils to furniture, and so on.) It might be a color promotion where all the clothing in one window is red, and the next display setup may consist of all-red household supplies and hardgoods. That presentation may be followed by a room setting in which red is the dominant color. Or, it can also be a display of lizard shoes, bags, and belts—all related because they are made of lizard skin. Red, white, and blue-striped hats, sweaters, scarves, and stockings would be a related merchandise display. The items go together and reinforce each other.

Variety, or Assortment, Display—A variety, or assortment, display is a potpourri of anything and everything. It is a collection of unrelated items that happen to be sold in the same store. It can be work shoes, silk stockings, tea kettles, Hawaiian print shirts, wicker chairs, red flannel nightgowns, and cowboy boots. It is a melange of odds and ends; a sampling of the merchandise contained within.

Promotional vs. Institutional Displays

A promotional display can be a one-item, a line-of-goods, a related merchandise, and even, for storewide

103

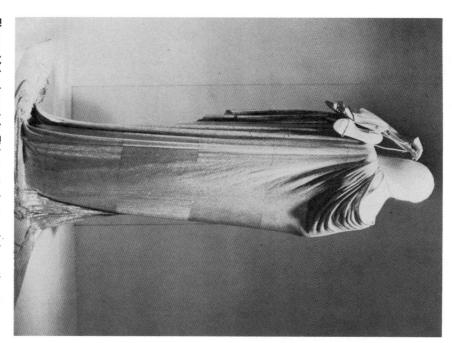

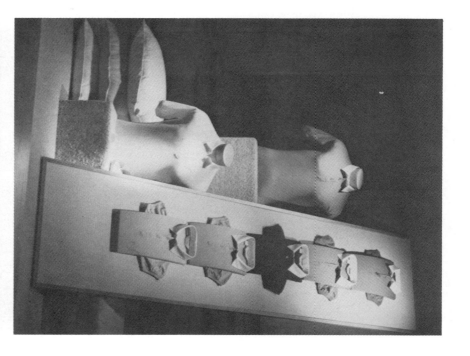

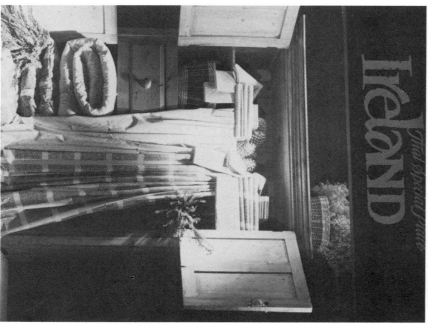

Figure 14-1, *above left*. This mysterious and dramatic presentation for a pair of golden slippers is an example of a one-item display. The back of the mannequin is covered with a gold cape. The drape at the shoulder, the long blond hair pulled to the left, and the use of pinpoint lighting, help emphasize the metallic sandals being held aloft by the mannequin. *Bloomingdale's, New York.*

Figure 14-2, *above right*. In this example of a line-of-goods display, the sport shirts are not only shown dimensionally on the shirt forms, but they are pinned onto a sloping board similar to a brightly colored totem pole. The pinned shirt, repeated over and over again, adds emphasis to the presentation of the wide color range. *Saks Fifth Avenue, New York.*

Figure 14-3, *right*. A window filled with Irish linens: bed sheets, pillow cases, quilts, comforters, towels, etc.—all coordinated by color and pattern to "go together." They are also just one part of a store-wide Irish promotion. Even the wooden cupboard, which holds and presents the assorted pieces in a unified design, is part of the related merchandise since it, too, can be found in a bedroom. *Bloomingdale's, New York.*

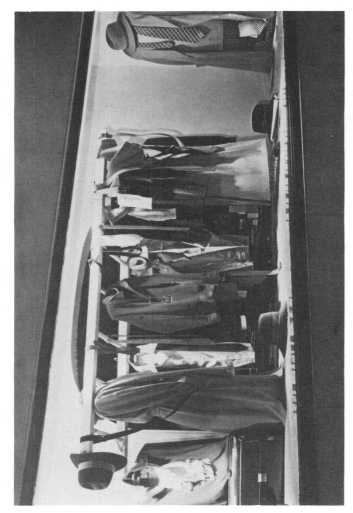

Figure 14-4. Hats, belts, briefcases, scarves, ties, sweaters, jackets, coats, and dresses—they are all here, but do not necessarily "go together," nor are they especially color or pattern-related. This window just shows the wide range of merchandise that is available inside. The horizontal ladder makes an interesting prop from which to hang and drape the merchandise. *Henri Bendel, New York.*

sales, a variety type of display. The display advances or emphasizes a particular concept, trend, or item. It promotes! As an example: Father's Day is coming up and is to be promoted by the store. A theme has been developed for advertising the event. That theme will be carried out in newspapers, on radio and television, and the displays (windows and interiors) will tie in with and advance that theme. If the store's promotion is "Dad—Our Kind of Man," then the displays would be related. In one window there could be a display for "Dad, the Athlete," with everything from active sportswear to sporting equipment, sports magazines, and even spectator sports items. Another window could have gifts for "Dad, the Connoisseur," consisting of a collection of dress-up clothes, classical records, wines, gourmet foods, and exotic cooking equipment. Each different "Dad" would be gifted with a variety of merchandise based on a particular type of man.

A sale can also be the basis for a promotional display. It might be a storewide sale, an anniversary sale, a pre- or post-holiday sale, or an end-of-season sale. As another example, if blue is the "in" spring color and the store is investing heavily in blue merchandise, then blue should be promoted inside and outside the store.

Often, a one-item type of display is used to promote the store's fashion image. The presentation is designed to tell the shopper where the store stands on fashion trends, what they think their customers want to look like, and just to whom the store is trying to appeal. So, even though a particular outfit is not being promoted as an outfit, the display is promotional in that it is advancing the store as something special.

An institutional display, on the other hand, promotes an idea rather than an item or a product. The display presents the store as a worthwhile and interested member of the community. If a national hero dies, a window may be set aside to honor his or her memory, and no saleable merchandise will be included in that display. If the Community Chest has a drive on, or any other worthwhile charity is in need of support, and the store promotes the organization and all the good it does, without including store merchandise, that would be considered an institutional display.

The local opera company or symphony orchestra may be starting its new season and needs more subscribers. The store might promote its cause in a small window or shadow box. Remember, this is not the same as using the posters and paraphernalia of a visiting ballet company to provide a background for a window filled with ruffle-frilled petticoats or ballerina-like dance dresses. That is a good example of the use of a current event or what is new in town to set the scene for store merchandise, but it is not an institutional display.

An institutional display helps further the store's image. It is a sign of goodwill toward its neighbors and the neighborhood. It shows the store as a concerned and interested party in the welfare of the community. The big Christmas extravaganza, full of animation, fantasy, and the delight of children eight to eighty, may not sell any special merchandise, but it certainly sells the store. People may travel from all over to see a store's institutional Christmas windows, and often, the "tourists" end up inside after having seen the "free show" outside.

Figure 14-5. An institutional window to celebrate American freedom. The replica of the Statue of Liberty, banks of live plants, a simple plaque, dramatic lighting—all combine to make a simple but strong, nonselling, patriotic window display. *Bloomingdale's, New York.*

TYPES OF DISPLAY SETTINGS

In presenting any display, there are some basic approaches the visual merchandiser can take to set the scene for the merchandise or the concept to be sold. These approaches include the following:

- Realistic setting
- Environmental selling setting
- Semirealistic setting
- Fantasy setting
- Abstract setting

Realistic Setting

A realistic setting is essentially the depiction of a room, area, or otherwise recognizable locale, reinterpreted in the allotted display area, either in the windows or inside the store. The realistic setting is best controlled and most effective in a fully enclosed display window. Here, the displayperson can do a miniature stage setting. He or she can simulate depth and dimension, and use color and light with great effect—all viewed, as planned, from the front, through a large plate-glass window. The scene can be a restaurant with wall-papered walls, carpeted floors, matching tables and chairs, flowers, ferns and potted palms, china and crystal, candles and chandeliers. It seems so real, so complete, so recognizable that the viewer can relate to it. To show formal or semiformal clothing, for example, in this setting seems so appropriate.

Sometimes, however, the cleverness and fastidiousness given to the details of the setting can work against the presentation of the merchandise. The viewer might get so involved in the settings and the background that the merchandise, the "star," is upstaged by the "set."

At certain times and in certain stores, however, a realistic setting can be most effective. Some holidays are just right for a true-to-life presentation. On Christmas morning, for example, mannequins wearing assorted robes and loungewear might be busily engaged in unwrapping more of the same merchandise. On New Year's Eve, a gala party is the perfect setting for gala clothes. Thanksgiving is a time to show tableware, while the family is "dressed" for dinner. Import promotions can be attention-getting displays when the settings are realistic, though foreign. People do want to see how other people live.

When realism is the thing, scale is of the utmost importance. The display area should not be weighed down with props or elements so large that the scale of the setting shrinks by comparison. A realistic setting

Figure 14-6. This complete room is so realistic that we are ready to step into it. The table is set for dinner; everything is shown. The store sells furniture, silverware, china, glassware, and rugs, as well as fashion, and they are all here in one Christmas gift-giving idea window. The realistic setting seems so appropriate for the formal fashions on display. *Abraham & Straus, Brooklyn, New York.*

Figure 14-7. This example of environmental selling is a vignette setting in the middle of a linens department. A coordinated grouping of linens is shown as well as the accessories that complement it. The background structure has openings to hold some of the featured stock. *Joske's, Dallas.*

requires the careful blending of color, textures, shapes, and the proper lighting to keep the background at a proper distance. It must still be attractive enough to be the "come-on" for the merchandise presentation.

Environmental Selling Setting

This is a merchandise presentation that shows an assortment of various related items in a setting depicting how and where they may eventually be used. In this form of realistic setting, the "background" is actually the "foreground" because the details that make up the realistic set are actually the merchandise being promoted in the display.

An example of an environmental selling setting is a display depicting a corner of a room with a bed, made up with matching sheets, pillow cases and comforter, a window with coordinated curtains and drapes, and an area rug of the appropriate color and design. A chair near the bed has a robe casually tossed over it, and there is a pair of slippers on the floor. The setting also includes a bedside table, on which is an arrangement of frames, boxes, a lamp, and a clock. Everything on display in this setting is for sale in the store.

Semirealistic Setting

When space and budget do not allow the time or effort for a fully realistic presentation, the displayperson may opt for the very popular, semirealistic or "vignette" setting. The visual merchandiser presents the essence, the tip of the iceberg, and leaves the rest to the active

Figure 14-8. In this semirealistic setting, the tile background and floor as well as the few lockers on the left suggest a locker room. The bench not only adds to the atmosphere, it provides an elevation or platform for a merchandise lay-down, as do the wall hanging units. Inside the open locker is more coordinated merchandise. This was a Father's Day window designed to promote gifts for the active dad. *Sage-Allen, Hartford, Connecticut.*

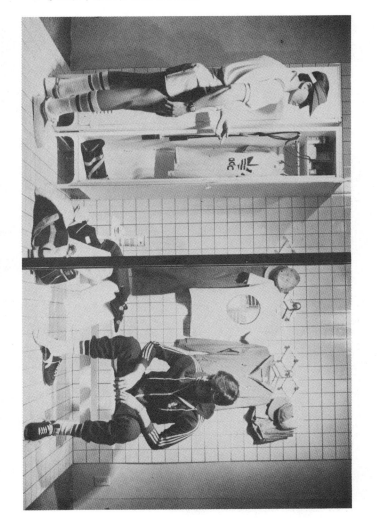

Figure 14-9. What could be more "earthy" and real than golf, but here the setting is surrealistic and attention-grabbing. A semi-abstract/semicomplete mannequin, on the left, is wrapped in stretched, white jersey fabric with a sporty and dynamic yellow band that leads the viewer to the yellow and white active sportswear displayed on the two sun-tan colored, semirealistic mannequins on the right. The effective lighting and the splash of white help keep the observers, who are outside, away from what is going on in the store just beyond the open-back window. *Descente, New York.*

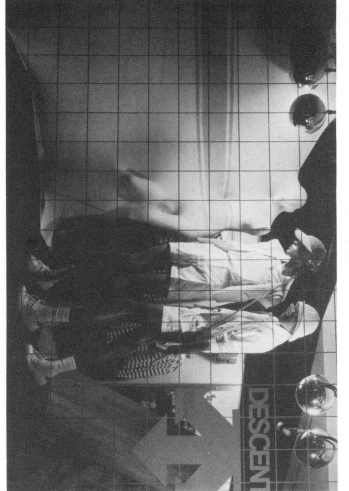

Figure 14-10. The black panel in the center of the background continues down onto the floor, creating a strong black and white setting for the dynamic, black and white striped swimsuits. Four black, semiabstract mannequins tend to disappear, while the boldly patterned suits stand out more clearly. The brightly lit mannequin in the center shows a different look. The jagged geometric shapes on the background add diagonals to what would otherwise be a vertical design. *Macy's, New York.*

imagination of the shopper. In many ways, this is a more effective but simpler approach to merchandise settings. The merchandise and mannequins do not have to compete with the "look-at-me" cleverness of a down-to-the-last-detail setting.

As examples of displays in a semirealistic setting: In a predominantly black or dark gray window (walls, floors, and side walls), imagine a small table covered with a red and white checkered cloth, two bentwood chairs with cane seats, a candle stuck into a straw-encased Chianti bottle already heavy with rivulets of melted wax, some breadsticks in a water tumbler, a brass hat stand, a potted palm. Couldn't this be any romantic, old-fashioned, neighborhood, Italian restaurant? Or, simply, a palm tree dripping heavy with green leaves, a mound of sand, an open, boldly-striped beach umbrella—anybody would know it was some faraway island in the sun. Who needs to look beyond this into the nebulous, no-color, no-detail background?

On ledges, in island displays, and in store windows with open backs, a semirealistic setting works most effectively. It is theater-in-the-round, but the viewer does not go beyond the fragment being shown. To the displayperson, it means getting to the heart of the setting, presenting that "heart," and then fleshing it out only as necessary. A park bench, a tree, some pigeons or a squirrel, the hint of sky, some grass and gravel—it's a park! An awning swagged off the dark back wall, a small metal table for two, two ironwork chairs, a bottle of wine and two glasses, a suggestion of a kiosk, over to the side, bedecked with French posters—it's romance, it's April in Paris!

Fantasy Setting

A fantasy setting can be as detailed or as suggestive as the displayperson, budget, and time permit. It is creative, it does require thought, energy, and lots of planning, but it can be very rewarding.

It may be surrealistic or just a "touch of the poet"; it is a strange "never-never" land, a fairyland, Oz, an enchanted forest, Alice's Wonderland. A fantasy setting can be tables on the ceiling and chairs on the wall. It can be 6-foot toadstools, or a mannequin drifting, in midair, on a magic carpet. It can be a world frozen in ice and icicles, or a trip in a space ship to visit a family of robots. A fantasy setting can be a stairway going nowhere with a crystal chandelier to light the way, or an underwater spectacular of swimsuited mermaids and giant sea shells.

These are just some examples of the touches of whimsy that can be a delightful change of pace after several realistic or semirealistic installations. A good imagination is the most important requirement.

Abstract Setting

An abstract setting seems to be the easiest to do, but is often the most difficult. The least amount of display often makes the biggest statement. In an abstract setting, the merchandise is the dominant feature and the setting supports and reinforces the message, often subliminally. For example, a viewer may look at some white ribbon streamers hanging down from an overhead grill and know that the classic gown in front of the

Figure 14-11. In this china department, the cubes and risers help create a beautiful presentation of the many different types, styles, and patterns of china. The eye easily moves along from level to level, reading a "setting" before moving on to the next. *Abraham & Straus, White Plains, New York.*

Figure 14-12. This display of shoes is more fun than a barrel of monkeys. It is a balance of barrels used as risers/platforms and of monkeys for interest and line. The vertical monkey on the right, over the low barrel, balances the monkey on the far left, submerged in the highest barrel. The monkey swinging in the middle bridges the two. The effective lighting, as well as the use of bananas and pineapples, lead the viewer from group to group. *Vittorio Ricci, New York.*

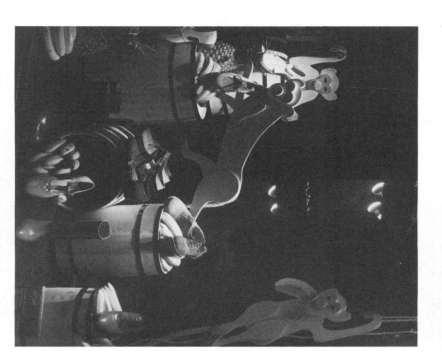

streamers is elegant. The viewer sees a mannequin wearing a lovely article of lingerie, stretched out on a long, lustrous divan—and knows this is the smoothest, sexiest, and most feminine piece of lingerie.

The abstract or architectural setting is predominantly an arrangement of lines and shapes, panels, cubes, cylinders, triangles, curves, arcs, and circles. It is like a nonrepresentational painting done in three dimensions, in various planes. The design does not really represent or look like anything in particular, but it does evoke certain responses from the viewer. An abstract setting is like a skeletal stage set in that there is form that functions. It divides the space; and the lines, shapes, and forms give a graphic message.

BUILDUPS

There is a vast difference between creating a one-item or line-of-goods display, and a mass display of a variety of items "related" only in use, material, color, or place of origin. To show, as an example, different dinnerware place settings, one is dealing with a group of objects that are similar in material, construction, and use, but are decidedly different in appearance. It is the difference in pattern, color, subtle variations in shape and size that will make one design of dinnerware more attractive to a customer than another.

In doing a display of five, six, or more place settings or groupings of different china patterns (or pots and pans, luggage, toiletries and cosmetics, or other "related" types of merchandise), there are certain methods of presentation that are more effective than others. The overall display must be balanced and easy to look at. There has to be a movement from grouping to grouping or item to item. Each group or item should be able to be viewed as a separate entity, somehow set apart from the others.

If, as in the case of the china, the displayperson is working with objects of the same general size or weight, he or she might use assorted size cubes or cylinders clustered together to create a stepup presentation. It is easy for the viewer's eye to travel upward, making a stop at each level to absorb what is being shown before moving on, up to the next level and the next showing. Thus, each group is separate and apart in space and the viewer's attention span, and each can be dominant as the viewer's eye climbs the setup. The topmost group, by its position, could be assumed to be the best or the most attractive—the most desirable. Therefore, if the displayperson wants to make all the items equally "best" or "beautiful," the top step could be reserved for a plant, a vase filled with flowers, or any decorative or related item or prop.

The stepup itself can be a series of forms of different sizes, arranged in a straight line with each cube or cylinder butting up to the next tallest one, but all flush in front. For the sake of interest and effect, there can be a combination of bigger stepups and smaller stepups. In a formal or traditional arrangement, however, each stepup will be exactly the same increment of height (e.g., 6 inches, 9 inches, etc.) until the next plateau is reached.

Where there is sufficient depth in which to set up the display, the buildups can go from front to back as well as from side to side. It would be like creating a pyramid with risers, cubes, or elevations building up from either end while at the same time, building from a low point out in front to the high point in the center.

When displaying merchandise that is related, but of different sizes and shapes (e.g., handcrafted ceramics which includes boxes, plates, bowls, decorative figures, and maybe even urns or vases), the stepup or pyramid buildup will work, but it requires a very deft feel for balance, especially asymmetrical balance. It is now a matter of building up one riser (or platform) with an object on it while balancing it with another riser that has a different size object displayed on it. The overall height and look of the riser plus the merchandise must be visually weighed against the other riser and merchandise. It might, therefore, require a lower platform or elevation to hold a tall vase, for example, if it is to balance with a low, squat bowl on a taller riser. This asymmetrical buildup must be arranged so that the viewer's eye will still move comfortably, through the various levels, to the top.

15 Floor Plans

An architect does not simply buy thousands of bricks and then start to erect a building. An engineer does not take a crew of bulldozers out into a field and say, "Let's try here." And a displayperson does not walk into an empty window or onto a cleared-off ledge and say, "What shall we do here today?" What they all do is *plan!*

They plan, they make drawings, they consider the details, the special requirements, and the limitations. Most of the problems are usually solved before the start of construction or installation. The displayperson, like the architect and engineer, is a professional and should not be given to whims and fancies that will not come to terms with reality. He or she must communicate with coworkers, consult with buyers and fashion coordinators, and get construction done through the carpenters and painters before ever stepping into the window or onto the ledge. It takes planning, plotting, and programming. It takes *preparation.*

Just as architects and engineers work with blueprints and mechanical drawings to correct errors before they become full-grown and costly mistakes, the displayperson should also work with scale drawings of the areas for which he or she is responsible. The displayperson can place figures, fixtures, props, etc., onto a scaled floor plan and, thereby, see what will and will not work in the allotted space. It is also possible, using these preliminary drawings, to estimate the amount of background or flooring material required; the sizes of the platforms or risers; the partitions, dividers, or screens that will be used. It is also possible to preplan the lighting requirements.

It is simple enough to prepare one sharp, clean, basic plan of each area to be arranged and displayed, and then make dozens of photocopies for use, as needed. Sometimes, for a really ambitious undertaking, a model is made in proportion to the actual finished design. This is done to get a "visual" image of how things will look, how things will fit, and how they will work. By planning and preparing properly, the investment of time, money, and effort will more than pay for itself.

SCALE

When we speak of scale, we are referring to the relative proportion of one object to another. When we say something is "overscaled," we mean it is too big, too overwhelming, too dominant in relation to the objects around it. "Relation" is the key word here. A real, live, 7-foot-tall basketball player visiting a kindergarten class would be overscaled in relation to the children. True, the ball player would be noticed—he would be an attention-getter—but he would also, by contrast, show how very small the children are. Scale, in mechanical drawing or in the preparation of floor plans or models, refers to the proportion that is used by the designer or draftsperson to designate the future actual size.

If an architect is going to build on a plot measuring 100 feet x 300 feet, it would be absurd to paste up a single sheet of paper to that size, then lay it out on a football field, and start to draw the foundation in the actual measurements. Instead, a scale is selected—a proportion—and the designer works on the assumption that each foot of actual construction will be represented on the drawing by 1/8 of an inch or 1/4 of an inch, for example. The contractor or engineer looks at the corner of the designer's finished drawing—in a special box usually found on the lower right-hand side—in order to find the proportion or scale used in the drawing. Thus, at a scale of 1/8" = 1', the plan drawing of a plot measuring 100' x 300' will be drawn at 12½" x 37½". Using this size paper makes it easier to make corrections, overlays, or even prepare new drawings, and it is certainly more convenient to carry around.

DRAWING A FLOOR PLAN

The displayperson should not only know how to read and interpret a floor plan or building plan, but should also be capable of drawing a plan—in scale—and with the special "hieroglyphics" used by architects, engineers, and designers. Today, the displayperson is often given a set of blueprints for a new store, or a revamped department, or the marked off space for a shop-within-a-shop, and told to lay out the fixtures, counters, counter fixtures, furniture, etc., to be used, and/or asked to plan the aisles, the traffic flow, and the display areas. He or she must be able to render these ideas in scale, in a plan, and sometimes with an elevation (see page 119), so that the area can be finished by contractors or carpenters.

It should be obvious by now that the visual merchandiser or displayperson has to be able to draw a simple floor plan. Let us, first, be sure we understand what a floor plan is. It is a flat representation of only two measurements—the length and width (or depth) of an area or object as seen from overhead. It is as though one were viewing the area from far up in the air, and all that could be seen is a flat, graphic representation with no third dimension, with no indication of height, and with everything flattened out.

By using a scaled floor plan, it is possible for the visual merchandiser/displayperson to experiment, on paper, with platforms, fixtures, display cases, etc., of assorted sizes and shapes, without ever actually having to lift or push them.

Materials Needed

Some basic materials are needed to draw a simple floor plan. It is a good idea to start with a *drawing board*, an essentially flat, rectangular surface, usually made of wood, with absolutely straight and true sides. The four corners should be perfect right angles.

In order to draw straight lines, one should have a *T-square* which looks like a 24-inch to 36-inch calibrated ruler with a head on top perpendicular to the ruler part, forming a "T." When drawing, the top of the T-square lines up with the edge of the drawing board, and thus any lines drawn along the ruling edge will be parallel to one another and perpendicular to the sides of the drawing board.

A *triangle* is a tool having three sides and three angles, used to draw right angles, other specified angles (30°, 45°, 60°, etc.), and to line up vertical and horizontal lines on the drawing board. They are usually made of plastic or metal, and used in connection with a T-square.

If a T-square is lined up with a drawing board and the base of a triangle sits flush on the ruling edge of the T-square, the straight, vertical edge of the triangle will work as a guide for vertical or perpendicular lines. Thus, with a drawing board, a T-square, and a pair of triangles, it is possible to draw straight or angled lines that are true and even.

A *compass* is used to draw circles and arcs of various sizes. This drafting tool consists of two rigid arms—a needle point and a marker arm—hinged to each other at one end. The wider the spread between the arms, the larger the circle or arc that can be drawn.

A *French curve* is a flat, plastic or metal drafting tool consisting of several scroll-like curves and arcs. The desired curve is drawn and reproduced by following the edge of the form at the selected curve. French curves are available in a wide variety of sizes and shapes.

Especially useful in mechanical drawing and essential for reading plans done to scale, is a triangular-shaped *scale ruler*. It is slightly over 12-inches-long and calibrated in assorted scales. One edge is marked off in 1/8-inch spaces; each line is equal to a single unit in the 1/8-inch scale. On the edge that is marked off for the 1/4-inch scale, the spacing is in 1/4-inch modules; therefore, the designer knows that each 1/4-inch space is equal to a unit, whether that unit be an inch, a foot, or a yard. A scale ruler is also marked off in the following scales: 3/32, 3/16, 3/8, 1/2, 3/4 (which are all fractions of an inch); and 1, 1½, and 3 inches. One face is usually calibrated as a traditional ruler, i.e., with markings of sixteenths of an inch. Scale rulers are also available in metric scales.

If you do not want to use a ruler, all is not lost! It is possible to do scale drawings on *graph paper*, paper which has been lightly marked off into squares. Until such time that the United States formally adopts the metric system, be sure to select graph paper that has been divided into four or eight boxes to the inch. Four boxes to the inch means that each box is equal to a ¼-inch. Using graph paper that has eight boxes to the inch gives a ⅛-inch scale. If you want a scale of ⅛-inch = 1 foot, and there are eight boxes to the inch on the paper, then each box is equal to 1 foot, and half a box is 6 inches. If you want to use the same paper for a drawing with a scale of ¼-inch = 1 foot, then each box is equal to 6 inches, and it takes two boxes to make 1 foot.

In addition to graph paper, it is recommended that the displayperson have a good supply of *tracing paper* to try out variations, moves, and changes. Once a plan is carefully drawn, any corrections and changes deemed necessary can be made on tracing paper laid over the finished drawing. Then, when the final design is approved, the final, corrected scale drawing can be done.

Have a lot of *sharpened hard pencils* designated (4H to H) on hand, not those with soft points. Soft pencils (No. 2 and B) make fat lines that smear and rub. A good *ruby eraser* (for erasing lines) and a *kneaded eraser* (for removing smudges) are also necessary adjuncts. It is a good idea to keep a *clean rag* on hand to wipe off the edges of the T-square and the triangles as the drawing proceeds. The lead of a pencil adheres to the edges of the instruments and can make a drawing messy.

Also, to make scaling and drawing floor plans simpler, there are dozens of kinds of *templates* (also spelled *templet*) available in art supply and stationery stores. They are thin, plastic or metal plates containing the patterns of specific symbols and shapes precisely die-cut out of the plate, leaving an opening one can trace in order to produce a perfectly scaled object. There are templates for home and office, using engineering and architectural symbols as well as basic geometric shapes (circles, ovals, rectangles, and triangles). Templates are available in assorted sizes and scales.

With the materials assembled and scale ruler in hand, the designer is ready to draw. The following are the symbols and "short hand" of architectural drawing as they relate to display and store planning.

READING A FLOOR PLAN

Figure 15-1 (see the following page) is a composite of a store floor plan, but it does give us the opportunity to point out some of the usual and unusual symbols and markings found in floor plans.

Basic Architectural Symbols

A: A heavy solid line (or two lines that are not filled in—see **AA** in Figure 15-1), indicates a structural, exterior wall. It is a part of the basic construction of the building. (This can also be a common wall that is shared with an adjacent building.)

B: A solid line, thinner than A (sometimes two lines that are not filled in, but closer together than AA), indicates a floor to ceiling interior wall, partition, or solid divider. The wall or partition may or may not be structural, but usually the columns or piers on the floor plan (see C) will indicate where the weight-bearing, structure-bearing elements can be found. This thin line indicates a division or separation between departments or areas, as well as where the on-the-floor selling operations end and the "behind-the-scenes" activities begin. In this way, it is possible to recognize how much space has been devoted to fixturing and on-the-floor stock, compared to the area reserved for back-up stock, dressing and fitting rooms, receiving, packing, offices, etc.

When the partition or wall does not go up to the ceiling, it is represented by narrow lines, partially filled in (**BB**). This is sometimes called a *partial* or *dwarf wall.*

C: A heavy, solid (or shaded) rectangle extending out from either the thin or heavy solid line, indicates a *pier*, a *beam*, or a *buttress*—reinforcing elements used to add strength to the wall's construction, or to help support the weight of the floors above. When the rectangle is attached to an internal or external wall, but is not shaded or filled in, it can represent a vertical conduit or duct for water pipes, electric or gas lines, etc. This is part of the building's functioning structure and cannot be removed or disregarded by the draftsperson laying out a store or a department.

D: A solid rectangle, out in the middle of the floor, usually in a set grid pattern with other such rectangles, represents a *column.* (A column stands free, out in the open and unattached, while a pier is actually a thickening or an extension out from a constructed wall.) In many cases, interior walls will be constructed to tie in with the independent columns, and thus make them appear as piers. A supporting I-beam will appear on the floor plan looking like the capital letter "I."

E: A rectangle with a "X" through it, will usually indicate a nonuseable area which is part of or essential to the construction and/or maintenance of the building. It is nonuseable floor space for the purpose of the draftsperson. It is a situation similar to the vertical conduits mentioned previously. (See C.)

F: A thickening at the end of a wall, indicates a door jamb, a molding, or a frame around a window. In either case, the thickening will be to either side of a break in a wall, thus indicating some sort of opening.

G: A thin line plus an arc, indicating a traditional door. The line represents the door in plan view; it is hinged to one side or the other of the door jamb or frame. The arc shows the direction and extent of the door swing. This is important to the space planner

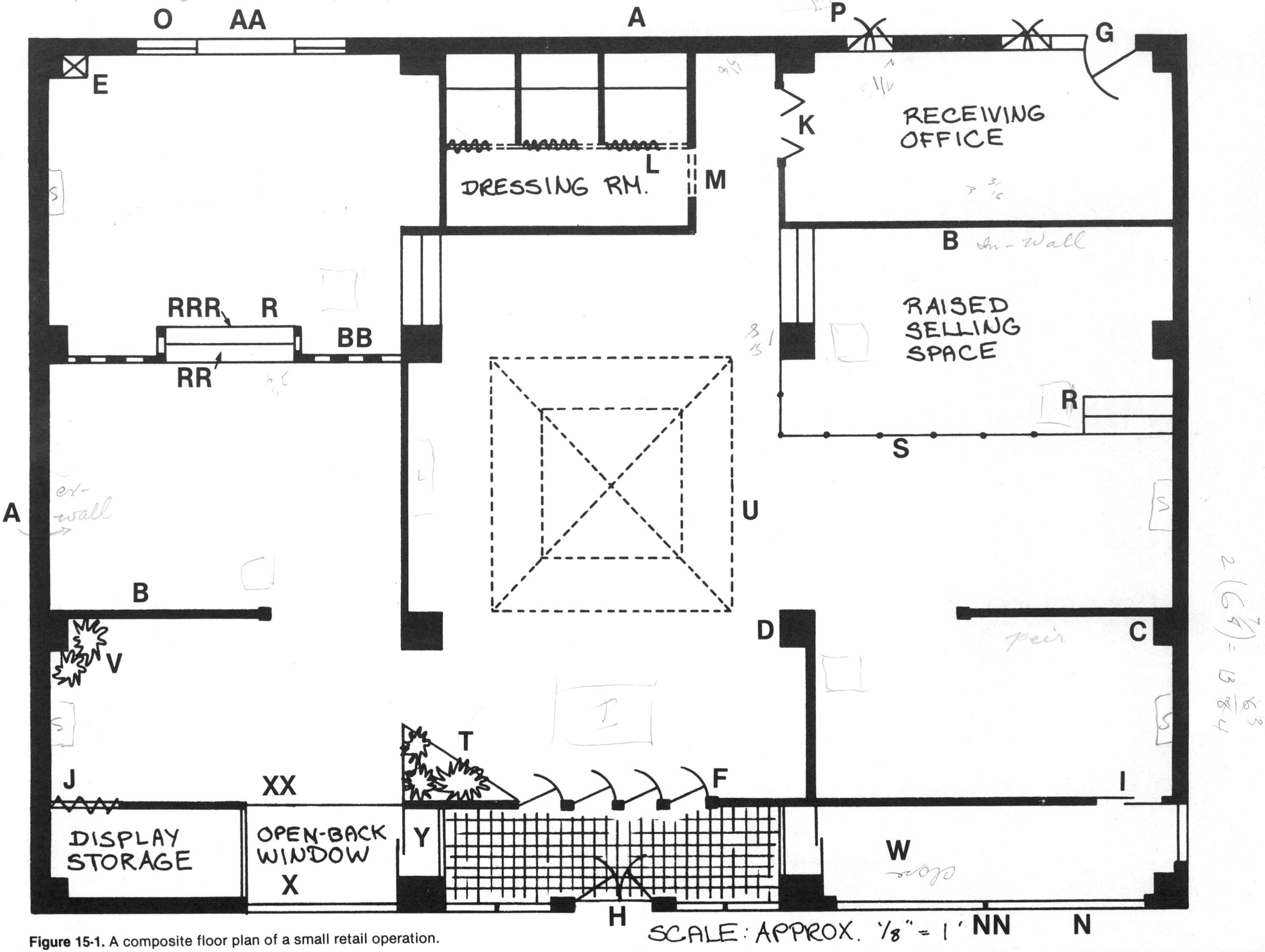

Figure 15-1. A composite floor plan of a small retail operation.

since it will limit what can be or should be placed on the wall onto which the door will swing back. Traditional doors will vary from 24 inches to 27 inches for closets and toilets, and from 30 inches to 36 inches for main entrances.

H: A double door—two doors that swing open, one to each side. The double arc indicates the two swings. If it is a foyer or vestibule and there are a series of doors—and they all open into the store—all the doors will be hinged, usually swinging in the same direction.

I: A sliding door. Since one panel slides behind the other, there are two lines shown, one for each panel. There is no loss of wall space with this type of door. It is usually used to cover closets or storage spaces.

J: An accordian fold door—a corrugated vinyl or slatted wood screen that folds back over and over again on itself and often does not extend out beyond the door frame. The same symbol could represent a movable, folding wall or partition between areas.

K: A pair of folding doors, hinged to fold back on themselves. These can be solid panels or louvered doors; they may be used as a single pair or two pairs to the single opening. Each pair folds back to the side of the door frame to which it is hinged. Because they fold back on themselves, they take up less back wall space then a traditional door.

L: A curtain closing over a doorway such as might be used in a dressing room area. The double dotted line indicates a hang-rod; the snaking line is the curtain. (At this point, it should be mentioned that a broken or dotted line usually indicates something that is above ground or floor level, i.e., does not rest directly on the floor, but is still an integral part of the floor plan.) The broken line indicates that there is some wall space above the opening and below the ceiling. If sliding panels or a corrugated screen were installed inside the wall opening, it would be indicated on the floor plan as they appear in *I* and *J*. (As previously mentioned in *F*, the thickening at the end of a wall could indicate a window frame as well as a door jamb. It is much more likely that windows will appear in perimeter or outside walls rather than in internal walls or partitions.

M: An archway or wall opening that has no door or any other covering or closing device. It could also be a pass-through from one area into another, similar to a pass-through between most kitchens and dining rooms.

N: A plate-glass window, similar to a "picture" window or a display window. It cannot be opened. It is represented by two fine lines that abut and fit inside the heavy line representing the exterior wall. Sometimes, three fine lines, close together, will represent the glazed unit inside the thickness of the wall. In architectural drawings, where the wall is not shaded in, the non-opening windows (*N*) are represented by three lines within the two lines indicating the exterior wall. (See AA.)

NN: A *mullion*, a metal divider between a run of several plate-glass windows. Mullions facilitate the replacement of glass, when necessary. It is represented in the floor plan by a solid area between the two fine lines of the plate-glass window.

O: Windows that can be opened, usually represented by three fine lines set inside the wall construction. The three lines actually make up the two window frames that can be raised or lowered. (In a casement window, it takes an upper and a lower frame to cover the window area.) The framed windows are usually 30 to 36-inches wide.

P: A casement window with two vertical frames, hinged onto the window frame. The windows swing in and out rather than ride up and down. This symbol is similar to the one for swinging doors (*H*) since the action is basically the same.

Q: A tiled floor. It could represent vinyl, asphalt, ceramic, or even marble squares set in a geometric pattern.

R: Steps. In this plan, only two treads (**RR**) are indicated. Since a riser is usually 8-inches high, the three risers (**RRR**), the elevated area or platform, are 24-inches high.

S: A balustrade or railing with stanchions or uprights set 3 feet apart.

T: A planter containing plants.

U: A skylight or glazed ceiling. The dotted line indicates something above ground level.

V: Plants.

W: A closed-back display window area with a full wall and a sliding door (*I*).

X: An open-back window with a full view of the store beyond. The thin line in the back (**XX**) indicates the end of the raised platform. If there were no line, it would mean that the display window was at ground level, not elevated at all.

Y: A shadow box display case with a glass front and sliding panels in back.

STORE PLANNING SYMBOLS

Figure 15-2 (see the following page) is part of an actual fixturing floor plan of a department in a large retail store. It is drawn and reproduced to a scale of 1/8-inch = 1 foot. The architectural symbols are the same as those used in any architectural floor plan.

As shown in the previous section, the basic construction elements are:

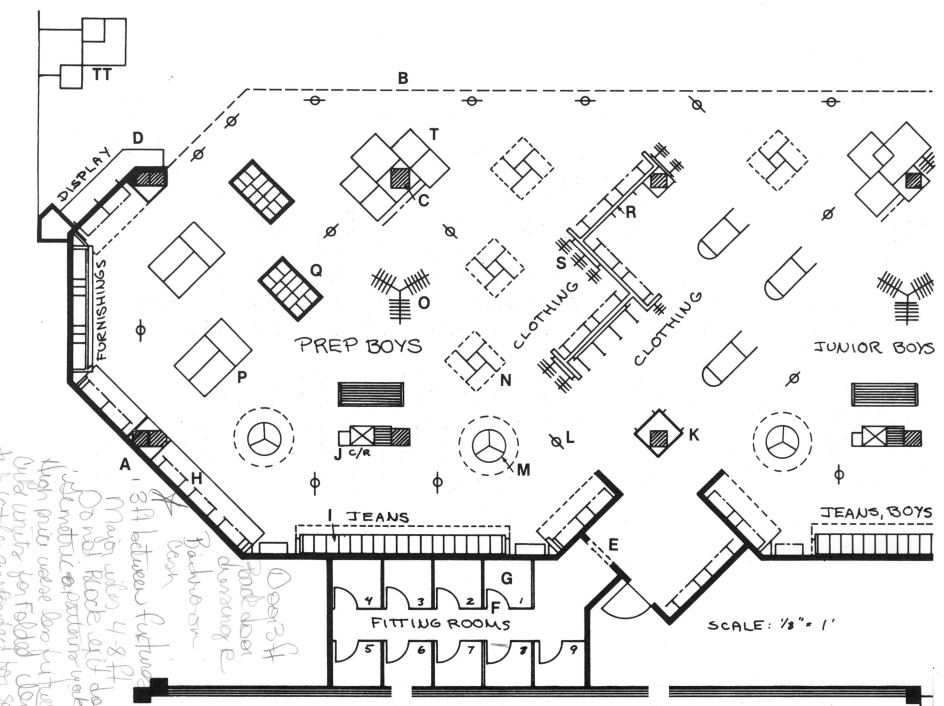

Figure 15-2. A section of an actual department store floor plan with the floor and wall fixtures drawn in.

A: The heavy line represents a constructed wall that serves as the perimeter or enclosing wall of a particular area or department.

B: The thin, straight, broken line is the boundary of the department and the delineation between the selling area and the walkway or aisle. In the store layout, that line could also indicate a change in flooring materials: hard floors (wood, ceramic, asphalt, or vinyl tiles) for the aisle, and soft floors (carpeting) in the department.

C: The shaded-in rectangles represent the columns necessary to the building's construction. As one looks at this plan, it is simple to see the pattern and spacing of the columns.

D: A platform, facing the aisle, designed to hold a display setup. Directly behind are two columns enclosed within a semitriangular partition.

E: The two dotted lines indicate an archway or opening in an otherwise straight wall. This is the entrance into the fitting room area.

F: The traditional symbol for a door, a thin line plus an arc.

G: The individual fitting rooms.

The fixtures on the floor plan are represented as follows:

H: Wall-hung merchandise. The two thin lines, perpendicular to the constructed wall, are probably brackets that are connected into a slotted system set in or on that wall. It is a safe assumption since so many perimeter walls have slotted uprights. The broken line between the two brackets indicates the hang-rod. It is depicted by a broken or dotted line because it is above the floor level. The dotted line that is spaced about 1 foot out from the hang-rail is an overhang or valance extending out from the wall. It covers over the hang-rods and is probably equipped with secondary lighting for merchandise and the back wall.

I: Binning on the perimeter wall. The dotted line in front of it is an overhead fascia or canopy with lighting.

J: A cash register and wrapping station, known as a C/R or cash/wrap desk. It is often combined with a column, as shown here. The latter provides an electric outlet, necessary for most new registers, as well as visibility. A shopper can see a column from across the floor, and thus, more easily find the cash/wrap station.

K: A column enclosure. It is a shield or mask built around an actual column and used either decoratively or functionally. Sometimes, the sides are mirrored to provide ambience as well as mirrors to enable shoppers to examine the merchandise. Sometimes, they are used as a backup for a mannequin platform (see N) or to hold merchandise from attached hang-rails or waterfalls.

L: A T-stand, the small, special item or featured attraction displayer often used to line the aisle as a "come-on." They are also used throughout the department as "reminders."

M: A round rack, in this instance, on a "Y" frame. Depicted here is a standard unit, 3 feet in diameter. The broken circle that extends out another foot from the inner ring indicates where the outer edges of the hanging garments will extend beyond the fixture itself. Thus, a 3-foot round rack will actually take up a space on the selling floor measuring 5 feet in diameter.

N: A quad rack, or four-armed fixture which shows four face-out groups of merchandise. Again, the broken square encompassing this fixture indicates the outer edges of the hanging garments extending beyond the floor unit itself.

O: A "Y" rack. It takes up a large area on the floor and does not hold nearly as much merchandise as might be fitted into that same space on a different fixture. It does, however, present a different look, a different directional setup in merchandise presentation. The short bars extending from the three major arms of the unit are the "hangers," and again suggest the amount of space they will require.

P: A group of three tables in a cluster. Sometimes, these tables will have drawers or cabinet space below the table top for extra stock.

Q: A multiple binning unit raised up on a base or a table.

R: A low partition, not a floor-to-ceiling, constructed wall. The short lines that are perpendicular to the "wall" suggest that they are brackets that fit into slotted uprights.

S: Waterfalls or a "face-out" arrangement for merchandise. The three arms that extend out are crossed with "hangers" to show that the merchandise will face forward.

T: An arrangement around a column of platforms, pedestals, or cubes for a mannequin presentation.

TT: Another cube or pedestal buildup.

OTHER TYPES OF DIMENSIONAL DRAWINGS

It is also recommended that the displayperson learn to make an *elevation* of an object or area. Whereas the plan view gives the length and width (or depth) of an area, the elevation, or flat, front-on view, is another two-dimensional view that shows the width and the height. The elevation is used in conjunction with the plan. It supplies the missing measurements and answers questions like these: Does the table have drawers or cabinets below? Does the unit have legs, or does it sit directly on the floor? How many bins or shelves will fit on the wall?

Figure 15-3. A 30°/60° isometric projection of a counter-top point-of-purchase unit (*right*). An isometric projection must start with a scaled floor plan (*lower left*). An elevation (*upper left*) drawn from the plan will then show the proper heights of the various elements. The isometric projection is drawn, in the same scale, from the floor plan, using the heights indicated in the elevation.

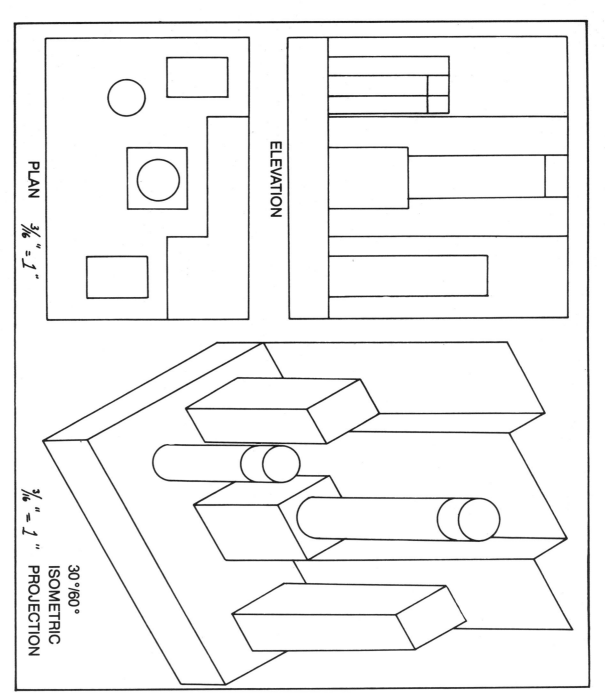

ELEVATION

PLAN ³⁄₁₆ " = 1 "

30°/60°
ISOMETRIC
PROJECTION
³⁄₁₆ " = 1 "

The displayperson can also attempt to master a simple *isometric perspective* or *projection* which is a type of mechanical, scale drawing that gives all the measurements (height, width, and depth), thereby providing a more natural, three-dimensional representation of an object or area. It is actually a form of shop drawing, and a carpenter or builder could take the measurements directly from the drawing, and at the same time see what the unit will look like. This type of dimensional representation starts with a correct and well-drawn floor plan.

16 Visual Merchandise Planning

A good display is the result of planning, coordinating, and cooperation. The displayperson must know, in advance, when a particular display will be installed, where it will be installed, and what will be shown and promoted. He or she needs some sort of schedule (which can be altered) or, at least, a master plan.

The execution of a good display comes from knowing, in advance, what trends, what colors, and what type of merchandise are scheduled for future display so that some thought and preparation can be made for the eventual visual presentation of that new merchandise. It also requires a close working relationship with the retailer or buyer, the promotion department, advertising people, and display manufacturers and suppliers.

Good displays come from the displayperson's knowledge of what is available and where, what is in stock or in the warehouse, and what can be borrowed or "begged" from neighbors or institutions in the community. It requires an awareness of what is going on in the community, in the city, in the country, and in the world, and then being able to draw on that awareness to create attention-getting, image-building, and merchandise-selling displays.

THE DISPLAY CALENDAR

A well thought out time schedule keeps displays and merchandise moving freely, in and out of the windows and on and off ledges and platforms. These predetermined time slots keep the store looking as new, fresh, and exciting as the new merchandise that keeps coming into the store. The change of windows may be set for every ten days or every two weeks. However, it should most emphatically *not* be any longer than one month between window changes. Even in the smallest store, there should still be a frequent change as well as variations with each change.

The schedule should be worked out with merchants and buyers, determined by when they buy new merchandise, seasonal and holiday promotions, and yearly sale events. There should be built into the plan the flexibility to switch or change a scheduled trim in the event of unexpected problems with merchandise delivery or happenings in the community or in the world. If there are only one or two display windows and several different classifications of merchandise (daytime dresses, evening wear, fur coats, lingerie, active sportswear, etc.), then the schedule should apportion which classification or type of merchandise will be presented, where and when. It can be based on the selling period (e.g., Mother's Day gifts, Christmas and New Year's Eve formals, etc.), or on the arrival of new merchandise (e.g., spring dresses, fall separates, winter outerwear).

The display schedule should be roughed out or

PLANNING A DISPLAY

The following are some of the points to consider in planning a display:

1. Is there a theme or an idea that will not only stimulate sales, but stimulate the displayperson to create an exciting, eye-arresting display based on that theme and idea? Are there to be newspaper advertisements; store mailings; national campaigns in magazines, on radio and television to tie in with the theme for greater impact and exposure? Is the theme new or timely?

2. Will the promotion or display presentation be limited to a single garment; a single classification of garments or merchandise; a single pattern, color, or featured designer? Is the promotion to be store-wide or will only one department or type of merchandise be featured? Will the window display be coordinated with the interior of the store: on major ledges, on columns, platforms, counters, and along the traffic aisles? How will the displayperson unify all these areas into a cohesive, dramatic, and dynamically flowing presentation? Remember, the simpler and more direct the approach, the easier it will be for the shopper to comprehend the message. Too many ideas, too many "stories," too many items or unrelated colors, can end up in confusion as well as clutter.

3. Ideally, the whole idea or theme of the display should be summed up in a copy card or reader that appears somewhere in the display area. It can be placed on a streamer or consist of raised, cut-out letters resting on the floor. It can be on a card raised up on an easel, or even spread across the front glass or all over the back wall of a window. This is the "key" copy, the catch phrase that tells—and sells—the story. The key message is told in the fewest words and in the most memorable way. It is like a message on a poster: simple, direct, and punchy. If it has a "ring" to it—a sound that stays on one's mind—so much the better. (See Chapter 20, "Signage.")

4. If there is to be a series of windows, will the merchandise all have the same look? Will there be variations on a theme? Will all the windows show only loungewear and robes, or will it be an emerald green promotion and include men's, women's and children's fashions and accessories—in green—as well as home furnishings, linens, kitchen gadgets, gift items, etc., in

blocked out a year in advance, based on the previous years experiences, sales, and promotions. If there is no previous experience on which to base a schedule, the displayperson might want to refer to the calendar on pages 124-125 which suggests possible events and promotions for a typical year.

that featured green? The displayperson may want to use the same decorative theme in all the windows—no matter what the merchandise classification, or vary the decorative elements from display to display, but retaining a flow and easy movement from window to window. The store management will decide how many windows to give to a promotion, and how those windows will be apportioned among the various departments in the store. This is part of *scheduling*. The schedule will indicate which merchandise will be given emphasis and "star" exposure, up front, and which will be subordinated to the secondary windows (on a side or less trafficked street) or to the shadow boxes.

5. How can this display setup be different from the previous one? Can a different set of mannequins—or an alternative to the regular mannequins be used? Can the background and floor colors be changed for this promotion? Can something new be done with the format of a window? Could the window be masked or cut down in size? Could a valance or proscenium be added to create a "come-and-look-at-this" frame around the glass? How about an awning or a change of awnings? Plants added in front of the window or trees or bushes placed between windows could provide a change. Can the type and arrangement of light be varied? How do we get the customer to know that something new and different is going on before they are close enough to really see it? (See Chapter 18 for some suggestions on attention-getting devices.)

6. How do we reinforce the store's image with this display? Is it possible to enhance the store's reputation while promoting the merchandise? Some noted stores today show only image-promoting window displays, assuming that shoppers will be fascinated enough to want to enter the store in order to be transformed into what was promised outside—in the window.

THE VISUAL MERCHANDISER'S PART IN STORE PROMOTION

Big promotions and big sale events need advance preparation time. They should be developed for possible themes, concepts, slogans, and directions, in cooperation with retailers and the promotion and advertising staffs. It is a good idea to find out if an extra budget allowance exists for some of these promotions. Sometimes, a manufacturer contributes to the promotion and advertising of a product by the store, or the store may be able to tie in with another group, e.g., an airline, a foreign trade council, or an industry organization.

The displayperson should start searching, among his or her regular suppliers as well as elsewhere, for props and devices to be used in the coming promotion. Often, props are available just for the asking or for an acknowledgment card in the display. The visual merchandiser should also question, if he or she does not already know, how much lead time (advance planning time) is necessary in order to ensure the on-time delivery of props, backgrounds, and accessories for the promotions. It is then the visual merchandiser's responsibility to get the "go-ahead" and/or the additional funds to get these items into the store and the windows on time.

Ideally, the displayperson should see or know, in advance, exactly what merchandise is coming in and what he or she will be required to "show." It means knowing how many pieces of merchandise will be available to the displayperson, in what colors, patterns, and styles; and what accessories are to be used. It usually does not work out that way, however.

Some stores have a fashion coordinator who pulls or specifies the merchandise and the right accessories before the display is scheduled to go in. Often, however, the displayperson or a member of the display staff must wander through the store, requisition book in hand, writing out requests or receipts for shoes from one department, scarves from another, jewelry from still another area, and so on. Some stores or fashion coordinators will bring in special merchandise and/or accessories to enhance their display presentation. This is called *showpiece buying.*

Scheduling the Promotion

Let us assume that the basic schedule was blocked out a year in advance and that the theme, copy, and advertising for the promotion were already "roughed out." Three months before the promotion breaks, the displayperson will order whatever props or backgrounds are necessary from an outside supplier. He or she will then schedule those parts of the display presentation to be done in the display studio of the store (e.g., covering floor and wall panels, signs, posters, mounted blowups, etc.).

A week or two before "P-Day" (promotion day), there should be a checkout with the buyers to be sure that the promotional merchandise is in or on its way, and that everything is set to go as planned. The displayperson should also check those areas in the store to be tied in with this promotion: the counters, ledges, platforms, etc., to be trimmed. The necessary signage, the pads to be changed in cases and under counters, backgrounds to T-walls, .the walls over ledges, and the column treatments—also have to be considered.

The following is a suggested countdown listing for installing a display, be it part of a major promotion or a regularly scheduled display change:

1. *The merchandise.* Is it in the store? Is it ready for the display: selected, cleaned, and pressed? Is it the merchandise that was expected? Does it, in the full piece, look the same as it did in the color swatches or samples around which the window was designed? If not, will any changes from the original plans be necessary? Have all the accessories been pulled together? Are there any unexpected problems?

2. *Mannequins.* Have the correct mannequins been selected on which the merchandise is to be displayed? Do they have the correct line, the appropriate look? Will the body positions work with the garments? Are they clean? Have any chipped fingers been repaired? The nail polish restored? Is any emergency cosmetic treatment required on cracks or rubs on the finish? Are the wigs right: the right style, the right color, and in good condition? Will the shoes fit properly? Does the mannequin's base need any special covering or repair? Are all the parts in one place and ready to be assembled?

3. *Lights.* Are all the necessary lights working? Does anything need to be replaced? Have the right filters been found and set aside? Are any necessary extra extension cords on hand? (It would be wise to have a few additional spots available should the setup need more lighting than anticipated.)

4. *Props, fixtures, and backgrounds.* Are all the pieces necessary for the presentation in the store? Does anything still have to be picked up? The displayperson should refer to his or her floor plan and display checklist, ticking off the items. Are the props, platforms, and risers that are to be used in top condition? Are any scratches, rips, runs, or ragged edges visible? Can a quick paint job or "touch up" remedy the eyesore? What is the condition of the fixtures to be used? If need be, will camouflage or "display magic" work (e.g., the addition of some ribbons or trimming, some netting, tape, etc.)? Are the floor pads covered? Are the wall coverings ready? Will the display window be clean, inside and outside, on the day of the trim? If the walls of the window show, in what condition are they? If there is a permanent carpet on the floor, will a thorough vacuuming be sufficient, or should the displayperson plan for some decorative ground cover (gravel, pebbles, ground cork, flitter, scatter grass, and so on) to cover any badly worn or soiled areas?

5. *Signs.* If any price and copy cards will be needed, are they ready?

On the day of the *installation,* the previous trim is "pulled" (removed) and the merchandise is returned to the proper departments. The *final* countdown includes the following:

1. The merchandise to be installed is given a final check: wrinkles, loose threads, uneven hems, loose buttons, mismatched patterns, etc.

Display Calendar

JANUARY

SALES:
Post-Christmas
Pre-inventory
White sales (linens, blankets, towels, comforters, spreads, etc.)
Furniture, bedding, and home furnishings

PROMOTIONS:
Foundations and lingerie
Bridal showings
Resort and cruise wear
Pre-season (for spring)

TIE-IN EVENTS:
Football—Bowl games
Martin Luther King's Birthday (15)
Benjamin Franklin's Birthday (17)
F. D. Roosevelt's Birthday (30)

FEBRUARY

SALES:
Final winter clearances
Presidential birthday sales (Lincoln and Washington)
Housewares

PROMOTIONS:
Valentine's Day
New spring fashions and colors

TIE-IN EVENTS:
Thomas A. Edison's Birthday (11)
Abraham Lincoln's Birthday (12)
Valentine's Day (14)
George Washington's Birthday (22)
Bachelor's Day (27)

MARCH

SALES:
Pre-Easter
China, glass and housewares

PROMOTIONS:
Spring and Easter for the whole family
New season accessories
Children's shoes
Rainwear
Summer bridal fashions
Home and garden improvement: fabrics, floor coverings, curtains and draperies, slipcovers, etc.

TIE-IN EVENTS:
St. Patrick's Day (17)

APRIL

SALES:
Post-Easter
Pre-summer fabric
Sleepwear and lingerie

PROMOTIONS:
Easter
Summer wear
Fur storage
Early swimwear and sunwear

TIE-IN EVENTS:
April Fool's Day (1)
Easter
Pan-American Day (14)

MAY

SALES:
Baby Week.
Home furnishings and housewares
Spring apparel clearance
Memorial Day sales

PROMOTIONS:
Mother's Day
Bridal
Summer sportswear
Change-of-season ready-to-wear
Luggage and vacation needs
Outdoor living

TIE-IN EVENTS:
Mother's Day (second Sunday)
First nonstop trans-Atlantic flight— Charles Lindbergh (May 20, 1927)
American Red Cross (21)
Memorial Day (end of month)

JUNE

SALES:
Home furnishings and bedding
Furniture

PROMOTIONS:
Father's Day
Graduation
Bridal gifts
Summer formals
Camping clothes and supplies

JULY

SALES:
Independence Day sales
Summer clearance begins
White sales

PROMOTIONS:
First flurry of fall
Fur coats
Early back-to-school
Christmas in July
Outdoor living

TIE-IN EVENTS:
Independence Day (4)
Bastille Day (14)
First Feminist Convention in U.S. (July 19, 1848)

AUGUST

SALES:
Summer storewide clearance
Furniture and bedding
Fur sales

PROMOTIONS:
New fall fashions
Back-to-school and college
Career fashions
Bridal showing
Woolen fabrics

TIE-IN EVENTS:
Founding of Red Cross, Geneva, Switzerland (Aug. 22, 1864)
19th Amendment, Women's Suffrage (Aug. 26, 1920)

SEPTEMBER

SALES:
Labor Day sales

PROMOTIONS:
Fall fashions and accessories
School supplies
Home improvement (china, glass, etc.)

TIE-IN EVENTS:
Summer active sportswear
Bathing suits
Sporting goods, cameras
Men's wear and furnishings (with a Father's Day tie-in)

TIE-IN EVENTS:
Father's Day (third Sunday)
Flag Day (14)

Sporting and hunting supplies
Introduce coats, suits, outerwear

TIE-IN EVENTS:
Labor Day (first Monday)

OCTOBER

SALES:
Columbus Day
Import
Anniversary or special storewide

PROMOTIONS:
Introduce Christmas gifts
Layaway plans
Evening and dress-up wear
Furs
Ski shop
Women's coats and suits
Outerwear for the family
Gloves and millinery
Personalized Christmas cards
  and gifts

TIE-IN EVENTS:
Baseball World Series (might be late
  September)
Columbus Day (12)
United Nations Day (24)
Statue of Liberty dedicated in 1886
Halloween (31)

NOVEMBER

SALES:
Thanksgiving Day
Veteran's Day
Pre-Christmas
Election Day
Fur sales

PROMOTIONS:
Christmas gifts
Home furnishings for the holiday
  season
Evening wear
Stay-at-home dress-up

Women's coats
Men's clothes and furnishings
Toyland is open—Santa is coming

TIE-IN EVENTS:
Election Day (first Tuesday)
Veteran's Day (11)
Sadie Hawkins Day (16)
Thanksgiving (third Thursday)

DECEMBER

SALES:
Pre-inventory clearance
Clearance of holiday goods (cards,
  wrapping, trim, and novelties)
Pre- and post-Christmas sales

PROMOTIONS:
Christmas gifts and fashions
Institutional windows
Formals and holiday clothes
Bridal showing
Beach and resort wear

2. The tool kit is completely fitted, and all the necessary tools and accessories are in it. (See Chapter 17 for specific recommendations.)

3. The lights are clean and working.

4. The windows and floors have been cleaned.

Much of this preparatory work becomes "second nature" once the displayperson has had some experience planning, setting up, and trimming displays. The best professionals remember to check out and take care of all the *little* details; most of the "big" ones are obvious and will be easily seen and checked. Remember: Someone out there is looking—judging the merchandise and the store. It is the responsibility of the displayperson that everything being shown is presented at its best—in the best of all possible ways.

17 Setting Up a Display Shop

If one goes to work for a department store or a large specialty store, there will probably be an established display area or department with tools, tables, bins, and the assorted paraphernalia that gets collected over the years. In the event, however, that such a shop does not exist, one would have to be set up. An effective but minimal shop can be equipped in a minimum space, with a small budget for materials and machinery. This shop should provide the basics for a work area to facilitate the planning, designing, detailing, preparation, and the eventual storage of displays—and all that these processes involve.

PHYSICAL REQUIREMENTS

There should be enough space for a worktable, a desk, a drawing table, bins, storage cabinets, and possibly, a sign machine or even a sign shop. Also necessary is a sink or some other source of water for mixing water-based latex paints, for doing a watercolor rendering, and for clean-up. Good lighting and lots of electrical outlets are essential. The displayperson also needs a telephone to keep in close touch with store activities and also to provide a line to the outside world and to suppliers.

A decent ceiling height is important since props,

rolls of seamless paper, and mannequins cannot be bent. Although hard floors (vinyl or asbestos tiles) are not the most comfortable under foot, they are easier to maintain than carpets. An office apart from the actual shop—a place to plan and draw projects and keep files, is desirable. It can be screened or curtained off, or set off by a 4- or 5-foot partition, but the more private and the more soundproof it is, the better. Shops can and do get noisy.

FURNITURE

To conduct the business of the department, a desk or other writing surface (not a drawing board) will be necessary. It will be a place to figure costs and work up budgets, to file away paid bills and find unpaid ones, to open mail and write correspondence, to study upcoming promotions, peruse fashion magazines and other periodicals relevant to the merchandise being offered by the store, and to check out the latest in *Women's Wear Daily*. A desk lamp and a good chair or two will also be very useful.

A file cabinet will be needed for the necessary files which must be kept. An organized displayperson knows what has been ordered, what has come in, and what has to go back. He or she should keep a log or calendar of

127

trims and coming events, and if possible, a record of past displays. Ideas for future displays should be filed away along with booklets, brochures, and other collected data which may be needed at some future date. Everything should be organized, labeled, and logically filed so that others, if necessary, can locate designs or data.

A drawing table or some sort of drafting setup should be a surface apart from the desk, and used for sketching, drafting, and designing. This surface can be at desk height (29 to 30 inches), counter height (36 inches) or higher, depending upon what suits the displayperson. He or she might prefer to sit on a posture chair, or to perch on a 24- or 30-inch stool, or perhaps stand to draw. A good light source which can be directed to the work surface is a must.

A *taboret*, or small drawer or cabinet unit (perhaps on wheels), should be close to the drawing table. It is necessary for the storage of drawing supplies, tools, templates, paints, pencils, and the other items necessary for the creative process.

A large, clean, unobstructed work surface is also a necessity. It should be 4 feet by 8 feet, at least, and approachable from all sides. This island in the display shop is used for cutting, scoring, constructing, and even dressing forms or children's mannequins. It should be at least 36-inches high. If possible, the area below the work surface could be a combination of cabinet space and shelf space. The cabinet could hold some of the tools that will be used at the table, and the shelf could be used for oversized cardboard or paper. This worktable should be under a good light fixture. There should be an electrical outlet close by for power tools. The tabletop could be covered with a piece of thick fiberboard or an inexpensive grade of plywood. There should be a roll of inexpensive wrapping paper on hand so that the tabletop has a clean and fresh covering on which to work. It is easier to put a fresh piece of paper down than to replace the tabletop. It also would be a good idea to use a clean, quilted cover (such as that used by furniture movers) to put over the table if it is going to be used for dressing mannequins or forms.

Adequate closets and shelves are essential for the storage of tools and hardware supplies, as well as for basic fabrics and trimmings. Also vital are bins for the storage of mannequins, their spare parts and wigs, and other forms. Ideally, the bins should be padded. Extra arms and/or action legs should be stored with or above the mannequin with which they will be used. If the bins are open, then a curtain should be installed to pull across the stored mannequins in order to keep them free from paint or sawdust while the worktable is in use. If the construction of bins is too involved, the displayperson could use a system of slotted uprights (standards) and brackets along one wall. Start these shelves about 6-feet high (i.e., just above a mannequin's head), and use them to store the parts and accessories that go with the figure placed directly below. Pieces of fiberboard, cut into 2-foot by 8-foot panels, can be used as vertical dividers between the shelves and act as separators between the forms. The mannequins could also be laid out on shelves, but they would have to be at least 24-inches wide for the mannequins to be secure. The shelf should be lined with a pad or felt, and a protective piece of plastic used as a cover over the reclining form.

The use of several fireproof, metal cabinets is advisable for the storage of inflammable paints, dyes, spray cans, etc. Paint brushes, rollers, and other painting equipment could also be stored in these cabinets, or nearby. When painting, adequate ventilation, may be a problem. Never spray paint in an enclosed or unventilated area. If need be, go on the roof, into the parking lot, or to any available space with an open window.

It is a good idea to have a simple, inexpensive pipe rack or two around to hold the merchandise to be collected, pressed, and/or steamed—and is ready to be displayed. A pipe rack can also hold the garments that have been "pulled" (removed from a display) and have yet to be returned to the proper department or area. An inexpensive shoe bag, with see-through pockets, could be attached permanently to the pipe rack, and the pockets could hold not only the right shoes for the selected outfit, but the other accessories that will be shown.

A small "dump" wagon, or a box on wheels, facilitates the movement of mannequins, props, tools, and more from the display department to the area to be trimmed.

If the operation is small and the borrowing of fashion accessories is not feasible, a locked cabinet should be provided for the storage of "basic" costume accessories (e.g., shoes of the proper size and heel height, costume jewelry—chains, pearls, colored beads—solid-colored scarves, a few new purses, some neutral colored gloves, etc.). The locked cabinet might even include some basic hat shapes in straw or felt which could be trimmed with ribbons, scarves, or flowers.

TOOLS AND SUPPLIES

Displayperson's Tool Kit

Every displayperson must keep an adequately stocked tool kit containing a staple gun (with extra staples), staple clipper, diagonal cutters (nippers), scissors and/or shears, "X-acto" knife, claw hammer, screwdriver,

Allen or hex wrench, Phillips screwdriver, masking tape, cloth tape, cellophane tape, assorted pins (banker, dressmaker, and "T" pins) nylon fish-line, "invisible" piano wire, fine sandpaper (or any emery board), kneaded eraser, needle and "invisible" thread, white glue (Sobo or Elmer's brand), whisk broom, some clean rags, ruler, tape measure, and extension cord. It is desirable to have a compact clothes steamer and miniature vacuum cleaner to bring into the display area for a final touch-up.

Hand Tools in the Display Shop

The aforementioned kit moves from the shop with the displayperson. Therefore, a separate set of tools should remain in the shop.

These should include the following: hammer, mallets, assorted screwdrivers (including a Phillips screwdriver), Allen or hex wrench, Stilson wrench, awl, pliers, wire cutters, nippers, plane, brace and bits, hacksaw, coping saw, chisels, staple guns, staple clippers, C-clamps, vise, a Pantograph or blowup machine (to enlarge drawings), mat knife, squares, compass (for big radius drawings); assorted nails, brads, screws, and staples; white glue, rubber cement, Duco brand cement.

Power Tools in the Display Shop

A *cut awl* is a "must." This is a lightweight power tool that is designed to cut out intricate profiles from boards and fabrics of assorted weights. It works best on a padded surface so that the cutting blade, which extends below the flat base surface of the saw, can bite into something disposable after passing through the layer or layers it is cutting. It comes with a variety of blades and attachments, making it very versatile.

Another desirable power tool is the *Skilsaw*, a portable, lightweight circular saw for ripping and cross-cutting. It can be used anywhere within reach of an electrical outlet; therefore, with this tool, it is possible to bring the "shop" to the installation. A *jigsaw* is another hand-held power tool which is excellent for cutting curves, scrolls, and irregular patterns. It is possible to adapt this tool to make inside cuts as well as outside cuts. The following power tools are also useful in a display shop: sander, electric hand drill with assorted bits, a router, a power or table saw, an air gun, and possibly, a band saw.

Basic Supplies

Seamless paper, or *no-seam paper,* is useful, relatively inexpensive, available in many colors, and extremely versatile. A stock of colors should be kept on hand. Seamless paper comes in rolls 9-feet wide by 36- or 50-feet long. Storing these tall rolls can present a problem. Even if there is enough space to store them upright, it is best to store them parallel to the ground and not stand them on end. The ends could become crushed or wrinkled. If space permits, they could be placed against a long wall, one over the other, and supported on brackets, with the whole selection on view. Since seamless paper is sometimes the medium for a painted or drawn background in a window, a wooden frame should be kept near the stock of paper. If it were necessary to draw a sketch on the seamless paper, all the displayperson would have to do would be to unroll the desired length of paper, tack it up on the frame, and start to draw.

Panels of fabric, sewn into curtains, could also be stretched out on this open frame to be painted or decorated. The frame can be constructed out of 2-inch by 4-inch lumber, with three vertical members going from floor to ceiling, and one top and one bottom member to hold it all together. If there is sufficient wall space available, the frame could be set about 1 foot forward from the wall. The space behind could be used to store templates for wall and floorboards, and so on.

Other basic supplies for the display shop include: casein paints, latex paints, and cans of assorted spray paints; enamels, metallics, and transparent floral dyes; fixatives (varnish sprayed over pencil or chalk drawings to protect them from smearing); spackle and wood filler; flitter (tiny bits of finely chopped brass and tin which sparkles) and glitter.

Basic Trimmings

The list of basic trimmings is endless, but for starters, the shop should stock: ribbons in assorted colors and widths; cotton and hemp rope; dowels and cardboard tubes of assorted lengths and diameters; braid, fringe, and gimp (or guimpe); cloth tapes in assorted colors and widths; millinery wire and covered wire; wrapping papers; assorted yarns and ties; gift boxes and assorted empty boxes, cases, and small crates; tissue paper in a range of colors; felt in as many colors as possible (but rolled rather than folded, the fold creases being hard to eliminate); net, tulle, duck, canvas, etc. A couple of fonts of cutout letters could be useful as well.

Save anything architectural or dimensional that is nonspecific, but can be adapted to different uses. For example, corrugated boards and boxes can make interesting backgrounds. Grass mats and assorted types of floor scatter could be useful, too.

Lighting Equipment

Start with extension cords, plugs, multi-outlets, electrical tape, wire, and assorted gelatins and colored glass filters with housings to attach to spotlights and floodlights. Add clamp-on holders for spots and floods. A simple, revolving wheel would be useful, as would a mirrored globe, or "disco ball," and turntables of assorted diameters, heavy enough to hold merchandise and mannequins.

There is no end to the list of things one could collect to fill a display department, but it takes time and money to do. To fill in any missing items, it may be necessary to "beg," borrow, and improvise. (See "Props" in Chapter 18).

BOOKS, PUBLICATIONS, AND REFERENCE MATERIALS

Whether the displayperson has an office, a studio, a shop, or works out of an attic or basement, some books and publications should be available, always at hand, for ready reference. Collecting books because they look nice, or because they have pretty pictures, is not the answer. Books should be used. They should be handled, read, and studied. It is not necessary to memorize everything contained in these reference books, but the displayperson should be able to find the information when needed.

Select the books as you would your friends. They will be around for a long time. They can become your allies, your protectors. They are filled with good ideas, suggestions, and answers. They can keep you from looking foolish because of misspelled or improperly used words. A good dictionary is a very worthwhile investment. *Roget's Thesaurus* or another good book of synonyms will give you a choice of words so that you can say the same thing, but in a different way. You can find ideas to "visualize" as displays in *Bartlett's Familiar Quotations*. Also, an encyclopedia will answer all kinds of questions, and can be fun to peruse.

Anyone in the fashion business should have a picture-filled history of costume to trace the derivation of a "new" look, a style, or a "retro" trend. A history of furniture and home furnishings is helpful if one has furniture to sell. Also, because furniture can be the right setting for fashion, it is helpful to know which are the appropriate periods to use in a display. The *Dictionary of Interior Design* illustrates periods and styles of furniture and architecture, and also lists art terms, artists, and artisans. The *Language of Store Planning and Display* is a compilation and explanation of thousands of words the displayperson hears in the daily business of presenting merchandise in a retail operation.

Also recommended is a subscription to Retail Reporting's "Views and Reviews," a weekly photo service, which reports on current window displays. Add, too, a subscription to *Visual Merchandising* magazine, a monthly publication filled with articles, photos, and ideas as well as ads for new materials and products. *Inspirations* is the European counterpart of *Visual Merchandising*.

The displayperson can subscribe to or purchase fashion magazines to keep up with the "scene." Fashion ads are filled with presentation concepts. Read *Women's Wear Daily*, the "bible" of the fashion world, for the day-to-day activities in this changing field. The displayperson should also peruse newspapers for community, national and world news, and for what is happening in the arts, sciences, and sports.

Other useful references include: illustrated books on the history of art and architecture; and travel books or brochures (filed by country), with vistas and views of familiar and recognizable sights, scenes, or symbols for ready reference.

A displayperson should become addicted to books and never pass up a book sale. One never knows from where an idea can come. He or she should *never* stop looking, reading, and learning.

18 Attention-Getting Devices

Be it a one-window, one-item display in an ultra-exclusive shop, or a wild, variety assortment in the multiwindow display of a mass merchandiser, the display was put there to be *seen*! The basic concept of display is to *show* and to *see* what is shown. One of the main problems in setting up a window display is how to attract attention in order to bring the prospective shopper closer to the window and then to convince him or her to enter the store.

In the past, merchandise tumbled out from the shop into the street to greet and envelop the shopper. Or, as is still practiced in some bazaars and markets today, the salesperson physically "collars" the shopper and cajoles him or her into buying something. This is hardly the recommended approach for sophisticated, fashion-wise storekeepers.

The display must be the "pssst" that is loud enough to be heard on a heavily trafficked street, but not so loud as to scare off the shopper. How the display says "pssst" will depend upon the merchandise and the image the store is trying to project. The display of a very chic and soft-sell type of shop may politely "clear its throat," and the "ahem" may be enough to be noticed by someone tuned in to the sophisticated—and the soft-sell. On the other hand, the popularly priced "shock 'em and sock 'em" operation may yell out a "hey you!" What they both want is the shopper's attention for a brief but important moment.

Sometimes, the most effective way to get attention is by not raising one's voice at all. Silence, the absence of sound, can in some cases make a very loud "noise." Also, it should be remembered that getting the shopper's attention sometimes will depend on what neighboring stores are doing.

There are many devices that can be used to attract the shopper's attention. Some of these, discussed below, have been organized into the following categories:

- Color
- Lighting
- Line and composition
- Scale
- Contrast
- Repetition
- Humor
- Mirrors
- Nostalgia
- Motion
- Surprise and shock
- Props

Color, lighting, and line and composition have been discussed earlier, in greater detail, in Chapters 5, 6, and 7, respectively.

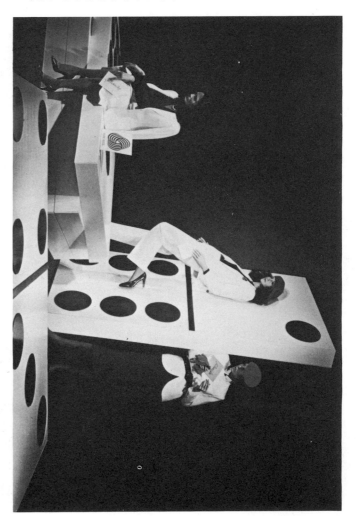

Figure 18-1. The black background makes the white dominoes appear even larger and whiter (providing greater contrast) and, thus, more eye-catching. The black and white fashions also become extremes of lightness and darkness thanks to the contrasts and the extremes. The bright red hats and gloves are a surprise and, therefore, add sparkle to the presentation. *Gimbels, New York.*

Figure 18-2. The use of spotlights and floodlights not only puts the mannequin into a brilliant pool of light, but the lights also become props and the scene-setters for this "fashion photo session." The copy card reads, "Black and white and light and...." *Carson Pirie Scott & Co., Chicago.*

Figure 18-3. A long horizontal line is broken with diagonals, easy and leisurely, but with a snap of difference. The face of the mannequin on the right is brightly lit. Her braid and her arm lead to the left shoulder of the mannequin seated on the floor. The light picks up the composition and leads down to the bowl, on the floor, in the foreground. *Saks Fifth Avenue, New York.*

Color

Color is still the big attraction. It is what we see first, what attracts us to an object. A big "hot pink" promotion can be dazzling in its intensity on a cool, gray day; the warmth of the color pink, flowing and gushing out from the window, can draw the passerby like a magnet.

An all-black-and-white window makes a really strong color statement even though the colors are neutral. Here, the power to attract is in the absence of color, especially since the display will be surrounded by a multicolor explosion of people moving back and forth in front of it.

Thus, a sharp color contrast will do it: black and white, red and yellow, and so on. Even in a window filled with dozens of related or assorted items, if all the merchandise is telling the same color story, in unison, the display will have the power to attract!

Lighting

Lighting is another device used to draw shoppers to both window and interior displays. Effective display lighting can be the jolt that catches the eye and carries it to the product. A forceful spotlight in a subtly lit display area can be as attention-getting as a yank on the collar.

A display bathed in fiery red or eerie green or dramatic blue light can effectively intrude into the gray environment of concrete sidewalks and building facades. Brilliantly colored lights can command instant eye contact. A window, or any interior display for that

matter, without lighting might just as well be a window with a drawn curtain or merchandise left hanging in a closet. Even a drawn shade can elicit more curiosity or interest than an unlit window.

Line and Composition

Line and composition can be valuable attention-directors after color and lighting have done their parts. The use of vertical, horizontal, curved, and diagonal lines can help determine the effectiveness of a merchandise presentation. Each type of line suggests something else (for example, vertical lines: height, dignity, strength; horizontal lines: width, elegance, tranquillity; curved lines: softness, grace; diagonal lines: action, force, dynamism). Each can be used in different ways to arrest the attention of the passerby to the display.

Composition is the arrangement of different visual elements in order to achieve a unity and wholeness. When brought together effectively, line and composition lead the eye around the design of the display, through the patterns created by the mannequins and the merchandise, around props and platforms, until the sales "spiel" is given and the scenic route is completed. In this way, the attention of the shopper is brought to the entire display as well as to each of its parts.

Scale

A change of proportion, an abnormal size relationship, is an attention-getter. Something overly large makes an average-size object appear tiny, while something tiny

Figure 18-4. Both the electric outlet and the whistle and string are way over life-size. They really call for attention. The orange and white merchandise plays against the orange outlet and floor and the white background. The whistle jumps out at the viewer because of its unexpected deep blue color as well as its size. The string leads the viewer through the display, while the whistle directs the eye toward the next window in the group. *Macy's, New York.*

Figure 18-5. The sharp, black vinyl silhouettes of place settings against a startling white background are sure scene-stealers in a series of five outside shadow-box windows. The china dishes are set off from the contrasting "bull's-eyes" behind them to gain full attention, while the diagonal lines of the composition add emphasis and a sense of excitement to what could otherwise be a staid and formal presentation. *Macy's, New York.*

Figure 18-6. It's a "hat trick"; hats on mannequins and hats hanging in midair, but it is the same hat that is repeated over and over. The mannequin on the far right wears the only red hat; all the others are black. A red circle on the wall, on the far right, behind the floating black hat, plays up the solid black dress. The other dresses are in assorted patterns of red, white, and black. *Macy's, New York.*

(e.g., miniatures or models) makes something average in size (e.g., a mannequin) appear to swell and soar to superhuman size. This is playing with scale and proportion.

Our eye accepts objects in relation to other objects. We know, approximately, how tall a door is because we know about where an average human being would stand in relation to that door. As the relationship between a known object and a known figure (e.g., a mannequin) changes, and slight differences are replaced with glaring differences, the look or size of the object to the figure, and vice versa, appears to change as well. Next to a door scaled up 12 feet, a 6-foot mannequin seems to shrink to about 4 feet. The human figure is dwarfed by comparison.

Place a full-size mannequin in a setting of child-scaled furniture, and the figure grows in stature and in appearance. The change from the traditional or usual proportion is the attention-getting technique. It is an "irritant"; the viewer "knows" the mannequin is not shrinking and that the door is overscaled, but the unexpected sight of a normal figure "growing" or "shrinking" will draw attention.

Contrast

Contrast accomplishes with light and color what a change of scale or proportion can do with line and form. A white gown against a black background, or a white spotlight on an otherwise dark display—these are the types of jolts that cause the eye to react and relay a message to the mind which says "something different"

is going on here, something special."

A beach or resortwear display, glowing with sunshine, blue skies, and palm trees is particularly effective when the street outside is mired in slush and dismal winter gloom. That is an example of contrast, too.

Repetition

Repeating an idea over and over again will make an impact—and the message will sink in. In a fashionable, but not *haute couture* operation, the same dress worn by three mannequins, each in the same pose but with different makeup and hairstyles, can be an attention-getter. Three different garments made of the same pattern or print, on mannequins in the same pose, will also score. A lineup of props of the same size and color, strung across a display and ending up with a single piece of merchandise, will be most effective, too.

Three windows in a bank, or group, reiterating the same color or promotional theme do so with more impact than a single, isolated window. It is also much more emphatic then three windows, each different, with different merchandise, each in competition for the shopper's attention. Seven coats (odd numbers seem to work better than even numbers) hung on hangers, all at the same height, will dramatize a coat story, especially if the different coats are all in the same color family, or presented in a dramatic, light-to-dark grouping of color.

If something is worth repeating, repeat it several times over. It could be just the attention-getting device for which the displayperson is looking.

Figure 18-7. In this marvelously clever window, six sheep are rolled in cuddly, warm comforters and stacked for greater effect. This display combines elements of repetition with humor and the sure knowledge that most people are pushovers for plush toy animals. *Gimbels, New York.*

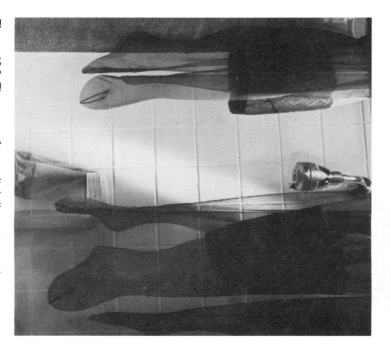

Figure 18-8. The cause for marital disagreement becomes an amusing presentation for limp, legless hosiery. Who does not recognize the scene: Hidden behind a shower curtain, hosiery is hung to dry. Not a pretty sight, but one that is sure to get a knowing and sympathetic smile. *Macy's, New York.*

Humor

A smiling shopper can be converted into a customer much sooner, and with much less effort, than a frowning or grumpy shopper. If a "show me" attitude can be replaced with a "that's funny" or "isn't that cute" outlook, a sale may not be far off. People will laugh at themselves and human foibles. Show the human and humorous side of life in display; show the "happily-ever-after" type of display. Freeze a moment out of the "soap opera"—an embarrassing situation or an awkward scene. Most people love to laugh at the harmless discomfort of others.

Examples of humorous scenes include a man in full evening dress, but also wearing sneakers or a T-shirt. Imagine a dignified woman in fur coat, hat, gloves, and "sensible" pumps astride a motorcycle; or floppy, soft-sculptured figures dressed like humans sitting at a realistic breakfast table and discussing a White Sale, with cartoon-type balloons over their heads explaining it all.

Eye-stoppers and smile-provokers that worked have included a male mannequin disrobing, down to his shorts, in what seems to be a doctor's examining room, being spied on by two "nurses" hiding in the shadows. Another people-pleaser is children playing at being grown up in grown-up clothes. All that the successful, humorous display need elicit is a smile and a relaxation of the tense feelings of some shoppers.

Mirrors

Mirrors are marvelous. They can add depth, width, and

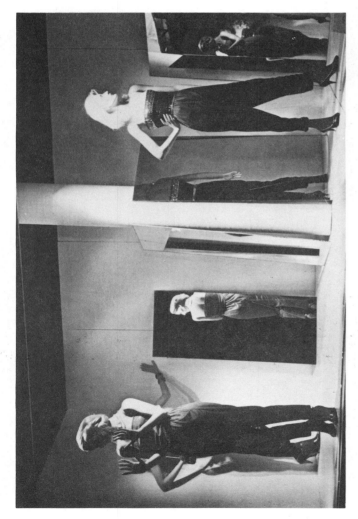

Figure 18-9. Cleverly angled mirrors add sparkle and interest to a window. They show many views of the garments being presented. The back of the mannequin leaning on the window glass, on the left, is reflected in the mirror behind it as well as in the mirror on the far right. The walls, floor, and the mannequins themselves are all purposely pale and washed out, in comparison to the black and red merchandise, by the carefully controlled and angled spotlights. *Macy's, New York.*

height to a display. They can reveal new angles and attitudes, show hidden backs and sides, and turn a setting into a full-round presentation. They reflect light and sparkle. They add flashes and unexpected splinters of light as a spotlight hits the surface of the mirror and sends out a spectrum of rainbow-colored sparks.

Mirrors, however, can also show the unfinished backs of objects and props, and the pinning and pulling together of nonfitting garments. They allow the shopper to see the backside of the window, the undressed, unglamourous side: the lights, cords, construction, and collected bits and pieces that perhaps never got swept out. Mirrors may also expose the shoppers to the overhead and side-lights that shoot back eye-stinging reflections into the viewer's eyes.

Mirrors can be the undoing of the presentation in other ways as well. People may become fascinated looking at their own reflections, completely overlooking the merchandise being presented. A good display-person will angle a mirror to show only that which is supposed to be seen. Mirrors should highlight, explain, repeat, or show a new fashion look.

Nostalgia

Nostalgia sells! Many people dream of the "good old days," which probably were not all that good and are not really so long gone. They find a backward glance to the fashions of the 1940's and 1950's as special as looking back to those of the 1880's and 1890's. We prefer to think that those were the golden days, days of charm and romance, when everything was "lovely."

The very old can be used to sell the very new.

Antiques and antique reproductions can add class and character to garments that still have to make their mark. By association with a "classic," a new classic is born.

People also love to see elements of "before and after." Show an old-time chemise, bustle, or crinoline in relation to today's teddy or other scanty undergarments. A line drawing, or a photo blowup of an etching, of a turn-of-the-century lady in the proper tennis attire of her day—all starched and buttoned up, from her high standing collar to her high buttoned boots, would make an interesting counterpoise for a long and lissome modern mannequin in an abbreviated tennis outfit. An old, wood-burning, kitchen stove as a backup for a microwave oven, could show how far technology has come.

Nostalgic props and scenes of the "good old days" can be used to lend their charm and acceptability to unknown and untested merchandise.

Motion

Motion or movement within a display area will get attention. A passerby is made suddenly aware, out of the corner of his or her eye, that something moved in an otherwise static setup. People of all ages will line up just to walk by and savor, for a few minutes, the delights of an animated Christmas display. An institutional spectacular does not become spectacular until some inanimate doll turns and bows, or a stuffed bear toots a horn, or an angel "sings" as part of a heavenly choir.

Motion can be created by a whole line of electric fans across a window, whirring and stirring up a small

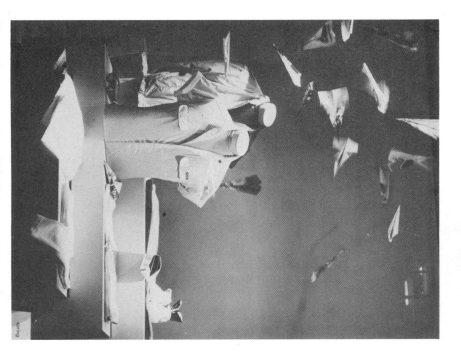

Figure 18-10. To sell new merchandise with memories of bygone times, the short-lived, but long-remembered automobile of the 1950's, the Edsel, appears right on the selling floor of this department store. This scene from a drive-in comes complete with trays containing gooey ice cream sundaes. It's *American Graffiti. Burdines, Sarasota, Florida.*

Figure 18-11. A squadron of folded paper airplanes zoom and twirl around the racing-style shirt and jacket. The wild motion of this aerial "attack" adds excitement and dash to exciting and dashing merchandise, which otherwise would be static. Notice the three-platform buildup used to show the lay-down merchandise. *Macy's, New York.*

hurricane to emphasize the cool, cool wonder of the clothes on the mannequin lined up behind the rotating fans. A single, old-fashioned ceiling fan, right out of the film, *Casablanca,* lazily spinning above a tropical setting, can move a palm tree or two below. (This display would be a combination of movement and nostalgia.) A fan, way off to the side and out of the shopper's view, can send a soft wind wafting through a window display just enough to play gently with the grace and lightness of a chiffon gown, or to set a scarf in motion.

Just as it can be attractive, motion can also be disturbing—irritating and distracting. Blinking lights and strobes have the impact of motion, but can be unpleasant and may do nothing positive for the presentation of the merchandise. The motion is intended to draw and attract the curious over to the window for a better view of the merchandise. It is generally not intended to be the whole show, except in those animated displays where no merchandise is being shown (Christmas institutional displays, for example).

A turntable will make a garment visible full round. It can show a variety of items as they come into view, each in its own space and each getting its moment in the spotlight. A turntable is relatively inexpensive to buy, easy to use, and versatile enough to use over and over again, in and out of the windows. Inside the store, it can add excitement to a gift display or individual place settings complete with linens, china, and crystal on a feature table, for example. A mannequin on a turntable which, in turn, has been set on a platform, will move around and show off some back interest. Shoppers will be interested enough in the turning movement to stop

Figure 18-12. What better way to sell leopard- and tiger-patterned outfits than on "tigers" and "leopards"—even if they are "humans" with animal masks. The dowels against the glass suggest a cage in a zoo. The elegant fashion parade beyond the bars is amusing and different. Notice the repetition of poses and the play of patterns. *Macy's, New York.*

and watch the full 360-degree showing.

Although it requires careful supervision by the displayperson, a display filled with battery-operated, stuffed animals can be fun. They can be made to carry on and carouse all over the display area, but the batteries will eventually run down, abruptly causing an end to the movement in this motion-filled display.

What gets more "oohs" and "ahs" than that "little doggie in the window"? A word of warning, however: *please, please* use care and discretion with live animals in a display. Windows heat up from the lights and the sun, air usually does not circulate adequately, and it can be disconcerting for the animals to have people constantly tapping for attention on the glass. There are also sanitation and odor problems that must be controlled. Therefore, it might be wiser and kinder to use cute, furry reproductions of live animals.

Some stores, usually those with open-back windows, have found that a live mannequin, walking into, around, and out of the display window—like a mini fashion show—will draw crowds to the window. Any live action in a window—a mime, a juggler, a disc jockey, a demonstrator, or even the displayperson setting up a window—is a great attention-getter. All the store is a stage and everything that moves—or looks as though it might move—becomes a player, attracting the attention of an audience of shoppers.

Surprise and Shock

Much of what has been described in various techniques outlined above will succeed in attracting atten-

tion because it involves elements of surprise or shock. A "smashed" window with a "brick" flying through it will stop a viewer in his or her tracks. The controlled mayhem of an overturned table, broken crockery, and a mannequin standing on top of a chair to escape from a mouse that looks like it just escaped from a Disney cartoon—will be answered by a viewer with a smile or a grin. Windows, floors, and props splashed with paints of all colors can be shocking and confusing, but a "come-on" all the same. However, there is always the safety of the glass between the viewer and the display to separate the shopper from the "shocking" or surprising goings on under all those lights.

A surprise can be fun; it can be a pleasant or amusing, unexpected moment frozen in time. A surprising display can be one with chairs on the ceiling, or a 7-foot "take-out" food container from a Chinese restaurant (a combination of surprise and scale), or an elegantly dressed mannequin "wearing" a cream pie on its face, with more pie splattered against the window and on the floor below.

A surprise can also be surrealistic or a bit of fantasy—the juxtaposing of objects out of a proper place or time sequence. For example, imagine a zoo setting, "bars" suggesting a cage, and a mannequin seemingly stalking about in a fashionable fur coat. The sign or copy card would clarify the "mix-up." Grownups acting like children, or "flying" off the ground like Mary Poppins or Peter Pan, will also get a second look from a passerby.

Shock goes beyond surprise. It must be used sparingly and carefully; it is a shakeup that can work against

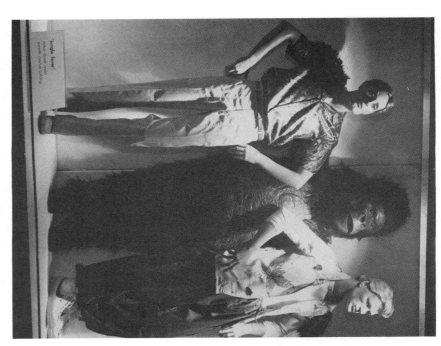

Figure 18-13, *above.* If you are promoting jungle or tropical patterns or fashions, why not introduce a gorilla? The shock of seeing the threesome presented in this display is sure to get a double take from the viewer. The "guy" in the fur suit in the middle is not selling what he is wearing, but he is certainly selling what his friends are wearing. *Macy's, New York.*

Figure 18-14, *above right.* This sleek, shiny turkey is a magnificent piece of sculpture fashioned out of knives, forks, and spoons to star in a window presentation of silverware for the Thanksgiving holiday. The use of the eating implements was more than clever; it was a great design and a traffic stopper. *Fortunoff, New York.*

the store and its merchandise even though it does attract attention. If not handled properly, a display aimed to shock can be upsetting, distasteful, or just plain, bad taste. Showing a mugger in the process of stealing a handbag, for example, will gain attention, but will it sell more handbags? How can a store benefit from showing a shooting in the window, with all of the realistic details, except to attract attention, and then generate unfavorable comments from long-standing, but now, irritated customers? Several years ago, a store on Fifth Avenue, in New York, showed such a window presentation, calling it "street art." Fortunately, it was reserved for a side window, and no merchandise was offered in that "murderous" setting.

Surprises can be delightful and ingratiating, capable of charming and amusing their audience. They can become topics of conversation: "Did you see what they did in X's window?" They can and will be remembered, and if the display is done well, the merchandise will be remembered, too.

Props

There is a whole industry that does nothing but produce props, devices, and gimmicks to enhance merchandise presentations. There are manufacturers who specialize in mannequins and forms; some produce fixtures and displayers; others create painted or photographically reproduced backgrounds; and still others collect tinsel, glitter, ornaments, and other assorted material from all over the world and supply them to the displayperson. There are some who are specialists in

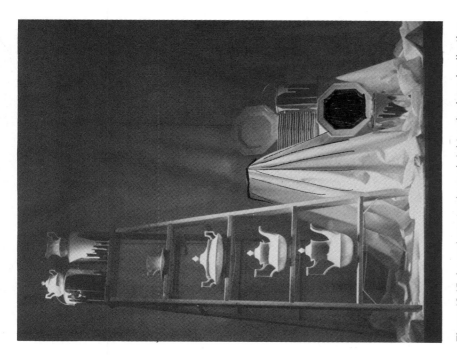

Figure 18-15. A novel way to show a bright, color-keyed collection of pottery: The stepladder supplies the necessary "steps" (risers) to show and separate the pieces. The dropcloth pulls the display together; hiding beneath it, the boxes used to create a different level for the dishes. The paint-stained cans restate the colors being promoted and also act as risers and separators. *Gimbel's, New York.*

foliage, while still another group supplies the raw materials, the decorative papers, and fabrics that become whatever the displayperson's imagination, time, and ability will allow him or her to create.

As members of the National Association of Display Industries and the Western Association of Visual Merchandising, these suppliers and manufacturers can be counted on to be reputable and reliable. Display trade shows are held several times a year. The NADI has one in early June and another in early December, while the WAVM has a major show in May. At these shows, the manufacturers and suppliers make their presentations of what is new for the coming seasons. In Dusseldorf, West Germany, once every three years, a "Euroshop" is held where hundreds of manufacturers from all over the world meet to present their latest designs and products. This is the industry that can sell the displayperson anything for merchandise presentation—from flower petals to palm trees, from elves to Santas, and from tie holders to floor fixtures.

There is, however, another world out there—one for the displayperson with little or no budget, but with imagination, drive, time, and the desire to be "different." Basically, it is a world of "beg, borrow, and make do." Even large retail operations must come over to this side of display when budgets shrink, which happens more and more often in times of inflation. Times like these test the displayperson's ability to improvise, be clever, creative, and see "splendor in the trash."

No store is an island unto itself. It is part of a street, a mall, a neighborhood, a community. Just as neighbors go next door and ask to borrow a cup of sugar or an egg, so the displayperson of a dress shop, for example, can step over and ask a noncompeting hardware store to borrow a stepladder, some unopened cans of paint, paint rollers, and dropcloths. The displayperson can then combine the ladder, paints, rollers, and dropcloths with mannequins dressed in bright yellow sportswear to promote a "Fresh Yellow Paint" story. A card in the window could give credit and thanks to the neighborly hardware store for its contribution. After the display is "struck," the unopened cans of paint and the clean dropcloths would be returned to the hardware store.

A Philadelphia store created a brilliant rainwear window by filling the floor space with clean, galvanized pails—the metal buckets traditionally used to catch leaks from the rain. The buckets were from a hardware supply house. And what could be simpler and more effective for certain promotions than artist's easels, paints, and brushes plus empty frames to accent and delineate merchandise or accessories? These useful props are only as far as the nearest art supply store. All one has to do is ask politely. Someday, the displayper-

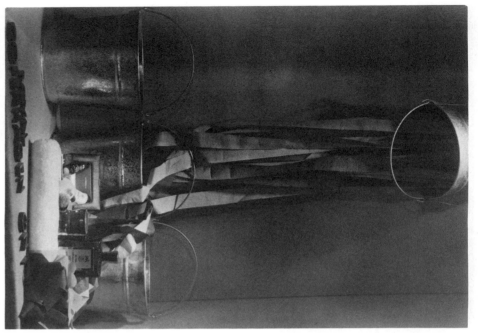

Figure 18-16. The galvanized metal buckets and "water" made of crepe-paper streamers of blue, aqua, and white suggest the cool and refreshing quality of the men's toiletries. They also are the colors that appear on the product packaging. The "downpour" leads to the buckets below and "overflows" over the grouped products in the foreground. The cutout letters supply the pertinent facts. *Macy's, New York.*

Figure 18-17. This spectacular array of ordinary folding chairs, used in a most extraordinary way, makes this large corner window even more dramatic. The height of the window is used and accentuated by having two of the mannequins each sitting and standing above eye level. The repetition of the pattern of chairs adds to the effective design and draw of this display. *Gimbels, New York.*

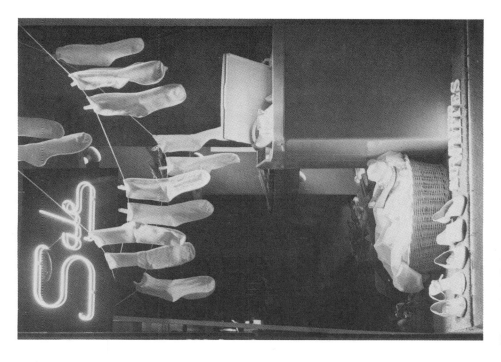

Figure 18-18. This washing machine prop is used to add new dash to a super-white summer promotion. The white socks and white shoes are hung on clotheslines, popping up out of the washer, and sitting in the wicker laundry basket. There is even a stepped-out line of footwear "walking" across the front line of the display. *Vittorio Ricci, New York.*

son may repay the "debt" to the art store with the loan of a be-smocked mannequin playing the artist, or without clothing—playing the model.

Cartons and crates can say anything from "import," "new arrivals," "open stock," or "ready for delivery." Brooms and shovels convey the concept of "clearance," "swept away with...," "getting ready for...." Brooms might even be used to supply a slightly giddy ride for mannequins on Halloween.

Ladders, of all kinds and sizes, are a great way to elevate a mannequin or even an assortment of small merchandise, like shoes "stepping up" in the fashion world or cosmetics "making the grade." Scarves, belts, and floral accents can cascade down the step. Planks, set horizontally between ladders, can become shelving units for sales promotions. Wire hangers, by the hundreds, can be woven into a fantasy that is still familiar—an abstract pattern created out of a fashion symbol. Shoe boxes can be risers, platforms, or spiraling stairways. They can also become building blocks or a big city skyline in miniature.

Other "sources" for props include: furniture stores which can be a great source for such props as beach chairs, bentwood chairs, ice cream and opera chairs, folding chairs, director's chairs, and all kinds and sizes of tables. "Raid" toy stores for stuffed animals, model railroad trains, planes, racing cars, building blocks, and pull wagons. There are also go-carts; supermarket shopping carts; golf carts, golf bags, clubs, balls, and tees; tennis rackets and tennis nets; bows, arrows, and targets—or anything from friendly and "giving" sporting goods, hunting, and camping goods stores.

Visit your local garden supply center for flower pots, rakes, hoes, lawn mowers, seed spreaders, packets of seeds, picket fences, plants and bushes in burlap bags, picnic tables and benches, beach and sun umbrellas, garden and patio furniture, barbeque grills and hibachis, firewood and logs. There are also clotheslines, clothespins, and clothes dryers. For travel and vacation promotions, use posters and giveaways from airlines, tourist offices, and foreign trade bureaus. See the importers in town who are looking for a place to show their wares. Luggage shops are a treasure trove of all those things that say "travel," "vacation," and suggest movement and direction. There are potential treasures in antique shops, secondhand shops, and clock stores. From building supply houses, "beg" bricks, cement blocks, terra-cotta blocks, gravel, rain drains, copper and brass pipes, joints, elbows, even the bathroom sink. Try tinsmiths, welders, ironmongers, and scrap metal dealers.

Even galleries, art shops, and handicraft stores might welcome some extra exposure. Explore art schools for young artists looking for a showcase; a store window might be just such a vehicle. Imagine the magic of a window filled with a display of military band instruments, gleaming and golden, and all courtesy of the local music store; along with collections of music boxes; music stands to hold sheets of music, copy cards, or fashion accessories; a metronome to suggest a timely move in fashion; and score sheets to play up a black-and-white sonata for spring.

Appliance centers have television sets and radios which will add color, light, movement, and interest. Fans, freezers, toasters, and coffee brewers can promote anything from cool summer clothes to beige or brown fashion colors. Extension cords, worklights, droplights, emergency lights—all spell "highlights."

There can be a display in a barber's chair, a dentist's chair, or a child's high chair. Piles of old newspapers can be as timely as the headline on the top sheet. A real refrigerator or ice maker can set a cooling pattern in a merchandise presentation. A water cooler, a desk, and some metal office files are all it takes to make an office setting—and they can all come from the office supply house. An architect's table, some high stools, a drafting lamp, and a taboret have the makings of a career scene for men or women. Store shopping bags and boxes make marvelous sales and clearance displays.

A housewares department has the ingredients for dozens of merchandise presentations: pins, brooches, or earrings in plastic egg storers; cooling balms and toiletries in vegetable crispers; hot-colored accessories in steamers. Why not a "sizzling hot" item in a frying pan? How about using colanders filled with spaghetti to show Italian imported shoes and bags. The possibilities are limitless! A few loaves of bread may last a week or more and add color and interest; slice one apart and make a "hero-ic" presentation with all the trimmings. A spray coat of lacquer may keep the bread looking fresh a little longer and retard any mold. Some fresh fruits and vegetables will have a window life of a week or two, but a few pounds of produce can go a long way in creating an effective, interesting display.

Do not pass up garage sales, "white elephant" sales, auctions, or house razings. Potentially, there are dozens and dozens of window displays and display props in all those objects that others want to dispose of. All you have to do is have the imagination and creativity to see the glitter amidst the ruins. Do not look at things for what they are, but for what they can be. Buy "classics." Buy things that can be used again and again and that always look different and can do different things. Buy objects that can be repainted, retrimmed, and/or rearranged.

When a house is being torn down, go prospecting. There is "gold" in "them thar ruins." There are doors, mantels, railings, architectural details, and even old bricks. A window frame, for example, has many uses. It can be used as a surrealistic, architectural frame, or realistically curtained and draped to create a vignette setting; a painted landscape could be inserted behind the open frame; or it can have drawn blinds, with perhaps a slat or two askew, to provoke the interest of some passerby. The outlined window could also become a framework for a geometric presentation of merchandise and accessories with some colored pinup panels placed behind it. In an open-back window, the

Figure 18-19. These file cabinets might come directly from the display office or an office supply house, but they certainly set the stage for career fashions. The opened drawers add interest, the scattered papers add vitality, and the mannequin atop the center file is unexpected, but highlights the whole composition. *Gimbels, New York.*

suspended frame will supply the background for the mannequin as well as the desired see-through presentation. As an additional touch, a few flower pots sitting on the "ledge" could be added for a seasonal accent.

Imagine what could be done with a segment of a row of seats from an old, torn down movie house. Think of all the vignette settings in which those seats could be featured. Old-looking, but not necessarily antique, curio cabinets and closets, strange and odd pieces of furniture with doors, drawers, and/or shelves—can be revived and rejuvenated quickly with a coat of paint. Investigate what is available from local theaters, theater groups, and movie houses. There can

be a potential display in the king-size poster for a current movie or a play, ballet, concert, or opera that is passing through your city. It can add a touch of culture and more than a smattering of what is current and special in town. There are local, municipal, and state institutions like museums, libraries, and historic preservations that can supply material on loan. Search out the local sources—and ask. How about traffic and road signs, bus and train signs, directionals and such?

You never know what can be had for the asking until you ask! Remember, the possibilities are limitless. The only real limitation is a lack of initiative, creativity, and imagination.

19 Familiar Symbols

Because they are used over and over again, certain familiar symbols used in display presentations are so commonplace that they have become clichéd. Clichés are the symbols and images that telegraph the message, sometimes more readily than the copy. One has to read to understand copy, but these symbols are like old, familiar friends; they announce and explain themselves. We have previously mentioned how certain colors or color combinations are recognizable as representing holidays or events; for example, red and green for Christmas; red and pink for Valentine's Day; red, white, and blue for presidential sales or the Fourth of July, and so on.

The following are everyday—and not so everyday —things that can be used to set a display scene; to trim a case, to accompany a mannequin on a ledge or platform, to accent a column or fascia trim, to illustrate a copy line, or to illuminate an event or promotion. They are simply ideas and "word-pictures" which hopefully will stimulate the displayperson's imagination.

Anniversaries

Anniversaries can be symbolized by anything old or antique, from bicycles to ice-cream makers, from brass headboards to foot warmers and kerosene lanterns. Birthday cakes and wedding cakes, multitiered and many candled, say "anniversary," as do wedding bells

and old-fashioned belles and costumes, fashion drawings, and etchings. Songs and song sheets from out of the past and the musical instruments of bygone days, the old gramophone and the player piano, can set the theme with musical overtones. Old kitchen appliances, coal stoves, iceboxes, ice tongs, mangles, hot irons, coal scuttles, and such are also reminders of bygone days. The toys and games of the past can be dusted off and revived for another go-around as can the tintypes and daguerreotypes of an anonymous ancestor.

Antiques or reproductions of period furniture from another century can create truly period settings. Whatever one might hope to find in some long, undisturbed attic can be used, with or without the cobwebs: ornate picture frames, trunks, carpetbags, strapped satchels, discarded clothes, hats, and hatracks. Blow up some line illustrations from old newspapers or fashion catalogues, or original store brochures or broadsides from years long gone. These are attention-getters and scene-setters. Check through the lettering books and the catalogues of the pressure-sensitive type suppliers for those typefaces that suggest "The Gay Nineties"— gaslight, tassels and fringes, red velvet swags and drapes. Suggest the wasp-waisted or shirt-waisted beauties of that period—the bustled, bosomy, bowed and buttoned-up belles of almost one hundred years ago. People looking in may not actually remember "the good old days," but they will definitely recognize them.

Figure 19-1. A new classic look is introduced with an antique bicycle—a touch of nostalgia, a perfect touch for anniversaries. The bicycle becomes the focal prop in the window and unites the two mannequins on the left with the leaning figure on the right. *Macy's, New York.*

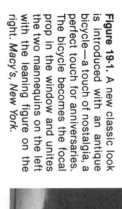

Figure 19-2. It's back to school, and books overflow in this window. They are stacked, packed, and racked. They are the risers and platforms. The antique library ladder not only holds and stores books, but the steps provide different levels on which to show the strongly colored knit shirts and pants. *Macy's, New York.*

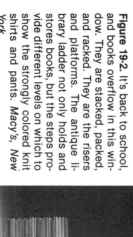

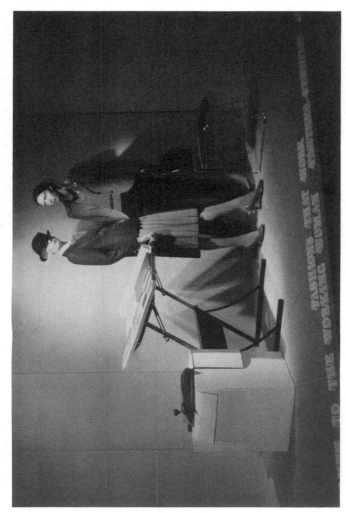

Figure 19-3. "Fashions that Work" and "Salute to the Working Woman" are spelled out on the floor of this suit and separates window. This vignette suggests a career woman who is more than "just a secretary." The sleek, simple, professional scene is right for the smart and sophisticated clothing. *Gimbel's, New York.*

Back to School and College

It happens every fall, starting with alphabet blocks and advancing to busts of Caesar and Shakespeare. Symbols of school also include owls, foxes, and squirrels storing up knowledge, and blackboards, chalkboards, and mortarboards for the graduates. It is the little red school house complete with a smiling sun and an unfurled flag, the school bus, the dunce cap and the stool in the corner, an apple for the teacher, teacher's pet, and teachers of all sizes and shapes. Don't forget pencils, pens, rulers and erasers, nursery rhymes and easy-to-read readers, the old school bell, books, pads of paper, notebooks, desks and chairs, and the inkwells that are now no longer used—these are all still symbols of school.

And then the student grows up: halls of ivy and walls of red brick. This can be the time to show spiral pads, date books, records, and intramural sports. And speaking of sports, don't forget banners, pennants, cheerleaders, megaphones, and the ever busy telephones. Try pompoms, confetti streamers, the football hero, "the most likely to succeed." For setting: the scene, there is the ice cream parlour, the junior hop, and the senior prom. In the classrooms are the classics: dictionaries open to the right word for fall fashion, books, bookcases, and the calendar to mark off the time.

Bridals

Bridal symbols include: "Here Comes the Bride" and "The Wedding March," the bridal aisle, the strains of an organ, love songs, and golden rings; hearts are entwined; white roses and lilies of the valley become nosegays or bridal bouquets flowing with ribbons and streamers. A petal-strewn carpet leads the way and is outlined with woven baskets billowing over with floral and foliage cascades, heroic-sized candles in gleaming golden candlesticks, lattice work, gazebos, or even a rose-covered bower. Floating wisps of net and tulle fill the air as do white doves and white plaster cherubs. Louis XV and Louis XVI tables and chairs set the scene while a rococo standing mirror is used to frame and reflect the bride's gown.

If a groom is not in evidence, suggest him at least with a supply of top hats and canes. Try a blow-up of a wedding invitation; or the garden party setting for the reception that follows: green grass, blue skies, and a pink-and-white awning or marquee. A stained glass window, an arch, a column—these are some of the minimal appurtenances necessary to suggest church architecture. The display can be set in a forest fantasy of entwining branches that form a leafy arcade. It can be a true-to-life setting with the mother-of-the-bride fussing with the veil, or Dad beaming, or a vignette of the bridal procession with flower girls, train bearers, and dainty gold chairs lined up to review the romantic affair. A bridal window should always imply: "and they lived happily ever after."

Career Fashions

This is the world of "9-to-5," of getting to work, coffee breaks, of lunchtime, personal and business calls, and

Figure 19-4. The merchandise is white, the mannequins are soft sculpture, but the oversized, red Santa hats and the brilliant red poinsettias, sitting on a red floor, say "Christmas" with wit and charm. The surprise of seeing the hats pulled down over the faces does it. *Courrèges, New York.*

Figure 19-5. A real mess! "Swept away with spring jeans," says the copy card, and the brooms, cartons, wrapping paper, and such add spirit and surprise to this sale window. This is a traffic stopper because the window is so unexpected and "unfashionable." *Macy's, New York.*

dinner dates. It is filled with desks, chairs, files, and typewriters, and a cluster around a water cooler or a coffee brewer. Career fashions can appear at an architect's table, an operating table, or the conference table for the chairperson of the board. Computers can take over the window, or a ticker-tape machine can spew out yards and yards of impresssive looking data. Graphs and charts look very professional as do doors with impressive titles lettered on them.

A law-office setting can be depicted by stacks of thick volumes and a stepladder to reach the top. A designer can be recognized by an easel, palette, drawing boards, swatches and swatchbooks covering the floor, and drawings pinned up on the walls. A giant phone or super-scaled Rolodex file means business. Portfolios, envelopes, briefcases, and attaché cases mean business, also. The world of big business is made up of newspapers and headlines; adding machines, slide rulers, appointment books and calendars, clocks and watches, timepieces of all types to tick off the business hours and the appointed times. Careers that can be depicted in displays include: commerce, law, medicine, engineering, designing, computer programming, politics, and theater—and it is all unisex.

Christmas

The Christmas list is endless. It starts with Santa Claus, a sleigh, elves and deer, and then continues with trees, garlands, swags and drops of evergreens sprinkled with snow and "diamond dust" or glittering with ornaments, paper chains, or strings of cranberries and popcorn. It is a "sweet" time: peppermint canes, bonbons, and candies gay with stripes and swirls. It is cakes and cookies, gingerbread boys and girls and little houses, all iced and sugarcoated. This holiday can shimmer with snow and snowflakes, ice and icicles, stars and comets, the fireplace and the hearth, families and friends, and gifts and gifts boxes, opened or ribbon-tied.

Christmas is the poem, "A Visit from St. Nicholas" by Clement Moore, a hundred children's fairy tales, and the sweetest dreams come true. Christmas can be "sung" with songs, carols by characters out of Dickens' England; "Silent Night" or "Rudolf, the Red-Nosed Reindeer"; musical instruments, music boxes, dancing ballerinas, and toy soldiers. It is a time for stuffed animals falling out of overstuffed stockings, model trains and planes, old-fashioned baby dolls, and chrome-plated computerized robots. Set the scene with chimneys or roof tops on which red-suited strangers can prance about.

For the religious emphasis of this holiday, try stained-glass windows or a crèche, organ pipes, oversized candles, and a choir of angels or angelic choirboys holding sheets of music dotted with familiar songs.

Santa is Père Noël and Father Christmas. It is also time for piñata parties, Mrs. Claus, signs directing the viewer to the North Pole, letters to Santa, and endless lists of gifts. It is a party time as well as a time for "Peace on Earth" and "Goodwill to All."

Clearance Sales

The posters say, "And away it goes" or "Gone with the wind," but not necessarily with antebellum houses and magnolia trees. The cleanup of a clearance sale can be represented by brooms, mops, pails, shovels, big plastic bags, oversized crates and cartons, wrapping paper, and twine. It also could be shopping bags and store boxes "walking," "riding," or "flying" out of the display area loaded with the sale goodies. A window filled with assorted mannequins and forms, stripped down to fig leafs or palmetto fans, for modesty's sake—or dressed in big brown paper bags because everything is gone—can be fun.

A few pipe-rack fixtures festooned with a few forlorn and naked hangers—some already lying on the floor—says "Going, going, gone!" Giant scissors cry out that "prices have been cut—or slashed" as does a setting of shelves or bins, denuded of merchandise with boxes scattered helter-skelter. The big iron ball used to smash down buildings could be "breaking" into the plate-glass window—with "cracks" beginning to appear, and announcing, "We're making way for the new season." "Clearance Sales" demand dynamics—action and movement—diagonals and direction. It's the only way to go.

Cruise, Resort, Sun and Swimwear

Summer is a time for the great out-of-doors: blue skies, picture-postcard scenery, green grass, and blue water. Over all sits a big, bright, yellow ball of sunshine to spread its warmth over everything. Cover floors with green grass mats or sandy stretches (the dunes can be painted on the background), and add some sea grass, seaweed, and seascapes. Palm trees and palmetto leaves, rain capes, thatch, tatami mats and tapa cloths—are the textures of summer and resort wear. It is the South of France and the South Seas. Get playful with beach umbrellas, beach blankets, beach balls, and beach chairs; yacht chairs and canvas sling chairs; outdoor furniture; fishnets and tennis nets. Try travel posters, steamer trunks, steamboats, sail boats, model boats, and boating supplies; or anchors, oars, lifesavers, rubber rafts and rubber ducks, gangplanks and boardwalk planks.

Summertime is sports time and spectator time—baseball innings and outings, golf and golf carts, bleachers and poolside sitting, tennis matches, lemonade and

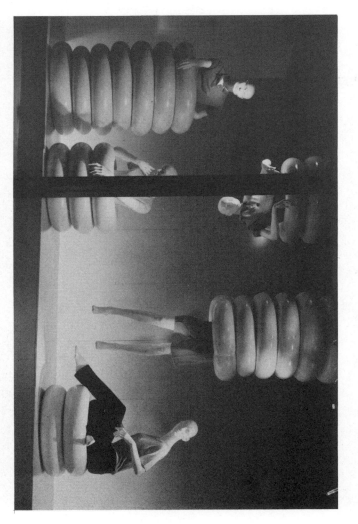

Figure 19-6. This window is filled with novelty, interest, and lots of the unexpected. The inner tubes "hide" and "feature" the sporty separates: the red shorts floating in midair, the upside-down mannequin wearing a new-look shirt. This much-used prop, used here in a new and different way, works especially well in displays featuring summer sportswear. *Gimbels, New York.*

Figure 19-7. A different approach to the familiar symbol of the Easter egg: Simple, naïve drawings of lavender eggs fill the background while more of the same are painted directly onto the front glass. The stepladder and the cans of lavender paint add a high point to the composition while directing the viewer's eye down to the two mannequins on the left. *Gimbels, New York.*

Figure 19-8. A very fashionable scarecrow sits in a shearling coat on a rustic fence decorated with a rich fall foliage. It all says "autumn." Burlap is wrapped around the mannequin's face, and straw is overflowing from the neck, wrists, and ankles. The mannequin has become a fully formed scarecrow. A warm, amber light fills this October/November setting. *Saks Fifth Avenue, New York.*

ice-cube coolers, picnic benches, barbeques, and grills. Daisies and cucumbers are considered to be "coolers," as are electric fans, ceiling fans, and hand-held fans, air conditioners and body conditioners. It is all part of outdoor living.

Easter

What would Easter be without soft, cuddly, pastel plush bunnies (the more the merrier), decorated eggs in a rainbow of colors, or stately, elegant, and pristine white lilies on slender stalks? What would this holiday season be without daffodils, tulips, and gift wrappings in yellow, pink, and lavender? What about Irving Berlin's "Easter Parade" and the "Easter bonnet with all the frills upon it"?

Easter is also fluffy yellow chicks, ducklings, and other baby denizens of the farm and forest. It is the time of rebirth and renewal.

There is also the spiritual side of Easter: sunrise services, pipe organs, stained-glass windows, architectural vignettes of a church or cathedral, choirboys, and the essence of the Renaissance. Easter may have its origins in pagan lore, but today it is a Christian holiday which sometimes shares the calendar with the Jewish Passover holiday. It is a time for dressing up and getting out, a time for families to gather and dine together.

Often Easter gets absorbed into the general spring trim, but it could rate an institutional window—in memory of what the holiday is all about. The window can be "religious" without using religious symbols. Show the beauty of nature and the natural growth of plants and flowers, which is spiritual yet nondenominational.

Fall

Fall is the "ripest" season of the year, the time for harvesting fruits and vegetables of rich, warm, and earthy colors; vines and vineyards, grapes and wines. Fall leaves are painted all red, gold, and glowing. The season is a bouquet of asters, mums, marigolds, and other flowers of rich ambers and rusts.

People expect to see pumpkins, gourds, jack-o'-lanterns, scarecrows, squirrels, and owls. It is the time for rakes and hoes, bushels and baskets, and all sorts of earthy materials and textures. Fall is a medley of music: "September Song," "Autumn Leaves," and "Autumn Serenade"—and everybody is "Falling in Love." It also happens to be the time for going back to school and when career fashions make their statements.

Father's Day

Make it a celebration for George, "Father of His Country," or to that "Great Guy," dad, pop, poppa, pater, or

Figure 19-9. A traditional/nontraditional Father's Day display using familiar masculine symbols and materials (Victorian cutout heads, wooden cabinetry, brass, director's chair, etc.) in a smart, assymmetrically balanced presentation which would be effective any time of the year. *Saks Fifth Avenue, New York.*

Figure 19-10. The three crystal chandeliers hang at different levels and suggest elegance, romance, and drama. The soft, "candlelight" against the sophisticated black background frames the richly dressed figure. The copy card says, "Big evenings call for a little Christian Dior drama." A small vignette that intimates a lot. *B. Altman & Co., New York.*

Figure 19-11. A black-and-white photo blowup of an orchestra makes a delightful background for an elegant, black evening dress. A folding chair, on the left, has been laquered jet black. Resting on the seat is a single red rose and a program for the local symphony. The neutral window is given a special glow from rich, pink-filtered floodlights and spotlights. *Sakowitz, Houston.*

father. Dad is everything: male, macho, sentimental, and amusing. The sentiment should not be treacley, but touched with humor. Familiar symbols associated with Father's Day are: chess pieces; oversized playing cards (with dad as the king); trophies, medals, awards, citations, and certificates for years of service and years of giving. Dad is shown as "Champ," as a winner, a leader, "tops." Dad can be portrayed on a facsimile cover of *Life* or *Time*. He can be the super-sportsman, the breadwinner, the careerist, and also a cartoonist's delight.

Father's Day can be remembered by marking the day on a calendar or in an appointment book. Show dad right out of an old photo album. Dad can bring back memories of the "good old days," bicycles built for two, Model T's, and barbershop quartets, even though Dad's father probably was not even a father back then!

Formals—New Year's Eve

Dressing-up can be classy and classically formal or fun and frolicsomely formal. It can be an elegant, smart, and sophisticated dinner party, complete with crystal, silver, lace cloth, prismed chandeliers, candlelight, rosebuds and baby's-breath centerpieces, and potted palms in the background. It can be a realistic setting with fine boiserie panels or flocked damask wallpaper and oriental rugs, or a vignette setting that suggests as much but does not include all the details.

Formalwear could mean a night at the opera or ballet, a charity concert, a fund-raising celebration. A few well-selected posters and props could set the scene: railings, balustrades, columns, arches, stairways with red velvet runners, brass stanchions swinging velvet-covered ropes, marquees or canopies, photomurals of famous opera houses or concert halls, or some gold opera chairs set about to simulate a box at the opera, with the addition of some velvet swags and drapes and a program or two.

A formal setting is a view of a skyline at night, a midnight sky scattered with diamond-like sequins, a garden with ghostly pale sculpture, a fountain, clipped and shaped plants. Furniture can be formal in a setting done in Louis XV, Louis XVI, or French Empire antiques or reasonable reproductions. The scene can be Versailles, Monte Carlo, the Cannes Film Festival, or a suite at the Ritz in any continental capital.

Antiques may also suggest formalwear. Coromandel screens, oriental lacquerware, and fine porcelain vases sparingly and artfully filled with branches and blossoms can bespeak formalwear. A man's top hat and cane resting on a small velvet chair says it, and so do opera glasses, theater programs, dance cards, and over-sized menus. A champagne cooler and two champagne glasses on a long skirted table can imply the start of something big.

Figure 19-12. Sheer netting billows across the front windows of this corner window. Tiny bee lights flicker beneath the "snow" that covers the floor. The figures, dressed in lingerie, lounge in their white garments in the all-white environment. Pink lights add warmth to this Christmas gift scene. *Filene's, Boston.*

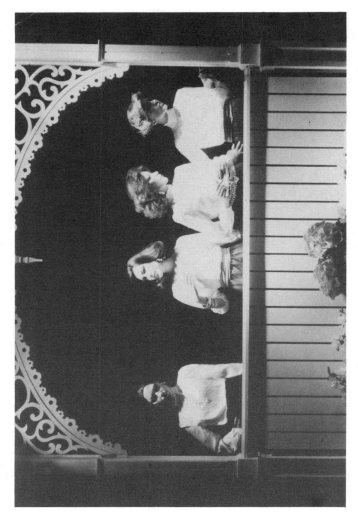

Figure 19-13. This display has all the makings of a traditional Mother's Day display. The front of the window is filled with blooming pink and white plants, while the gingerbread-style porch adds more than just a touch of Victoriana and nostalgia. The setting is so right for the "romantic" blouses being promoted. The porch railing comes up high enough to hide, yet still show, the skirts, with the emphasis remaining on the ruffled and frilly blouses. *B. Altman & Co., New York.*

"Formal" can also be disco, jazz concerts, or jet-setting to "in" places. Dress-up clothes also belong at a New Year's Eve gala with balloons, confetti and colorful streamers, champagne, party hats, party favors, a clock and a countdown to midnight, "Auld Lang Syne," "cocktails for two," and more. Father Time and Baby New Year appear together—for one night only! It can also be a gambling casino, roulette tables, rouge et noir, blackjack, croupiers, dice, and chips galore. Formalwear is synonymous with "going out," gala, grand, gracious, the arts—how the "other half" lives. Formal is fantasy and dreams.

Lingerie and Underwear

Lingerie is lovely and sexy. It is hidden and secret, but designed to be seen. Show it in the boudoir, sheer and all ribbons and ruffles; sheer curtains can be drawn partly across the window and tied back so that the viewer can get a good look at what is going on underneath. Or set the scene in a leafy bower, a gazebo in a garden, a powder room, or a bedroom all rococo or faded French provincial.

Lingerie usually suggests pastel colors: pinks, creams, pale lavenders, and other fashionable delicacies. A period screen can suggest privacy or a barrier behind which a woman can change. Use a vase filled with pretty blossoms set on a festooned table which can also show some choice pieces of merchandise. Lingerie is right for Mother's Day, Valentine's Day, and rates high in Christmas gifting.

Lingerie can be set against a midnight sky and blanched classic columns, or a billowing tent and soft satin pillows filling the floor. Provide a setting for a modern-day Scheherazade in which she can tell her thousand and one tales, or make it the tent of the Sheik of Araby. With a bit of imagination and the merest suggestion of props, the lingerie-attired mannequin can be a fairy princess; a long, long blonde wig to turn into a ladder (Rapunzel); a red apple and a wall mirror (Snow White); a spinning wheel and a floor full of pretty slips, bras, and panties (the fair captive in Rumplestiltskin). With a crown, a long velvet cape, a satin streamer across her chest, and an armful of red roses—it is the American choice, Miss America.

For attention value, for a touch of humor, or to show how things do change or never change, juxtapose a modern, scantily clad figure against a period piece of furniture. Turn the lingerie display into a ballet setting—*Les Sylphides, Giselle,* or any other romantic piece—with the mannequin on *pointes* to show the freedom of movement, the drape, and the shape of the feminine garment. Use a ballet bar and a large mirror to suggest a practice setting; or let her hold a pair of ballet shoes, with some flowers and sheets of music on the floor. Or, try a theatrical trunk spilling over with more lovely "unmentionables." Add a poster for a ballet company, and say "grace," "charm," and "feminine." Lingerie should be lovely, sexy, and definitely seen.

Mother's Day

Pink carnations may say it all, but it can also be said with pink roses, ribbons, ruffles, laces, lavender, and

Figure 19-14. Three red-lacquered, semiabstract mannequins salute the Fourth of July in red, white, and blue outfits. The red and white striped background sets off the box of oversized sparklers. The sizzlers that have "fallen" out of the box add some more diagonal lines to the composition. The sharp white spotlight hits the blue and white garments and the torch in the middle of the box. *Macy's, New York.*

Figure 19-15. Potted flowers, the watering can, and gardening tools complete this fantasy setting for "new-for-spring" fashions that are sprouting out of a flower box and are being shown on dressmaker forms. (The dressmaker form also happens to be part of the logo of the manufacturer of these garments.) The seed packet in the apron pocket adds a touch of color and reinforces the spring message. *Bloomingdale's, New York.*

Figure 19-16. For Valentine's Day, lots of chalky white cherubs are sitting it out on spindly gold ballroom chairs. The delicate, lacy garments are white as are the background and the shiny tiles on the floor. The repetition of chairs and cherubs and the broken pattern of mannequin placement makes this a Valentine's display with a difference. This is an interesting use of a corner window. *Bloomingdale's, New York.*

lilacs. Mother's Day is *Whistler's Mother* and all the other famous mothers of history. It is represented by cameos, lockets, velvet-covered photo albums, tintypes, and ornate, rococo frames. A bell jar protecting a fragile floral arrangement on a moiré or velvet-skirted table or a pink and white boudoir setting can say "mother." Chicks in a nest can be reaching out to a providing mother bird.

Mother's Day is the time to bring out the Victoriana and turn-of-the-century devices that usually enhance anniversary promotions. Even though mother may be smart, sophisticated, and ultra-chic, on Mother's Day she can become all "lavender and lace," fragile, feminine, and frou-frou. Turn a display setting into a bonbon dish or a plate of petit fours, all strawberries and cream. Add a giant, lace-edged card dripping with sweet sentiments; mother will be served, as will the gift merchandise that is usually promoted for her day.

Patriotic: Presidential Sales, Fourth of July, Elections

This is a time when flags are unfurled; it is hooray for the red, white, and blue, and Stars and Stripes forever. Now is the time to show pictures of George Washington and Honest Abe, hatchets and cherry trees, log cabins and log fences. Bring out the eagles, the White House, the Capitol, victory wreaths, Columbia, and the Statue of Liberty. Add fireworks, firecrackers, and the light of the "rockets' red glare." Show Betsy Ross sewing away at a star-studded flag, Washington cross-

ing the Delaware, or the three weary Revolutionists fifing and drumming in a cloud of dust.

The setting can be a map of the United States, the Declaration of Independence, the Bill of Rights, or the Constitution. Musically, it is any song by George M. Cohan going from "It's a Grand Old Flag" to "Yankee Doodle Dandy"—or Irving Berlin's tribute, "God Bless America."

The Fourth of July or any patriotic promotion could stress brotherhood, liberty, and equality—the "melting pot" concept that is America and its citizenry. Surround the promotion with striped bunting, white stars spattered on a blue field, and gold fringe; shields and frames; campaign buttons, banners, and election-type placards and posters; and balloons—red, white, and blue, of course—confetti, and streamers. The viewer will get the message and salute your efforts.

Spring

Green is busting out all over, and the early bloomers are daffodils, jonquils, crocuses, tulips, and hyacinths. Trees are budding and ready to bloom. Grass and shrubs are sprouting and "the red, red robin is bob, bob, bobbin'," all over the place. Spring is the time for seeds, rakes, hoes, and lawn equipment; April showers and May flowers, and May poles. It is a period of renaissance and rebirth. Baby birds appear in nests, and bunnies hop onto the scene. All kinds of soft, caressable animals announce "Spring is Here."

Spring could be represented by a clock made of branches, flowers, and ribbons that say "Spring-Time," or by an oversized song sheet with flower-headed notes to suggest a sing-along of any of the hundreds of spring songs. Try butterflies, dragonflies, and flying kites; flowers and flower pots, vegetable gardens, lattice work, garden hoses, and "Everything's Coming Up Roses." Spring can be a woodland nymph, a forest fantasy, or an enchanting setting for a fairy tale. It is a state of mind, a reawakening, and a return to nature.

Valentine's Day

After red hearts, pink hearts, and cerise hearts, it is "sweethearts" all the way: Romeo and Juliet, Tristan and Isolde, Scarlett and Rhett. This is the time for cherubs in pink, white, and gold. Make a hero of Cupid with bow and arrow; or simply show the bows and arrows dripping with ribbons, rosebuds, and lover's knots, and heart-shaped targets to hit.

An oversized deck of playing cards will win a lover's heart, if the display shows a suit of hearts—all kings and queens. Deliver the message with Valentine's cards, both sentimental and humorous, trimmed with ruffles and scrolls, flourishes and furbelows. For a sure reminder, use stuffed animals with arms entwined, and red, red roses on extra long stems. There are love songs and serenades; madrigals to be accompanied by lutes, lyres, harps, and flutes; and minstrels to sing them.

Tell a fairy tale with a happy ending, or show love poems, love stories, and love letters tied in red ribbons. Valentine's Day is a date on the calendar circled with a red heart and surrounded with lipstick kisses, chocolate kisses, and love birds. It is a day lovers remember, and a ribbon tied around an elegantly gloved finger would serve as a lovely reminder.

20 Signage

A store's signs, both inside and outside, have a great effect on the store's image and the customer's understanding of what is going on. A sign, large or small, is judged on legibility (i.e., how easy the copy is to read, as determined by the size, color, and type used) and on comprehension of the message (how understandably it has been stated). A store can have a well-recognized logo which does not "read," but is so familiar and has been publicized for so long that it has become a known symbol. That may be fine for a logo or a decorative symbol which is used over and over again, but when a copy message is to be delivered, it has to be readable!

COLOR AND CONTRAST

Some colors "read" better than others. The greater the contrast between the color or ground of the board or paper and the copy printed on it, the more readily the copy will come across. Black on white and white on black are two good examples of contrast. The former is more traditional, and, therefore, is usually more acceptable. Black on yellow makes a strong statement. Mention has already been made of using red and green as contrasting colors; this combination can and will be a disaster for a sign that has to be read. The proximity of the two colors creates a vibration; the letters jump and

jitter over the printed surface.

Metallic paints and inks can be elegant and lovely, but become almost invisible when light strikes the metallics in a certain way, or when there is a glare on the window or the picture. Metallic boards look marvelous and super-rich under controlled lighting arrangements, but because of highlights, white lettering can "disappear" from a metallic surface. Black or dark-colored inks or paints do not hold up well on the metallic backgrounds either.

Sometimes, a light colored or white letter with a darker outline or shadow will survive under window lighting. Though they may lack excitement, white or pale tints make the best grounds for signs, and black ink, which is so convenient and available, can, at times, be replaced by more fashionable or interesting colors which do tie in with a theme or promotion: red for Valentine's Day, green for spring or St. Patrick's Day, royal or flag blue for a presidential sale, brown for Father's Day, and so on.

POSTER AND CARD SIZE

The size of a sign will depend on the location or end use of that sign, and how much copy or information the sign has to carry. Following are some of the stock, or standard, sizes. *Stock* refers to the usual sizes to which the boards or cards can be cut down. The cardboard is stored in these sizes or can be purchased precut in these standard dimensions; frame-holders and easels are available in these same sizes.

Stock also refers to the material (paper or card-board) to be imprinted. The thickness or rigidity of the stock is designated by *points*. The larger the number of points, the thicker and usually more rigid the material. Of course, the displayperson can vary from these standard sizes if the new or unusual dimensions will satisfy some special design requirement.

Standard Stock Sizes

The *standard full sheet*, or poster size, is 22 inches by 28 inches. Most floor frames are designed to accept that size board, usually in 14 pt. stock, a fairly stiff board which is not too thick or too rigid. This size poster can be used in windows and on or off columns. This is the popular choice for storewide promotions, sales, and holidays. The 22-inch by 28-inch sign will usually carry some sort of graphic design or illustration, and a banner or caption indicating the event. A sign of this size will often be silk-screened (see the following page) for use throughout the store and for use in branch stores, if there are any. The poster will also tie in with ads, commercials, and other media, like store mailings and handouts.

A *half sheet* measures 14 inches by 22 inches and is used for window displays or to identify merchandise in an interior display. A *quarter sheet*, measuring 11 inches by 14 inches, is a smaller, more restrained window reader or feature copy sign. It can be used effectively on the selling floor to explain certain larger pieces of hardgoods or furniture. This size is also used in elevators and dressing rooms for signs about store policy, special events, fashion shows, etc.

Small *copy cards* come in a variety of sizes—7 inches by 11 inches, 5½ inches by 7 inches, and 3½ inches by 5½ inches—in order to fit standard easels and frames for merchandise identification within the store and in windows. The smaller ones usually appear on counters in cosmetics and accessories areas.

An easel may be a plastic holder that is self-standing at a slight angle, or it can be elevated on a metal upright to extend above the merchandise described. A frame can also be mounted onto a wall or fixture, and the proper copy can be dropped in and changed as the merchandise or the event changes.

Card toppers, usually long and narrow—about 11 inches by 3½ inches or 7 inches by 3½ inches—are used to tie in with storewide events, themes, and promotions. They often have the same color and graphic concept as the promotion's 22-inch by 28-inch store poster, and the same caption or tag line, acting as a reinforcement, for the shopper, that this merchandise is part of the ongoing sale or event. The card topper emphasizes the limited-time concept of the promotion. The sameness and the repetition of the colored and designed card topper on the selling floor can be an effective point-of-sales technique as well as a way of adding a seasonal or holiday look to the area. Card toppers should be short-lived. They should disappear from the floor as soon as the event is over.

This standardization of sizes is convenient for the displayperson or the store's signmaker. The material can be precut and stocked in specific sizes. All the sizes listed above can be cut from the regularly available 22-inch by 28-inch board without waste. This standardization also helps keep the interior of a well and fully signed store looking neat and orderly. The customer can find and recognize the signs by their shape and size and not be bombarded by a confusion of assorted cards and cardtoppers.

Other sizes can be used for store signs, but the ones given above are traditional and easy to purchase in various colors and finishes.

TYPES OF INFORMATIONAL SIGNS AND CARDS

A *selling sign* is a promotional sign, in that it promotes the sale of a particular item on the selling floor. A good sign should be clear, concise, and comprehensive. If it is "selling" an item, it should say what the item is, what it does, why it should be purchased here and now, and how much it costs. In the fewest possible words and in the most understandable language, it should cover the questions a customer might ask.

When preparing a selling sign, remember the following points: Print only three or four words on a line. Be sure of the facts, the spelling, and the punctuation. Be sure that the overall effect is neat and not crammed with copy. If a relatively great amount of information on the featured merchandise is to be included, use a larger card or two signs next to each other. Shoppers on the selling floor do not read "encyclopedias."

If the back of the copy sign will be visible, back it with either another sign or a graphic design. Try to keep all signs that appear in the same area or department consistent in color, size, and layout, so that the customer is not confused by too great a variety of conflicting signage. Be sure the choice of type is clear and readable, and in keeping with the merchandise and the store's image.

A *category card* specifies the major classification of the collected merchandise rather than a specific design, pattern, or price. It could read, for example,

Figure 20-1. The store's 22-inch by 28-inch store-wide poster for Valentine's Day appears in the upper right with the following message: "February 14 is as close as a kiss." The giant, heart-shaped candy box is filled with loads of small gift ideas set in white cupcake holders. The "lips" motif, from the poster, makes a big satin-pillow appearance in the midst of the "variety" gift selections. *The May Co., Cleveland.*

"Women's Wool Sweaters"; and under that one sign there could be a binned assortment of varying prices, colors, kinds of wools, and manufacturers. As with the selling sign, neatness, accuracy, and simplicity count.

An *institutional card* lists the services provided by the store: its hours, refund and exchange policies, delivery charges, alteration setup, and so on.

A store should not have too many signs, but items and categories should be identified to provide ease of recognition and relevant information. The more fully a store is "self-service," the more important good signage becomes. The signs help to supply the answers the salesperson would ordinarily provide.

SIGNAGE TECHNIQUES
Silk-Screening

Silk-screening is one of the oldest and most dependable stencil reproduction techniques for making signs and posters. With this process, printing is achieved by means of paint or dye forced through a screen which is covered with a fine silk (or synthetic) mesh. Silk-screening is especially effective where there is a considerable quantity to be produced (a *run*), but not enough to warrant the use of expensive plates and lithography.

There have been tremendous advances in the silk-screening or hand-screening processes, including photographic methods for producing the screens, or stencils. This technology eliminates the hours required to cut each stencil by hand, including all the letters needed for the signs. The hand-cutting of the stencils is an art and a craft, requiring much more than just a steady hand. Many books are available on how to do silk-screening. Briefly, this is the technique.

For each color that is to be printed, a separate stencil is usually prepared. The stencil is actually a true and rigid wood frame over which a very fine denier of silk (or a synthetic fabric of a similar type) is stretched and pulled taut. A lacquer film is applied to the fabric screen. Only the parts of the design that are to be printed in the specific color are cut out of the film, leaving exposed those areas of the fine screen through which the paint or dye will be forced. The area that is not to be reproduced is left with a protective coating of the lacquer which will resist the paint.

After the screen is prepared, it is carefully set down on the surface to be printed (i.e., the stock). If more than one color will be used, special care must be taken to ensure that the succeeding screens—for the overlaying colors—will be lined up with each other, so that there will be a minimum of *bleeding* (colors seeping through beyond their intended outline). A "puddle" of paint is placed at one end of the screen and a *squeegee* (a hard, rubber-edged tool, similar to a wind-

Figure 20-2. In this smart white-on-white window, where the only touch of color is the silvery gleam of the silver settings arranged on the floating hoops, the copy is readable only because of the shadows cast by the dimensional letters. The whole window display is understated and gently lit; even the sale image is subdued and restrained. *Gumps, San Francisco.*

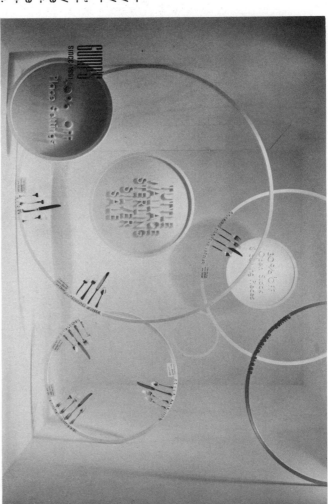

shield wiper) is pulled across the screen, forcing the paint through the openings in the fabric. For each color, this process is repeated. All of the stock to be printed is "screened" in the first color before proceeding to the next color.

For smaller runs (several dozen of a single kind), one might make a less sophisticated form of screen, or stencil. The area that is to be printed is left exposed, and the rest of the screen is "printed" with a blocking solution which will not be affected by the paint, lacquer, or dye used for the screening.

Another silk-screening technique involves the use of liquid *tusche* (a substance similar to a crayon that has been dissolved in turpentine) which acts as a blocking agent. In this method, the area that is to be printed is painted with the tusche and allowed to dry. The remaining surface of the screen is sealed off by a glue that is not water-soluble. When the glue dries, the tusche is washed off with water, leaving exposed to the paint only the design to be printed. This is a simpler, more manageable technique because no cutting is required. The results are not as sharp and slick as they might be from a real silkscreen, but posters and card toppers printed in·this way can still look good and deliver the message in color.

Sign Machines

Some stores have made an investment in sign machines, especially when signing and pricing play an important part in the store's promotional attitudes and selling techniques. For the retail operation with a full sales force, which provides help and answers for shoppers just for the asking, signs may tend to clutter or create confusion on the floor or with the store's image. The more popular-priced the store, the more often the customer will "self-select" and the greater will be the need for the clear, clean, and precise merchandise and pricing information supplied by signs.

There are basically two types of sign machines on the market today. One is a *punchboard* machine, which is similar to a "giant" typewriter. It has a flat surface, or "bed," on which is placed the stock to be printed. An alphabet of type, on a roller, is designed to ride up and down and across the bed of the printing machine. A hand press, or punch, brings the selected letter or symbol onto the exact desired location on the stock. Rollers with ink cross over the typeface and keep the letters inked.

After being lined up exactly where it will appear on the printed card, a letter is punched. The ink rollers coat the letter; the letter descends and is imprinted on the card. The next letter or symbol is lined up and the process is repeated. This technique is fast and simple enough to use for one or two signs, or where there is a great variety of signs and prices needed.

A store that uses a dozen or more of the same copy card or price card would do better with a *proof press.* This is a more traditional type of printing press. There is a flat bed or surface on which the copy is set down in bars of type (held in place by a magnetic force); and a roller sweeps across the bed below. The card is printed by placing the face of the stock down on top of the type which has been inked either automatically or manually, and pulling the roller across the back of the card stock, thus causing the inked type to make an impression on the face of the card.

When using a proof press, many cards or readers can be made from the same setting of type. It just takes another pull of the roller over a fresh piece of card stock. With this kind of machine, it is possible to have an insignia or logo plate made which can be incorporated with the type for a personalized touch.

The punchboard machine is cleaner to operate than the proof press and is generally considered to be more versatile and adaptable. With the punchboard, it is possible to print on fabrics, plastics and, in some cases, wood or laminates.

Other Signage Techniques

Cutout letters are available in many fonts (a *font* is an assortment of type all of one size and style), in diverse sizes, thicknesses, and colors. Some cutouts are reusable and, thus, can be a worthwhile investment. There are also rub-on, *pressure-sensitive letters* which are inexpensive and can be purchased in most art supply houses. They, too, are available in a tremendous assortment of styles and sizes and can be used to make signs with different looks conveying particular images.

With the printing machines described above, the displayperson, due to the financial outlay, is wedded to a specific style or type of letter. With the pressure-sensitive letters, the displayperson can use different types for different products, from very elegant, elongated, and ultra-thin letters for fine jewelry and furs, to strong, dark, condensed letters for lawn mowers, power tools, and auto tires. Even in a store that sells only fashion merchandise, different lettering styles for swimwear and bridals, for example, could be used.

Hand-lettering, or *calligraphy*, is almost a lost art. It requires a steady hand, infinite patience, and talent. There are many brushes and pen nibs on the market which will assist the letterer in his or her work, but the tools alone do not ensure the desired end result.

The art of calligraphy can enhance special events or promotions, or it can be used to create a look for a logo, a headline, or for an original store signature (a "sig"). In many cases, however, a pressure-sensitive alphabet can be found which "will do." It may lack the color option that is possible in hand-lettering, but it does have the advantage of being predictable, sharp, precise, and mechanically reproducible.

Typewriters with oversized type can also be used for small signs and price tags, or for explanatory copy that can be added to a reader or card.

21 Point-of-Purchase Display

Point of purchase (abbreviated *P.O.P.*) means just that—display or merchandise presentation of the product at the point where the sale is made. The display is designed to sell or promote a particular product or brand name. Point-of-purchase displays are usually produced in large numbers for vast distribution and are paid for by the manufacturer or distributor of the product.

The counter in a store is a prime point of purchase, and so is the checkout area in a department or in a supermarket. Hopefully, the point-of-purchase display will catch the shopper's attention, pique his or her curiosity, maybe offer a sample, and eventually bring about a sale.

In a cafe or lounge, for example, the point-of-purchase display might be the neon sign outside recommending a particular brand of beer, the advertiser's name on the clock that sends out rainbows of color over the bar area, or the name on the coasters that are slipped under the drink. It might be the brand name or logo on the rubber mat on which the change is delivered, or the receptacles put up by various charities and organizations in which to collect some of the customer's spare change at the cash register. A window display with a cardboard poster or three-dimensional cutout bearing the supplier's name is also an example of point of purchase.

The point-of-purchase display, therefore, is not necessarily relegated to appear on counters. It can be used in windows, on ledges, at the end of gondolas, or free-standing, out in the middle of an aisle. What separates P.O.P. displays and fixtures from specialty and department store displays and fixtures is the quantity in which they are produced, the usual appearance and promotion of a particular manufacturer's name or brand name, and the wide distribution and use. The same P.O.P. displayer or fixture may appear on a counter in a fine department store, in a drug store window, or jammed onto an already crowded counter in a discount operation where price is more important than image.

TYPES OF POINT-OF-PURCHASE DISPLAYS

The point-of-purchase display can be anything from a banner flapping outside a store, to a well-stocked, permanent fixture inside the store. The various categories of P.O.P. displays are discussed below.

Outdoor Displays—Outdoor displays include electrified signs, fabric and/or plastic banners and pennants, window posters, and window displays—all promoting a product or a brand name. It can also be the

Figure 21-1. This complete and compact counter unit, made of molded plastic, is a cosmetics P.O.P. stocker/displayer. There is product identification as well as actual products enclosed in see-through cases. Below is a "selector" which explains how the various cosmetics can be combined and by whom. Additional packages can be contained in the back side of the unit.

decals that are affixed to the glass window or door. All of these devices are used to attract the potential customer and to inform him or her that these manufacturers and their products are represented and available inside. The same banners and pennants can appear inside a selling area as overhead decorations. The same posters can also be used inside the store to reiterate the message and, possibly, direct the shopper to the item being promoted.

Counter Displays and Fixtures—The counter display may be regarded sometimes as the window display brought inside, only more compact. It may be used to introduce a new product, show the range of merchandise available, or supply testers, samplers, or coupons for the product illustrated. Some counter units will contain an actual stock of the product and thus facilitate self-selection on the part of the consumer. Some of these stockers/displayers are designed to be disposed of after all the merchandise on the unit is sold. Other units, often made of wood, wire or plastic, are more permanent, designed to be restocked with more of the same product. In this case, the design of the unit will often include a storage area for the refills.

Floor Fixtures—Larger P.O.P. units are designed to be free-standing on the selling floor. They are often constructed of more permanent materials and function as self-selectors for the customer. This is convenient for the retailer, too. The merchandise is stocked by style, color, or size; it is intended that the displayer/fixture will answer any questions the shopper may have.

These units are usually constructed of wool, metal, or plastic. They are given or lent by the manufacturer to the retailer to show the manufacturer's products only. Since selling space on the floor and counter is so valuable, the design must attract, inform, and sell the shopper, using the smallest amount of space. The brand name will appear prominently in the design. (The famous egg-shaped fixture, which was designed to hold the plastic eggs containing L'eggs hosiery, is a noted example of a P.O.P. stocker/floor fixture.)

Accessories—There are many small accessories that may be added to a P.O.P. display concept in order to enhance the promotion of a product inside a store. It can include, in addition to overhead banners and pennants, ledge signs, dump bins for temporary merchandise stocking, lapel pins for the salespeople to wear, and sample or demonstration setups. Food tasting, cosmetic testing, and fragrance sniffing are effective ways of getting the consumer's attention and promoting the product.

Media Tie-In—P.O.P. is most effective when it is tied in with other media promotions. Ideally, it should follow through on an idea or motif that has been

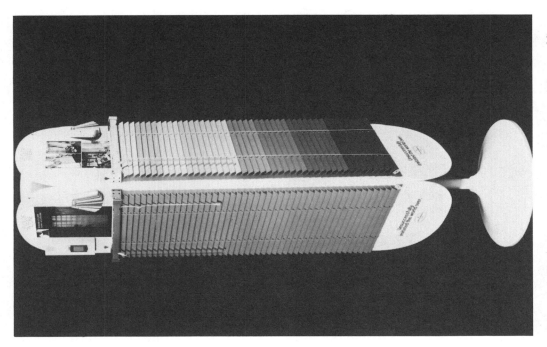

Figure 21-3. This smartly styled unit takes up a minimum of floor space and shows the variety of colors and styles of Levelor Blinds. The fixture was featured in television commercials, and on the upper portion of the displayer are reprints of ads from magazines specializing in ideas for the home. The viewer may also operate the sample blinds. This unit is constructed of metal, hardboard, and molded plastic.

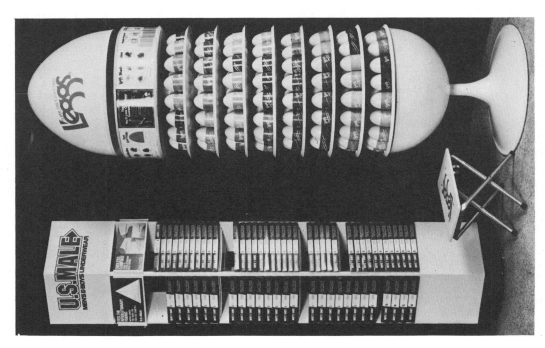

Figure 21-2. Two excellent examples of space-saving P.O.P. floor fixtures. On the right, L'eggs is a prize winner which was used to introduce a new product in a new package (the plastic egg), stocked in a molded plastic, egg-shaped unit. U.S. Male underwear on the left, is packed in triangular containers that fit into the pie-shaped stocking areas of the hexagonal unit. Both units are easily identifiable on the selling floor.

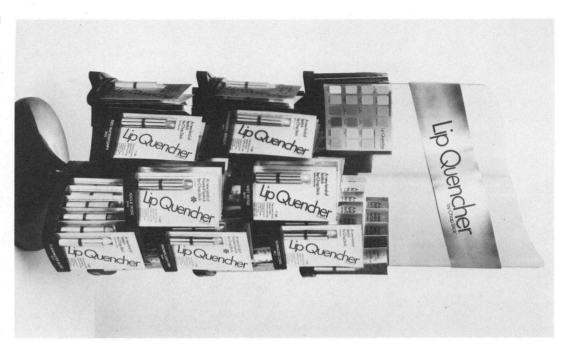

Figure 21-4. A stackable and stockable counter unit made of molded plastic with a changeable copy streamer. The narrow, rotating fixture takes up a minimum of space and carries a maximum of prepacked products (lipstick) in a stepped-up design, showing the variety of colors available. The color card, on the upper left, shows the many shades available.

SOME POINTS TO CONSIDER WHEN DESIGNING P.O.P. DISPLAYS

introduced to the consumer on television, in newspaper and/or magazine advertisements, or store mailings. The P.O.P. display or fixture can be the ultimate and important reminder, at the point of purchase, of the message that has been relayed through other media.

Counter Space—As previously stated, the counter is the prime location for point-of-purchase displays. Counter space is limited and, thus, very valuable. A counter is often only 24-inches deep and anywhere from 3-feet to 8-feet long. It is where the salesperson communicates with the customer; it is where items that are usually out of the customer's reach are presented to the customer for closer examination. Sometimes, several different items have to be set out for comparison. Often, this is where an item is wrapped, money is taken, and change is made. It's a busy location. With all this activity taking place on this limited, hip-high tabletop, is it any wonder that there is a constant battle raging to get a P.O.P. displayer, sampler, or fixture on this counter? Thus, a successful design must be light and easily portable, low enough for the salesperson to see and reach over, and narrow or shallow enough not to impede the selling action on the counter surface.

Product Identification—A good point-of-purchase display must attract (just as any good display must). It should quickly inform the shopper what the product is, what it does, and who makes it. The brand or trademarked name should be easily seen. Some industries are restricted from using their names right on the displayer. The brand name will appear only on the product or the product package which is presented in the display unit and, thus, the customer will still get the message.

Customer Involvement—Displayers that are also samplers will often get preferential treatment when it comes to meting out counter space. Samplers mean customer involvement. The shopper will come closer to see the various shades of lipstick or to squirt and sniff a new cologne. This interaction with the actual product can lead to an impulse sale, and that is what point of purchase is all about.

Shipping and Assembly—P.O.P. displays should be sent to stores as completely assembled as possible. One of the big expenses in point-of-purchase design is the individual packing and shipping of the displays. The display designer, working with the manufacturer, will endeavor to create a unit which is as compact and safe for shipping as is possible so as to avoid unnecessary shipping charges and breakage. If the display unit is shipped "knocked down" (K.D.), in

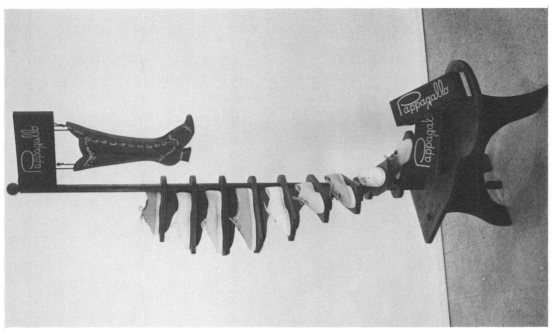

Figure 21-6. A simple, but effective, shoe displayer constructed of wood with a silk-screened logo and design. The unit is easily assembled; the bench is constructed in two parts that notch together, and the upright has shelves that fan out once the pole is in place. The wooden boot hooks into the predrilled holes in the sign.

Figure 21-5. In the busy notions area of a supermarket, this well-designed and clearly identified "Center" becomes a shop within a store. The molded plastic units are made with hooks for the "blister-packed" items; there are shelves as well as dividers. Depending on the amount of space that is made available, the unit can be anything from a single stocking module to two, three, or more. The unit can be free-standing on the floor or used, as shown, revolving on the base of a gondola.

prefinished parts to be assembled in the store, then the assembly must be as simple and minimal as possible. Too often, the harried and hurried storekeeper will just toss the unit away rather than fumble with Piece A slotting into C, after B and D meet at Point E which has to be folded back at a 73-degree angle.

Wherever and whenever possible, parts should be prescored (i.e., the line to be folded is lightly cut to enable a neat, clean fold without breaking the finish of the board) and all parts numbered or tagged. The instructions for the assembly should include a simple, clean diagram of the unit with all parts, tabs, and slots numbered. The written instructions have to be as concise as possible and supplemented with "how-to" sketches. A good P.O.P. unit, when the product and the end use permit, will almost pop up and out like an illustration in a child's pop-up book. The assembly should require no great manual dexterity or great mental prowess.

Light and Motion—Light and/or motion can greatly enhance the effectiveness of a P.O.P. display. In experiment after experiment, it has been shown that shoppers are more attracted by a unit that has some element of motion. The movement can be as simple as the rocking back and forth of a cutout of a child or the spinning of the hands on a printed, make-believe clock face. Besides being attracted by the motion, tests have shown that the shopper is also more likely to remember the name of the product being shown.

Blinking and flashing lights have the same effect. They are attention-getting devices. However, be it light or motion, ideally it should be gentle and easy, rather than hysterical and nerve-racking. The people who are in the store all day can be negatively affected by frantic motion or firework-like lighting. There are many simple and inexpensive motors available which are battery operated, and some can even be set to a desired number of revolutions per minute (rpm).

If the unit is to be animated or have a light as an integral part of its design, battery-operated motors or lamps should be specified and supplied. Do not expect the storekeeper to pull wires across his or her counters or go searching for extension cords that will reach the nearest outlet and possibly create an obstacle course for the saleshelp.

If the unit is to include pamphlets, forms, coupons or "give-aways," the refills and extras should be included with the unit. A storage area could be provided in the construction of the unit to hold these extras.

If "dummies" (facsimiles that look like the real thing, but are not) are part of the design or if actual products are to be used in the unit, it is wise to recess, cut out, or devise a slip-in pocket to hold the containers. It will keep the box, bottle, or package from slipping or from "disappearing."

CONSTRUCTION

Depending upon the product, the intended use, the time it is expected to be on view, and the budget, the displayer or fixture can be made of a wide variety of materials: paper, cardboard, foamcore, various thicknesses of wood, pressed board, plastic, or metal.

The smallest units are usually not much more than posters. These are often constructed of cardboard (14-ply stock) and held upright by means of a prescored, bend-back, cardboard easel which is attached to the back of the poster. The poster may have some appliqué on it: a bit of fabric, a flower, paper lace, etc., or it can be made up of several levels of board to simulate greater depth.

The unit may have its own flat base, or an elevated platform to raise the merchandise off the counter surface. The closer the product is to the viewer's eye level, the more effective the presentation. Sometimes, there can be additional decorative cutouts, panels, or sides arranged to add dimension to the design as well as to separate it from adjacent displays. Depth adds drama to the presentation.

When the displayer is also a stocking unit, like a lipstick case which holds several dozen tubes in assorted colors, the unit probably will be executed in a more stable and durable material than cardboard. Since this type of unit is expected to have a longer counter life, and be handled by more people, it might be made of Plexiglas or metal, and have less pizzazz and flash than those which are short-lived and designed to "hit and run."

Another less glamourous example of a stocking unit is a type of dump bin. This is frequently of a heavy cardboard or corrugated board construction which may also be the actual shipping container for the display poster or sign and the stock to be promoted. This type of P.O.P. stocking unit is associated with sale items or promotional merchandise. It can appear free-standing on the selling floor, used to line an aisle, or placed at the end of a gondola. The shopper is invited to dig in and take some of the "special" merchandise. After the promotion, the dump bin is discarded, and so the heavy cardboard construction is usually sufficient for the limited time this P.O.P. unit will be in use.

Some manufacturers, as previously mentioned, will supply their customers, the retailers, with well-built, fairly permanent fixtures to house their merchandise. These fixtures will hold a large number of units of merchandise and are designed to be restocked by the retailer or a representative of the manufacturer. In the latter case, the manufacturer or the distributor (the middleman between the manufacturer and the retailer) will have one of its people come to the store where the fixture is located, check the stock on hand, and fill in

Figure 21-7. A slick, well-designed and constructed metal and molded plastic floor unit which carries a large selection of merchandise compartments that are easy to see and to flip through. The copy sign, across the top, identifies the manufacturer, but the merchandise can vary with changes in product design, promotions, etc. This is a prize-winning, P.O.P. permanent fixture.

where stock is needed. These permanent, restockable fixture-displayers are often made of wood, wire, or plastic and remain the property of the manufacturer. They are on loan to the store as long as the retailer continues to sell the merchandise.

Always, as in all point-of-purchase displays and fixtures, the two major considerations are space and cost. The well-designed P.O.P. unit is economical and efficient on both scores. No retailer wants to lose valuable floor or counter selling space to an oversized unit that just stands there and does not earn its way in the selling space it consumes.

PROCESSES USED IN PRODUCTION
Printing

Most large runs of cardboard point-of-purchase displays are printed by a process known as *four-color lithography*, or *offset printing*. It is a fast and economical technique to use where a large quantity of the same design is to be reproduced in full color. In color lithography, the artwork is reduced to four separate plates, one for each of the three primary colors plus black. In full-color printing, the four standard colors are yellow, cyan (a blue-green), magenta (a blue-red), and black. Other colors are produced by printing one color over another; for example, to reproduce green, yellow is laid down and the cyan is printed over it. The color separation, the individual plates for the four colors, and the four separate runs (one for each color) are basically expensive, but become extremely practical and economical when the cost is amortized over a large number of units.

When a large run of a displayer or sign is required, but the number is not large enough to warrant the expense of four-color lithography, the display manufacturer may opt for silk-screening. (This technique has already been discussed in Chapter 20.) It is an efficient and effective graphic reproduction technique when there are not too many colors involved and the design to be reproduced is not a photograph.

This screening technique has many advantages to offer the P.O.P. designer. By selecting the proper inks or paints, it is possible to print onto a great variety of surfaces: wood, glass, fabric, cork, plastics, and, of course, paper and cardboard.

The offset process, on the other hand, is limited to a certain range of papers. This makes it necessary, at times, to mount the material that has been offset onto a heavier stock board, or some other material—a costly, time-consuming operation. The offset process requires plates and a printing "bed," and so the size of the stock used will be determined by that plate and the bed, which is the surface in which the paper will rest during

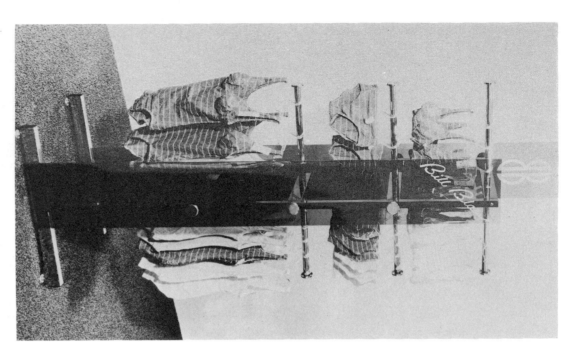

Figure 21-8, above. An elegant swimwear floor unit designed to show a designer's collection. The designer's logo and signature were silkscreened directly onto the lucite panels which were then combined with the metal base and pierce-through rods. The rods are adjustable and the unit can be used for other Bill Blass designs.

Figure 21-9, above right. The silk-screened, heavy cardboard panel is die-cut to create an interesting silhouette and also to provide a slot with a perfect fit, through which the sand toy can be slid into place. The toy supports the selling card and becomes the easel. The sample "sand flipper" is electrified to show how the toy works as well as providing an attention-getting appeal to this P.O.P. display.

the printing process. This is usually limited to an area of about 30 inches by 40 inches. With silk-screening, the only limitation on size is determined by the screen, which can be as large as 5 feet by 10 feet.

With offset lithography, the great economy is in a fast, total run of all the pieces. In silk-screening, it is possible to make a short run, clean up, and store the screen for possible reuse.

Also, with silk-screening, it is possible to print white and pastel colors on a dark surface or reproduce glittery metallics. Fluorescent colors can be used for added emphasis, and flocking or texturing can also be accomplished while the color is being applied. Since the silk-screening technique can be done in short runs, it is also feasible to change colors and thus, using the same artwork, print some pieces in red for Christmas and then do the same design in green for spring.

Die-Cutting and Scoring

The die-cutting technique is similar to cutting cookies out of rolled dough. Steel cutting blades are shaped into the outline or profile to be cut, and then sunk into the surface of a thick wooden plate or panel. The blades that are the most exposed will make a complete cut, while those that are somewhat further recessed, will make score lines (i.e., creasing, bending or fold-over lines).

This panel, together with the blades, in effect, are the "cookie cutter," or die. The die is placed into a press and brought down, under great pressure, onto the paper, board, or fabric which has been screened or

SAND FLIPPER

Hours of FUN in the Sand

action action action

lithographed with the design. The die stamps out the outline and makes whatever interior cuts are required, discarding the excess or trim paper.

Sometimes, only a perforated outline will be die-cut, making it possible to protect a rather intricate and fragile outline while in transit. When the piece arrives at its destination, the unnecessary part can then be removed by simply tearing around the perforated outline.

Die-cutting is used to cut out silhouettes or make inside cuts on P.O.P. units. During the same die-cutting procedure, it is also possible to make score lines, slots, and tabs necessary for assembling the unit.

Cut-Awl or Bandsaw

In smaller runs and where the cuts or silhouettes are not too complicated, the display producer may use a cut-awl machine, or bandsaw, with a template as a guide. It is possible to get a fairly accurate cut, but there will be slight differences from stack to stack due to the human element involved.

The cut-awl operator may be able to cut only a few boards at a time or paper about an inch thick. The result can be fairly crisp and clean, but when precision matching between slots and tabs is essential or where intricate interior cuts may be required, this technique is decidely limited in its effectiveness. Under these circumstances, die-cutting is preferable.

superimposing different shapes, one atop the other, to add a sense of depth to the P.O.P. display. These layers can be set directly one upon the other, or they may be separated from each other by blocks and tabs. Using a tab or a fold-back flap to attach a layer will give the effect of greater depth, but the P.O.P. unit will still pack fairly flat.

Embossing—A raised, embossed, or relief impression can be made on a piece of artwork when, during the printing process, specific lines etched into a die appear on the printed surface. Sometimes, a die is placed beneath a piece of artwork and pressed up, from below, to create a raised pattern on the surface of the artwork. The embossing, in either case, creates a raised or textured surface.

Vacuum-Forming—Vacuum-forming is an "extreme" form of embossing. In this technique, a light-weight thermoplastic material (capable of being re-shaped when heated) is softened and then forced over a mold or die which is beneath it. Pressure is brought down from above, causing the pliable plastic to take on the contour and shape of the mold below. Suction, also from below, assures the skinlike fit of the plastic to the mold; it also helps cool off the plastic. When the shaped plastic is set (i.e., returns to room temperature), it will keep the shape of the mold. The process is repeated with the next piece of plastic.

Vacuum-forming is a relatively inexpensive way to get fully three-dimensional representations of a design. The major expense is sculpting the design and making the mold of the piece to be reproduced. As in offset printing or photolithography, the more units produced, the less the cost per unit for the making of the mold.

DIMENSIONAL EFFECTS

Appliqué—A flat P.O.P. display can be given greater depth and interest with the addition of some three-dimensional appliqué or attachment. A touch of paper lace glued down on the edge of a fan, a paper flower stuck behind the ear of a photographed Polynesian beauty, a corner of actual fabric sticking out of a silk-screened, pin-striped jacket—are examples of appliqué. Since this is usually a manual process, it can add quite a bit to the cost of manufacturing the unit, but because it is so effective, it can be worth the added cost.

The appliqué breaks the flatness of a design, making it more of a dimensional display and less of a poster. Sometimes, these softening elements are sent along with the unit, and the retailer is requested to add the boutonnaire or to lay down the satin squre or pin on the piece of bridal net. In this case, the producer does not need to handle each unit separately. The packing is simplified for the producer, and the appliqué looks fresher for the viewer. The retailer, however, must be agreeable to adding this final touch.

Layering—Dimension also can be achieved by

CONCLUSION: A CHECKLIST

The point-of-purchase unit should be considered and designed as part of an overall promotion and as the ultimate message of an advertisement. The P.O.P. displayer can support a shrinking sales force by answering customer questions, supplying the necessary information, giving prices, and by showing the available range and selection. It can offer a sample or supply a taste. It can be an asset to the merchant with limited sales help and limited sales space. The P.O.P. fixture can be a self-service, self-selector with simplified stock control. Most important, the P.O.P. displayer or fixture is where the customer is—where the sale is made.

The following is a checklist of questions to be answered before designing a point-of-purchase display unit:

1. When is the unit to appear? What is the timing?
2. Toward whom is the product or service directed? What is the target market?

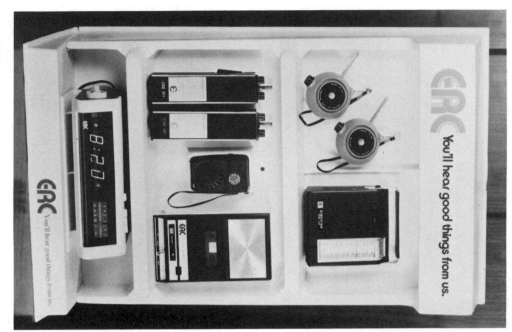

Figure 21-10. This vacuum-formed window display unit, counter unit, or ledge piece is molded, with shelves and compartments to hold specific items made and sold by the manufacturer, whose name and logo are screened on the lightweight and compact display piece. The store manager will have no questions as to which product goes where.

3. What is the purpose of this unit? Is it to introduce a new product? An improvement? A new style?

4. Is there an ad or TV campaign planned in conjunction with this unit? Will the P.O.P. design carry the same ad and message?

5. Does the unit have anything to do but carry the message? Is it a sampler? A tester? A stocking or restockable unit?

6. What P.O.P. units have been done in the past for this product or manufacturer?

7. What are the competitors doing with their P.O.P. programs?

8. In what types of retail operations will these units be used? Where will they be located in these stores? Will other P.O.P. units be used in coordination with this piece?

9. What quantities will be required?

10. What is the budget?

11. How long will this unit be used? Is it to be reusable?

12. Will the finished unit be bulk shipped or individually packed and shipped? Will they be sent by public conveyance or personally delivered by a company representative?

13. Should the unit include samples? Dummy boxes or bottles?

14. If the unit is to be stocked and prepacked, how many items should the P.O.P. piece carry?

15. Would the client like light or motion? Is there room in the budget for special effects: appliqué, vacuum-forming, embossing, complicated die-cutting, and so on?

16. What materials and/or techniques would the client prefer?

17. Who installs the unit? The customer? A sales representative?

18. Would the client like to see rough sketches? A comprehensive ("comp")? A model?

19. How is the client to be charged for the designs or comps?

20. Would the client like to see some auxiliary design concepts that would reinforce the message being presented in the P.O.P. unit; for example: table-tents, shelf readers, overhead banners or streamers, decals, buttons, T-shirts, and so on?

22 Exhibit and Trade Show Design—Industrial Display

Exhibits are the display and showing of special materials that have been collected and then edited for the presentation. The major purpose of an exhibit is to stimulate and create interest for a particular product, idea, or organization. The exhibit itself is organized and orchestrated for the enjoyment and enlightenment of a special audience or market, and may be used to educate, advertise, or propogandize.

A trade show is a commercial display of new products or concepts presented to a select group of prospective buyers or consumers. The "sale" may be direct (with purchases being made at the site of the exhibit) or indirect (may lead to eventual purchases). Please keep in mind that many of the principles of exhibit and trade show design, described below, apply equally to merchandise display and visual presentation.

TYPES OF EXHIBITS

Permanent Exhibits

The concept of a permanent exhibit should be abolished from the world of merchandise display and visual presentation, an area in which nothing should ever be considered unchanging and immutable. The idea of setting up an educational or promotional exhibit of a

project or product in an enclosed case or in a restricted area, and of allowing it to remain frozen in time and space—for an unlimited period of time—is against all that for which merchandise presentation stands.

Many museums have permanent exhibits in which paintings, sculpture, and other artwork are lastingly framed, hung, and encased. There is no surprise, novelty, or excitement in an unchanging, permanent display. The dioramas in museums of natural history are permanent, too; polar bears frozen forever on graying icebergs; Indians gathering dust and cobwebs in crumbling adobe huts. Though the preparation and installation of these extravaganzas are costly and time-consuming, they can become too familiar and even boring for the faithful museum visitor.

If the installation cannot be changed or relocated after a particular interval, it would probably be best for the viewer and the object being viewed, if it were curtained off or blocked off with another exhibit for "a pause that refreshes." Even a permanent exhibit should be a limited showing of something from the permanent collection which can then be replaced with another display. If the object is world-famous and many persons come especially to see it (e.g., the *Mona Lisa*, a Michelangelo sculpture, and so on), then the presentation and the area around the exhibit should be refreshed with a new attitude or look by adding changing floral arrangements, trying period furniture settings, experimenting with different lighting techniques, or using new background colors or textures.

Temporary Exhibits

A temporary exhibit is usually the presentation of an item or items that are on loan for a limited time. The showing schedule is announced and the duration of the showing is advertised and publicized. The arrival and showing of the treasures of King Tut at a local museum for a one-month showing is an excellent example of a temporary exhibit. The arrival and opening date is publicized and anticipated by the public. The limited stay creates the necessary impetus to have the public come and see the exhibit while the artwork is on loan.

A community room in a library, town hall, or department store might house temporary exhibits sponsored by local clubs, artists, or artisans of the community. A public service area in a large corporate building or a shopping center may also hold temporary exhibits which could be either educational or promotional (e.g., a Red Cross life-saving exhibit or an automobile show).

Trade Shows

Trade shows are commercial ventures wherein a manufacturer or distributor will show a line of merchandise, introduce a new product or an improvement on an existing one, exhibit for the sake of "goodwill" or "antique" versions of the products the company is producing today. It is the "soft sell" approach and the exhibit would be designed to show the historical perspective of the company and the product rather than to place the emphasis on the current product or line.

The company seeking goodwill (instead of showing its merchandise) may provide, in a setting of plants and seats, an arrangement of a very few choice objects; perhaps, the earliest prototypes of their product or company image, or do an institutional presentation (see Chapter 14).

Often, trade shows are produced in large exhibition halls in which several hundred exhibitors battle for attention in rather open and exposed areas. The management of the exhibit hall or the organization sponsoring the show may set restrictions concerning the height of a booth or exhibit, the use of opaque walls, fireproofed materials, lighting equipment, overhead signs, and sound equipment. The union regulations that govern the setting up, lighting, trimming, and the eventual dismantling of the show can be a serious problem for the trade show designer. Following these regulations can become costly and time-consuming. The storage of shipping cases and crating material may also present problems. This rather specialized subject of trade shows will be considered more fully later in this chapter.

Traveling Exhibits

Traveling exhibits is a broad, all-inclusive term for movable or portable displays. A traveling exhibit is conceived and designed to be moved from one location to another and to be assembled quickly, with few changes and a minimum of professional assistance. Some traveling shows are actually large buses or vans that have been converted into "galleries on wheels." The viewer enters at one end of the vehicle and exits from the other, after having seen the complete showing. Often, the government will produce a traveling show which will visit schools and libraries. The van or bus may be parked in the parking lot, or out in front of the institution, and the students will be invited in to see the special collection.

Other traveling shows are not designed to move "as is" in their own vehicles. These shows use collapsible panels, frames, or stands which can be reassembled and will adapt to a preestablished plan or pattern in an area of a specific size. Sometimes, the designer may have to supply several alternate arrangements for the panels or frames in order to accommodate variations in floor layouts or space allocations.

This basic concept of traveling shows capable of being reassembled is often the principle upon which many trade show exhibits are based. Since the manufacturer or exhibitor may have to show in several different markets (different trade shows in different cities) within the same short selling season, the exhibit may have to be assembled and used for a week or less, then be broken down, crated and shipped off to the next exhibit hall, where the following week it has to be reassembled and ready for the new trade show. The exhibit designer may have to add or subtract panels or frames from the exhibit depending, again, on the allotted space and restrictions set by the new exhibit management.

Outdoor Exhibits

An outdoors exhibition may take place in a garden, a park, a parking lot, on a closed-off traffic street, or in the middle of a shopping mall. Depending upon the material to be shown, this can be the most challenging type of exhibit. The garden or park setting is ideal for sculpture and other dimensional objects that are not affected by heat, cold, rain, or snow. The natural light and setting can be glorious "props" for these natural but "hard" materials. Other exhibits (art shows, craft shows, and such) may suffer from the uncertainty of the weather. Strong winds and strong sunlight (to say nothing of sudden rain) can be discomforting to the viewing public and play havoc with the show itself. Where the exhibit can be contained under a roof—a pavillion or a tent—the exhibit is more manageable. With an overhead enclosure, the designer can make plans despite the sun, gusts of wind, and an unexpected shower.

PLANNING THE EXHIBIT

The Audience

As in all displays, the market is a prime consideration. What is the age and intelligence level of the viewing audience that will come to see this show? Are they children, teenagers, adults, or all of the above? Are they knowledgeable on the subject or must they be directed and oriented to the material to be presented? Are they coming with a preestablished interest or curiosity about the subject (which is usually the case with trade shows), or must they be stimulated to rouse their interest in the show? What is their average interest span? How much material will they be able to absorb in one visit through the show?

Armed with the answers to these questions and other information supplied by the exhibitor, the designer can then plot the exhibit within the anticipated length of the visit to the show and arrange the material for its best acceptance and viewer stimulation. Depending on the material and the floor plan or the traffic pattern of the show, which will be discussed shortly, the designer can help set the pace for the viewer at the exhibit. This should permit the viewer to spend as much time where he or she pleases. Again, this is ideal in a trade show exhibit where the viewer is usually a potential customer, and the viewing is done with an eye toward buying.

The Subject

The better organized the exhibit, the more readily it will be understood and accepted. If the exhibit is based on a single, unifying theme and all the material is related (e.g., fashions of "Coco" Chanel), the background needs to be explained or illustrated only once, at the beginning. That one explanation then serves as a guide for everything that follows.

At a trade show, it is simpler and more effective to show one product or a related line of items rather than present a complete spectrum of unrelated and sometimes conflicting merchandise. Where many diverse items must be presented, the good designer will use some device or gimmick (color, line, dividers, graphics, etc.) to unify the dissimilar and individual pieces into a harmonious and controlled flow. At a recent trade show, the manufacturer of a diverse line of manne-

quins (from very realistic to very abstract, from child to adult) had all the mannequins dressed in black and gold. Though the fashions and styles were varied, in keeping with the type of mannequin used, the black-and-gold color scheme made a strong, unifying impact.

Whatever the subject matter of the exhibit, the exhibitor and the designer must supply an avenue of interest for the audience to follow, in which the theme, product, or premise is presented in an appealing, coherent, and compelling manner. There should be a point of view expressed, and that point should be presented up front, at the beginning, so that all that follows is an explanation and an elaboration on the basic theme. A good exhibit presents, stimulates and leaves an impression, but never confuses. Even if it is a goodwill, prestige, or institutional type of exhibit, the exhibitor still has the opportunity to publicize, either directly or indirectly, his or her product and to stimulate a demand for his or her services.

Size of the Exhibit

The size of an exhibit is commonly a great variable. When dealing with a particular gallery, museum, library, or exhibit area, where the space devoted to showings is relatively constant, the exhibit designer "knows the territory," what can be done and how much can be shown effectively. On the other hand, the designer of a traveling exhibit supplies panels, frames, and stands that will require a certain amount of space in which to set up the show correctly. The persons who receive the exhibit (the staff decorators) must then make the design work within their actual space.

A well-designed traveling exhibit will have a degree of flexibility drawn into the plan. The design will either expand or contract as space permits. Sometimes, that means adding some purely decorative filler panels, plants, or additional material. It might require omitting some secondary material in order to make the best presentation of the major items. A display that will travel and be set up in any number of different spaces should have auxiliary floor plans, alternative arrangements, and sketched recommendations accompanying the exhibit. The show that is "mobile" (i.e, set on a train, bus, or van), is already limited in size by the unit that houses and carries it.

The design of the individual trade show exhibit will vary with the particular exhibit hall and its space allocation. The exhibit floor is divided into booths that may be 8 feet by 8 feet, 10 feet by 10 feet, or 12 feet by 12 feet, depending on the module of space that is most economical for the hall's management. The exhibitor reserves a booth or a combination of booths, so that the exhibit area (based on a 10-foot by 10-foot module as an example) may be anything from a 10-foot by 10-foot space (one booth); to a long, narrow rectangle measur-

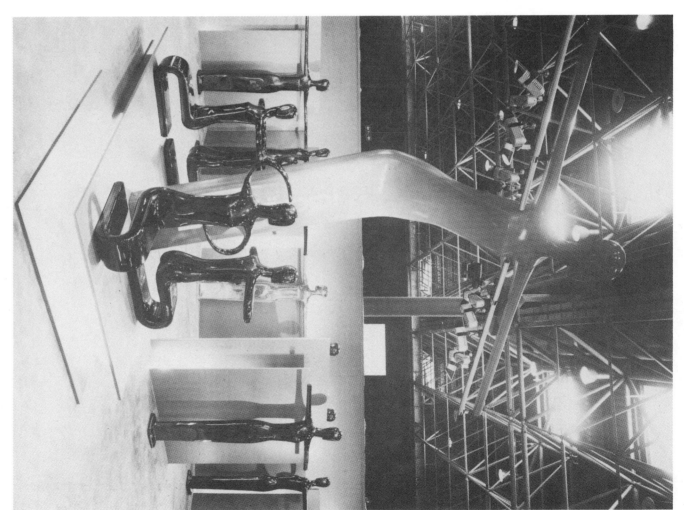

Figure 22-1. A spectacular presentation of abstract mannequins and fixtures in a no less spectacular setting. The ceiling is over 40 feet off the ground and this exhibit area is encased by an 8-foot wall. Five and 6-foot dividers are used on the floor to back up and separate groups of figures as well as to establish traffic patterns. The high metallic finish of the mannequins is enhanced by the powerful H.I.D. spotlights set along the outstretched "arms" of the colossal figure that dominates the display area. *Schlappi, Waldshut-Tiengen, West Germany.*

ing 10 feet by 40 feet (four adjacent booths); to a square block, 20 feet by 20 feet (two booths wide by two booths long). The size and shape of the total space will determine the layout and traffic pattern of the total booth area, the location of the entrance and exit from the display area, and the amount of material that can be shown.

Ideally, the space should be related to the subject matter. Statues and large architectural pieces need open spaces so that they can be viewed from all sides as well as from a distance. Coins, jewelry, manuscripts, and small collector's items are more effective in smaller, more intimate surroundings.

When space is "unlimited," the exhibit may show too much, in too diversified a manner. A very long exhibit is more likely to weary and confuse the viewer, and eventually lose his or her interest. Also, the intended impact can be lost.

When the amount of material (like a retrospective showing of Picasso's works or the full line of General Foods' products) is staggering and requires lots of space and material, it is advisable to have a catalogue or guidebook available for the visitor. As the viewer threads his or her way through the maze of myriad objects, the booklet will supply the basic information and the necessary background material that would have only cluttered the exhibit if additional signs had to be included. It also provides a route for the viewer to follow. The guidebook provides the viewer with a means to locate what he or she actually wants to see and to spend time where the viewer feels it will be most beneficial and instructive.

The size of the exhibit is especially important when the exhibit must be crated to be shipped to the next show place. The cost of crating and shipping is a very big part of the exhibit budget, and the designer must consider this in the original plan. It will affect the framework used for the show and the manner in which the show is set up and taken down.

Design and Layout: The Traffic Plan

Once the size of the exhibit is specified and the material to be shown is selected, the designer starts by plotting the traffic patterns within the booth. This is most important and may determine which structural materials are used.

The traffic plan is the basic consideration in moving people through an area. The layout may be in long lines following the perimeter walls. The latter creates a gallery effect with series of straight lines, panels, or "walls." The gallery effect may be accomplished with free-standing panels displaying exhibit material on both sides.

The path may follow a zigzag of screens folded into a series of V-shaped bays. These bays or alcoves may be used to separate or highlight certain material, contain a case or riser, or to create a setting for a dimensional object. Or, the floor plan can be a pattern that combines straight panels with an occasional "V" for emphasis or as a change of pace.

The maze is another option in exhibit design. In this case, the traffic flow is directed by "pointing arrows" and the viewer is swept along by a series of angles and turns. He or she has no alternative but to follow along the prescribed route. The maze allows more material to be shown because the aisles are usually narrower, the material is shown on two sides of the frame or panel, and the convoluted floor pattern permits the use of more panels in the allotted space. Although the viewer is shepherded through the presentation, there can be bunching or tie-ups with people getting "stuck" in funnel-like openings. A viewer who decides to go back to look at something previously passed can cause a problem in the traffic flow. Rarely does the maze layout allow the viewer the freedom of selecting a course through the show at his or her own tempo. Some viewers may resent the "herding" quality and the "closeness" of this type of exhibit layout.

Whatever type of traffic plan or floor plan is used, a change of pace should be built in. Long gallery runs, although exceptionally well-suited to certain material, can be enhanced when balanced with a few bays or aisles for added interest or emphasis. An occasional maze might supply just the right ambience for other materials, or work to separate groups of products. However, if the visitor feels restricted, inhibited, or confused, the purpose of the exhibit may be lost.

Theme or Story

A good exhibit has a theme or unifying element, e.g., "The History of Product X," "The Development of a New Product," "100 Years of Men's Fashions," and so on. The exhibit should start with the main idea and then elaborate and illustrate the premise behind the show. Something should get the visitor's attention or pique the curiosity, enough to make the viewer want to go on and see more.

If graphics are used, they should start out with an effective statement, up front. If the area lends itself to it, a dramatic and enticing entrance is always effective. It is like the overture to a musical comedy; stimulating and exciting, with just a bar or two of what is to come, and enough to set the feet tapping and the senses moving in the right direction. The opening statement can be heightened by means of light, lighting effects, a dynamic color, or animation. If there is copy, a headline, a quote that sets the theme, it should be easy to read and provocative. As mentioned previously, brochures or guidebooks should be available at the entrance or start of the exhibit.

Color and Texture

Color is always vital to a presentation, whether it be by its presence or its absence. If an exhibit is mainly black and white (i.e., printed materials, photographs, etc.), then the designer may have to use colored backgrounds to add pace and pizzazz to the show. A change of color may serve as a "punctuation mark" to indicate the end of one idea or phase and the introduction to the next one.

Colored or neutral backgrounds may be necessary to overcome the existing background color of the exhibition area. If the exhibit hall is white and airy, and the presentation requires deep, dark colors and dramatic shadows, the designer may accomplish this by means of colored panels, dropped ceilings, or special lighting effects. Optically, color can stretch walls, bring them closer together, open or close areas and, thus, seemingly affect the architecture of the show area. (See Chapter 5.)

Texture is also a tool that can be used by the designer. Color and texture can be used on the walls, panels, ceilings, and floor to set the traffic pattern of the show. The designer can lay a path of carpet or tiles which contrasts with the existing floor of the display space. Imagine a red velvet runner leading around a painting or sculpture exhibition, or a green "grass" matting used to set a crafts show inside a brick or stone enclosed space.

Graphics

Logos and Trademarks—A successful exhibit often will carry through its theme by means of an identifying and well-publicized logo. The logo or decorative motif appears on posters, in mailings, and in the ads for the show. It may be part of the catalogue cover design or on the brochures or giveaways. Souvenirs like T-shirts, pennants, posters, scarves, etc., will often be identified by the same logo. A dramatic, dimensional representation of the logo can be the entrance to the exhibit.

Lettering—Any copy used, whether for headlines, captions, or for general information, should be in a style that is consistent and in character with the material being exhibited. Various fonts are available for sign printing machines, which the designer can use to facilitate the making of signs. (See Chapter 20.)

Instead of being printed, the signs can also be made with three-dimensional letters. There is a great variety of these letters from which to choose. They may be made of plastic or stamped out of cardboard or foamcore. These "3D" letters are available in sizes ranging from about ½-inch to 6 or more inches in height, and in a wide range of styles and colors. Though, initially, they are more expensive to purchase, they are reusable if handled with care.

The dimensional letters do add quality and character to a display. The shadows created by their thickness improve the overall look of the show, especially when the material on display is flat and nondimensional.

The style of lettering can suggest what the exhibit is all about. Elongated, elegant sans-serif letters speak of refinement, classic qualities, and uniqueness. P.T. Barnum, a "Gay Nineties" type of compressed lettering, is right to evoke the "old-fashioned," with warm, pleasant feelings for "the good old days." Heavy, expanded letters are more contemporary, hard-hitting, and emphatic. Italics can be exciting and stimulating. Obviously, what the words themselves say is very important, but what they look like can have more impact.

Supergraphics and Line—A long, straight, unbroken gallery wall can become an exciting, moving, and dazzling background by means of a supergraphic pattern superimposed on it. The designer may plan a dynamic line design full of sharp angles, crisp turns, and abrupt movements to become the background for what might otherwise be a rather staid and pedestrian showing. Visually, the supergraphic, done in a bold, contrasting color scheme, becomes the actual eye-arresting background, while the neutral gallery wall seems to fade away. The dynamic movement suggests the "path" for the presentation, and the viewer is "led" along by it. The supergraphic technique also works on self-standing screens, frames, or modular constructions.

The linear quality of the design affects the emotional response of the viewer. (See Chapter 7.) A vertical presentation is more likely to suggest strength, dignity, elegance, and the classic look. Horizontal lines are easy, gentle, and restful; and angular, diagonal lines are dynamic and exciting. A good exhibit designer can "write a score" with these lines; going from a mighty vertical opening into a calm and quiet stretch of horizontal, to climax in a crescendo of clashing diagonals.

Photomurals and Blowups—The use of over-sized photographs and enlargements of detailed drawings and printed material can be used effectively in promoting the theme of an exhibit. A greatly enlarged, graphic, over life-size, adds impact to an idea and turns a minute phrase into a mighty statement.

In a showing where crowds are anticipated, the photographic enlargement makes it possible for the viewers in back to see what is going on up front. The surprise of seeing a 6- or 8-foot closeup of a face or pattern, as one turns from one aisle into another, can be just the thing to add impetus and tempo to the next group of objects to be viewed. A grainy or grayed photomural may be the right tone and texture for appliquéd cutout letters with a message.

In a crowded exhibit hall, where many exhibitors are striving for attention, photomurals can be very effective. The buildings in which commercial trade shows are held often have ceilings high above the show floor, and the large graphic design helps scale the exhibit area to its surroundings. Numerous, small objects can become nervous, fussy patterns when the space is wide open and "sky high."

Murals or long continuous pictorial illustrations can serve as a bridge between groups of ideas, explain the passage of time or a change of locale, or supply an historical setting. The mural can supply the atmosphere or background that will make what follows more readily understood. A giant map can set the scene for what comes next. A regatta of ancient sailing vessels entering a port can explain the change from the "old world" to the "new." A greatly enlarged etching or line drawing of a street fair in Eighteenth Century London can set the mood for an exhibit of the everyday utensils and handicrafts of that time and place.

Where words may be difficult to read or where too many words would be required to explain the "why," "what," "where," and "when," a pictorial representation may do it best. The exhibit designer will find thousands of picture books and line illustrations which can be blown up photographically or printed as ozalids or blueprints (or as black or brown prints).

Any exhibit that uses too many blowups can be dull and pointless, with no variety, no highlights, and no shadows. When using any device or gimmick, discretion is required. Special effects should be reserved for where impact and stress are needed.

Heights and Elevations—Eye level is a very important consideration in planning an exhibit. It is not enough to simply place material to be viewed at 5 to 5½ feet off the ground. Where it is anticipated there may be crowds or several layers of viewers lined up for a glimpse of the material, the designer should hang the work above regular eye level. This is an accommodation to the people in the back who may have to look over the heads and shoulders of those in front. It also adds a change of pace to what otherwise might be a routinely hung show.

There is no hard-and-fast rule for the height or level of presentation at a showing. Basically, it should be determined by the individual object being presented. Some things look better when viewed from above; that is, the viewer looks down on them (e.g., coins, jewelry, manuscripts, miniatures); other objects are best displayed when the viewer can look up to them; while still others need a straight-on view. Thus, the presentation will depend on the material, the type of exhibit, and the construction of the exhibit, and the main object or thrust of the show. If a dramatic story is being presented, or the development of a product or theme, then a straight-on showing may be best. If it is a showing of artwork of various materials and techniques, the exhibit can be made more interesting when a variety of heights is used in displaying or setting up.

Most designers who are involved with the displaying of graphics find that the overall appearance of the wall, or backing, is enhanced when there is a straight, horizontal line somewhere in the arrangement. Since the sizes of the frames or prints will vary, it is easier for the viewer to perceive the total showing within his or her eye span if all the frames or mats are aligned with the floor. For a walk-through type of presentation (for adults), 3½ feet to 4 feet off the floor is usually a good baseline from which to start. This baseline is an imaginary line on which sit the bottom edges of frames, mats, etc. Another option would be to have all the artwork leveled off at the top at about 6½ feet to 7 feet off the floor. In this case, the lower edge is broken and irregular. Interior designers will often use this imaginary line to "contain" a picture arrangement on a wall. For an exhibit that is essentially designed for children, the eye level should be lowered proportionately.

In any long presentation, whether it be a gallery run or an unbroken lineup of screens or panels, a "change of pace" is necessary. The viewer's eye needs a rest, a pause. It is quite monotonous to see object after object on the same background color, lit with the same intensity. In such a case, after a while, all the objects on view tend to blend together. Varying sizes can break this routine pattern. One large unit might be balanced by several smaller ones that fill the same amount of space. (See Chapter 7 for a discussion of balance and symmetry.) A break in the imaginary top or bottom line will cause the piece that extends above or below the others to receive more attention. It makes the viewer aware of the break in the routine. Interspersing an occasional panel of a contrasting color will also relieve the overall sameness of the presentation and focus in on the uniqueness of the one that has been treated with special emphasis. The copy panel or message can be especially effective when highlighted on a special background color. Using plants and flowers will also help reduce the potential for monotony.

The use of museum cases and pedestals can add momentum to the pace and rhythm of a show. If photos and manuscripts have been carefully mounted on a vertical surface (a wall, panel, etc.), then placing a book, manuscript, or photo on a pedestal, at a different eye level, will emphasize the importance of that particular object. The viewer is "forced" to look at this part of the show in a different way, switching eye level, the angle of the head, in fact, his or her whole concentration. Subsequently, it registers on the viewer that this is something special, different, more important.

In the discussion of buildups and risers, in Chapter 14, we have discussed how they can be used to show and separate groups of items into individual units. Clusters of platforms of assorted heights are effective for exhibiting three-dimensional objects. A riser can bring an otherwise unimpressive object to new "heights" of importance in the viewer's eye. For example, a vase on a pedestal is special and unique. A vase along with several others, at the same level in a display case, is just another vase. Separate and apart, it becomes extraordinary.

A dimensional cube or riser can also become an island in an aisle and serve as a separation in a traffic pattern. The riser can also be used to direct traffic around a run of panels or frames. The platform serves to break away from a flat gallery presentation, or to fill in the bay or "V" formed by a folded screen. For a traveling exhibit, cubes can be designed with open bottoms and made to fit one inside the other so that they will stack and ship more easily.

CONSTRUCTION AND MATERIALS

Gallery Walls

When the exhibit is to be set up against the walls of an existing gallery, or in an area that has been designed for presentations, the exhibit designer is limited, to some extent, as to what can or cannot be done. In most cases, the wall is painted or covered in a neutral color—anything from stark white to pale beige, to muted gray and on to deep taupe tones. Supergraphics, colored panels, risers, platforms, and museum cases will help add interest and variety.

If the wall surface is hard (plaster, stone, cement block, brick, fine finished wood, etc.), items to be displayed may have to be wired and hung down from a molding which is usually located near the ceiling line. A soft wall (wood, cork, beaverboard, or any other material into which a pin or nail can easily be driven) is simpler to work on. Sometimes, the soft wall material is covered over with a natural, textured fabric, such as jute, burlap, nubby cotton or linen, or grasscloth, which "hides" the marks left by pins or tacks. The material "heals" itself and is fresh and ready for reuse. Four by eight panels of foamcore or other lightweight, porous materials can be treated with color and texture (i.e., painted or covered with fabric). The treated panel can then be hung or pinned onto the wall for greater interest and appeal.

Screens and Grids

Screens are a natural solution for quick and efficiently set-up exhibits. A screen is basically two frames or

rectangles hinged together or joined by means of hooks, clips, etc. The screen will stand on its own rather well when the panels are angled into a "V" and, usually, will fold flat for storage or shipping. Screens are adjustable; that is, the angle of the "V" can be changed. If space on the floor is limited, the angle can be sharper and closer to a 90-degree angle. Should space not be a problem, the angle can be opened up beyond the 90 degrees. Although one "V" screen will be able to stand, two or more linked together will be more secure.

The screen may be nothing more than a pair of wood or metal frames, 3 feet by 7 feet or 4 feet by 8 feet, having a surface within the frame upon which the exhibitor can display. The enclosed panel may be foamcore, Homosote, plywood, or any other soft surface which has been covered or treated with a decorative or textured surfacing material. The covering can simply be a panel of fabric attached to the inner surface of the frame or hemmed and hung from the top rail of the frame. In the case of a fabric divider, the material to be displayed would probably have to be wired and hung with picture hooks or S-hooks from the top rail of the frame. When a rigid panel is inserted in the frame, the graphics can be pinned or stapled directly onto the surface. In either case, the screen will be double-faced, and material can be exhibited on both sides of the screen.

Sometimes, a metal or plastic grid will be inserted into the opening of the frame, restricting the use of the screen to one side. There are many special attachments available for use with open grids, including a shelved unit which may be used to show dimensional objects at assorted heights. The grid affords the viewer a "see-through" into the next part of the exhibit which might be desirable. The openness of the grid not only makes the screen seem lighter, it also allows light to pass through. Again, in pacing an exhibition, it might be advantageous to alternate and intersperse grid panels with solid ones.

Grids can also be used without frames. They can be hung from the ceiling, either horizontally or vertically. The vertical panel (perpendicular to the floor) will become a divider or a carrier for some graphics. However, since the grid is open, it requires careful hanging and/or camouflaging of the back. If the grid is dropped horizontally (parallel to the floor) from above, it becomes, in effect, a dropped ceiling and an ideal vehicle from which to suspend display objects or from which to hang lights. In an exhibit hall of great height, the dropped ceiling can be a very effective device for closing in the exhibit and gaining a sense of intimacy and warmth in cold and impersonal surroundings.

Another device that works well with panels and grids, but does not require hinged screens to support it,

Figure 22-2. This exhibit area is, quite literally, a sea of pedestals—all the same height and laid out with mathematical precision. There are no surprises and no highlights; it is hard to tell if you have seen one of the exhibits or if you have yet to get to it. The lighting is way up in the ceiling, and the pages of the magazines secured to the tops of the various pedestals are barely lit. The mounted flags are the only vertical relief in the whole, rather dull exhibit.

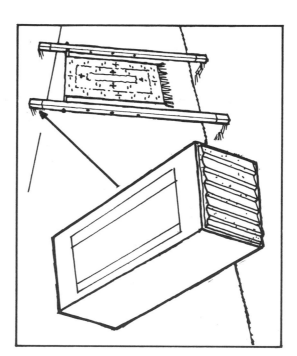

Figure 22-3. The detail on the left illustrates the construction of a *Timber Topper*, a trademark for tension spring mechanisms made to fit on the top and bottom of pieces of lumber, usually measuring 2 inches by 3 inches. The lumber is then wedged into an upright position between the floor and ceiling. The resulting rigidity, created by the tension of the springs against the floor and the ceiling, allows the post to support panels, frames, and so on.

is the spring-loaded post. This is a vertical member, often a piece of 2-inch by 3-inch lumber, with a retractable spring-like cap and foot pieces at either end. The top cap is retracted while the post is wedged into place on the floor; the top spring is then released. The tension of the springs against the ceiling above and the floor below supplies the necessary rigidity to make the post(s) capable of bearing or supporting panels, frames, and/or grids. This technique will work in areas where the ceiling is not more than 12-feet high. For shipping or traveling and, of course, storing, the post is easy to pack. The caps come off and are replaced when the posts are next erected. The posts can be decoratively surfaced or covered with fabric or vinyl, or painted any desired color. Here again, the color can make a decorative statement or help carry along the action or sequences of the exhibit.

Frames and panels can be secured onto these posts in various ways. Depending on the space, the subject matter, and the material to be shown, the 4-foot by 8-foot panels might be used in the "landscape" position (horizontal). In this way, the designer could place them 3 or 3½ feet up from the ground, like a floating panel, thereby permitting the viewer to see the legs of other viewers in back. If this presents a problem of aesthetics or style, the designer can use plants in flower boxes or an occasional platform or riser set below the panel.

Exhibit Systems

Systems used for store planning and display have been discussed in Chapter 13. Although they were intro-

Figure 22-4. The PPM exhibit at a trade show for its own product (a ball and rod structural system) used soft sculptured figures dressed as construction people to add a "human" touch to the exhibit—to show scale, strength, and the height of the structure. *PPM, Friedrichsdorf, West Germany.*

Figure 22-5. This Rieger System exhibit shows the product in use as a self-standing, independent, two-story structure complete with graphics, self-contained lighting, shelves, even a clear plastic awning. The graphics on the panels explain the system and its applications. *Rieger, Essen, West Germany.*

Figure 22-6. A free-standing and self-enclosed exhibit or shop which collapses down to "ladders," panels, shelves, clamps, and clips. The lighting can be self-contained and brought down to where it is needed. *Bruynzeel-Monta, St. Cloud, France.*

duced as a fixturing concept, many were brought on the market specifically to serve the exhibit industry. As previously mentioned, systems are available in steel, aluminum, wood, and heavy-duty, but brightly colored, plastic. Most systems seem to be designed with an infinite collection of joiners, end caps, and accessories. Some even come with built-in lighting. The systems may be super-sleek, ultra chic, high tech, or look like a warehouse construction. Some are designed to "disappear," be all but invisible, while others are meant to make a decorative statement. Systems go from simple ladder constructions, to tinker toys not meant for children, up to very complex webs and grids, such as the noted designer-architect, Buckminster Fuller, might conceive. Listed below are some additional exhibit systems that are available to the designer.

P.P.M. is manufactured in West Germany and is a strong but simple skeletal construction which can be equally effective indoors or out. With it, the designer can create multistoried constructions. It is basically a ball and rod building system in which the rods fit snugly into precision-drilled holes in the balls. It resembles a scaffold, and with the use of shelves and inset panels, becomes a dimensional, self-standing, partially see-through wall for the display of dimensional or flat pieces.

The *Quadro System* is another West German design consisting of round polypropylene plastic tubing 2 to 3-inches thick, which is available in assorted precut lengths in black, white, or red. These tube lengths are joined by means of precision joints that are simply shaped as a "T," "V," or "X," or a five-armed "star."

The *Quadro System* is available with clips to hold panels (vertically) or shelves (horizontally) in place on the construction. Wheels for mobility and end caps to close off tube ends are also available.

The *Rieger System*, also from West Germany, is similar to the Quadro System in that it consists of round tubes and joints. In this aluminum system, referred to as #65, the tubes are 2½ inches (65 mm.) in diameter. The joints are elbowed. These rounded corners give the complete construction a generally softer look. The #65 System comes with its own light fittings that work within the confines of the 2½-inch tube to provide long, gentle lines of light for general lighting in the area. Though the system is stocked in black, it can be ordered in colors of the designer's choice. Accessories, such as panel clips, hangers, and sign holders, have been designed to fit over the round tubes.

Monta is manufactured by the Bruyzeel-Monta Corporation in St. Cloud, France. This is a simple wooden frame, with the vertical uprights notched at regular intervals. Shelves, panels, and even drawers can be inserted into the notched openings and a slatted back panel can be fitted into the rectangular frame. Specially designed clamps and clips keep the assorted horizontal attachments in place.

Instand is a product of AB Adam Ltd. of Stockholm, Sweden. It is an expandable, lightweight, and truly portable wall exhibit system. When the unit is opened, the multitriangular web work will provide about 80 square feet of open, see-through, self-standing display wall (about 9 feet by 9 feet or 8 feet by 10 feet). The triangular elements combine to form rectangles, which in turn can be covered with graphics or panels. Shelves can also be laid across the triangles. The web can also be shaped into arches and used as a horizontal "ceiling" span or a grid for hanging or for lighting equipment. The special feature of this system is that it folds in on itself (like an umbrella), and when completely closed, it fits into a 30-inch case.

The *Radius Portable Panel System* is a "no-tool," easy-to-assemble idea from Hanna Designs of Toronto, Canada. It, too, is ideal for a portable presentation. The basic system consists of metal tubular frames and panels. The corners of the panels are equipped with hooks which can be inserted into predrilled slots at various intervals on the frame. There are different modules available to diversify the system and the panels vary in size from 10 inches by 36 inches up to 4 feet by 6 feet.

Kalutex of W. Germany provides a different approach to exhibit design. This is a ceiling track system (not unlike a track light system), which allows the carrier clips to move freely along the track and to turn at a right angle into crisscrossing tracks. Panels can be hooked on any place there is track installed. Graphics or frames can also be clipped into these tracks. The major drawback to this system is that it is fixed into the ceiling of the exhibit area. It can be restrictive.

The *Nemcon Modular System* from Ville St. Laurent, Quebec, Canada, is a simple, delicate-looking, 1/2-inch round tubular system that is similar in appearance to Abstracta (see page 99). It creates a light and airy effect, although it is strong and rigid once it is assembled. Nemcon is simple to assemble and dismantle. A stainless steel spring incorporated into the con-

nectors assures a strong union even after repeated assemblies. This system is also equipped with a variety of connectors, clips, and accessories.

Voluma is a panel-clip system without bars or frames. It is easy to assemble with only a simple tool which is often supplied with the system. The panels are connected to each other with clips. Almost any type of panel that is about 1/4-inch thick can be used. The construction is functional and economical, requiring a simple inventory of parts and a relatively small number of reusable connectors (clips). The system is easy to dismantle, takes up a minimum of storage space, and packs conveniently into inexpensive, transportable packages.

Exposystem is produced in the United States by Giltspur. It is one of several ready-to-use, multiscreen kits. This system consists of interlocking components of chrome-plated steel frames for dimensional stability plus textured, velvetlike, fabric-covered panels, and connectors, lighting fixtures, and shelves. The kits are designed to provide a practical starting point for the designer. With these, he or she can create many different variations. The designer can build up, out, or around with these self-standing screens. In addition to the fabric-covered panels, multiscreen kits are available with panels of Plexiglas or black or white hardboard. The manufacturer will supply the designer with drawings of many possible arrangements and a list of accessories that will extend the life of the kit.

Several *grid systems* are manufactured in the United States. They are usually made of 1/4-inch wire with 3-inch by 3-inch grid openings, in two stock sizes:

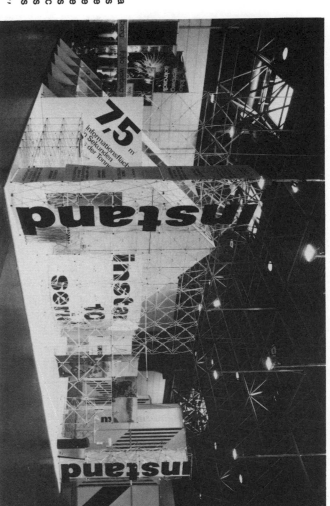

Figure 22-7. Instand makes a dramatic statement with its lightweight web of rods. The graphics are strong and get the attention they demand. The stark white floor separates this area from the regular traffic floor of the show and makes Instand stand out from its neighbors. *AB Adman Ltd., Stockholm, Sweden.*

2 feet by 7 feet and 2 feet by 8 feet. These grid systems are usually available in five baked enamel finishes or in brass, chrome, or nickel-plated finishes. Among the many accessories available are a wall clamp (for permanent installations) and assorted rectangular and triangular shelves made of a wire grid or of butcher block. Also provided is a 4-foot by 4-foot "roof" grid that can be used with the walls or screens to hold them together or as a free-floating, dropped ceiling panel. Many hook-on devices are also available. Grids are available in many module sizes and with various size openings. Sid Diamond, Inc., located in New York City, is one manufacturer of a grid exhibit system.

Die-cut board units are made by several manufacturers. They are basically simple, compact, fold-up, portable exhibit booths. Lightweight but rigid materials like foamcore or paper-covered styrofoam or honeycombed cardboard materials can be made into slot-together panels. No tools are required and the whole construction can be put together or dismantled in less than an hour. These portable booths are often available in their own carrying cases which are designed to fit into the trunk of a standard automobile.

The panels can be painted, trimmed, silk-screened, or finished with Velcro (a fastener consisting of strips of specially treated fabric which adhere to each other and can be separated simply by pulling them apart) for a quick, self-stick appliqué of graphics. Cutout letters can be applied directly onto the surface or pinned into the porous core.

Some of these system-like designs are preset regarding their use, and there is little the designer can do to alter the physical setup. Other "systems" offer a varied collection of modular, multisized, notched panels which can be creatively built into an intricate "house of cards" that stands, or into folding screens, cubes, and such. Exhibit designers would do well to check with organizations such as the Point of Purchase Advertising Institute (POPAI) in New York as well as larger trade show buildings for lists of current manufacturers of portable trade show booths.

In selecting a system, especially one that will be used for temporary setups and for traveling or trade shows, the following criteria should be considered:

- Is it compact?
- Is it light?
- Is it easy to assemble and dismantle?
- Is it easy to maintain?
- Is it flexible and adaptable?
- Is it modular?
- Are replacement parts and accessories readily available?

Dividers

When separating an area into exhibit space, and in order to provide the proper ambience and a sense of intimacy, or to add sparkle to the progression of a presentation, dividers can be helpful. Basically, dividers act as separators and backgrounds; the objects to be viewed are the "stars"; the dividers provide the setting. They can support or enhance the material to be seen by means of their texture, color, and possibly their

Figure 22-8. It could be a shop entrance out on a street, but it is an exhibit that shows the versatility of the Voluma Shop System. The walls, planters, risers, display areas, and even the electrified entablature overhead—all are basically panels held together with clips. A strong change of color indicates the entrance. The illuminated windows sell the product. Notice the height to which the Voluma logo has been raised over the display area. *Voluma Shop Technik, Friedrichsdorf, West Germany.*

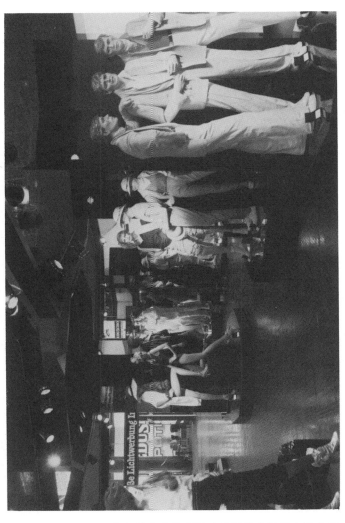

Figure 22-9. Hindsgaul introduces its new groupings of mannequins by setting them on octagonal platforms and backing them with dark gray, three-sided, Plexiglas screens. The vertical screens seem to support the octagonally framed "ceilings" of translucent fabric. The spotlights are attached to the ceiling frames. The ceiling cuts down on the light that floods the exhibit area, makes this area more intimate, and helps to dramatize the lighting and the product. Notice the traffic pattern created by the use of the octagonal platforms. *Hindsgaul, Dusseldorf, West Germany.*

pattern. A panel of fabric hung from the ceiling or a banner, hemmed top and bottom to hold a weighted rod, can act as a divider and also provide a welcome touch of color. If the show's logo is screened on the banner, it also reinforces the show's theme.

Bamboo rolldown shades can be effective with certain presentations. String curtains or macrame-type panels add interest without being "pushy." Plants clustered together can provide a delightful oasis of greenery and life in an otherwise flat, black-and-white show. Cubes, platforms, and risers can also "divide and conquer," depending on the theme and the material.

THEFT AND VANDALISM CONTROL

Unfortunately, theft and vandalism are problems which the display designer must help to control. The designer has to plan for the safety and protection of any irreplaceable materials on view. Sometimes, it does not require more than clear plastic shields hung down in front of the flat exhibit, or the setting of objects into glass- or plastic-enclosed museum-type cases. If the objects are especially precious, the shield or case may have to be wired into an alarm system.

Security guards may become part of the exhibit landscape, not only as symbols of authority and guardians of the material on view, but also to admonish viewers who touch and stroke. In some cases, the appearance of security in the form of television cameras, sensor equipment, and locks on cases may be enough to protect the exhibit. Ropes and stanchions

can also be used to keep the exhibited material out of arm's reach. The rope and stanchion combination can also be used to control and direct traffic.

An electric eye may be necessary in some extreme cases, but they are usually not activated until after show hours. Good lighting, which is discussed below, can also be a means of security. Things are much more likely to disappear from dimly lit rooms or heavily shadowed areas. Nooks, crannies, and culs-de-sac may make wonderful display areas, but they can provide the mischief-maker with an out-of-sight spot to work some potential maleficence.

Trade show exhibits are often conceived as vehicles for testing and sampling products, and it is difficult for the visitor to realize that the material on view may not always be taken as a sample. The designer, therefore, must arrange to protect what is only for show and make clear by the location and the container used what legitimately may be taken as a sample or a souvenir. A collection of brochures and pamphlets for distribution can be set up, in front, with a sign to the effect that the visitor is welcome to take one. If the printed material is not for the taking, it could be matted and framed and set under glass. (A booklet or pamphlet that is wired or chained to an exhibit wall looks less than professional.)

Most trade show buildings do keep a security staff on duty throughout the night. This is included in the cost of renting exhibit space. Still, merchandise does disappear. Ideally, the exhibit or the exhibit area will be locked after hours. Whatever is valuable and not locked into the exhibit should be removed nightly and returned the next morning. This may be a nuisance, but

it is often necessary. As a further security precaution, the designer who specializes in trade shows may conceive a presentation that is enclosed. For this, the visitor must walk through the entrance and leave through a designated exit. With this arrangement, it may be possible to seal off the two openings nightly. (Theft control has also been discussed in Chapter 11.)

LIGHTING

Lighting is such a crucial element that it often makes or breaks an exhibit. The kind of lighting used is determined by the type of material to be displayed. Too much light, as well as too little, too many spotlights, not enough shadows—can destroy some presentations, especially where a mood has to be created or where dimensional objects are displayed and shadows are necessary to give them form. A dark, dark show can be great for ambience and mood, but a serious drawback for seeing what is being shown. The exhibit designer, just like the retail merchandise presenter, must balance the primary or general lighting with the secondary lighting. It might be useful, at this point, to refer back to Chapter 6, "Light and Lighting," for a quick review of lighting techniques and materials.

Daylight

Daylight, or natural light, can wreak havoc with the overall lighting scheme of an exhibit. It is never the same. It changes during the same day. It changes with the locale and the time of the year. It may be too blue or too yellow. It may be gray and dull or filled with bright sunshine.

It is difficult for the designer to plan for and counteract the pervasive flood of natural light in an area that has many windows or a giant skylight. Vast, cavernous exhibit halls make it difficult for the designer to achieve a special atmosphere or mood. If budget and installation time permit, and if regulations allow, the designer may opt for screening off or blocking out windows. It is an added expense and there can be construction problems, but a "ceiling" might be lowered over the exhibit area to screen out overhead daylight where it exists. This "ceiling" does not have to be more than a dark, opaque fabric pulled taut across the exhibit space, or a series of paneled frames dropped from above or bridging the perimeter walls of the display.

Not all exhibits suffer from the use of daylight. For some, it is a plus. Flower shows, sculpture exhibits, craft shows—virtually anything that is appropriate for an out-of-doors setting—will be enhanced by daylight.

The designer should find out, in advance, if the

general lighting is mainly fluorescent, incandescent, or H.I.D., and what can or cannot be done with the lighting plan. It may be possible to turn off the overhead lighting in the particular exhibit area or change some of the lamps from cool to warm, or from warm to cool. A forewarned and prepared designer is never at a loss. "Magic" is still possible. The design may make use of ambient lighting.

Ambient Lighting

Ambient lighting is the mood-producing light used in an area or exhibit. Colored filters can be used, adding warmth and depth where needed, or strong, sharp accents of color can excite or stimulate the viewer. Ambient lighting is part of secondary lighting and makes use of floodlights, filters, and wall washers. It can include indirect lighting devices: lights hidden behind foliage, a riser, or behind a baffle or valance dropped from overhead. The designer may create a free-standing, out-in-the-open exhibit and bathe the bare perimeter walls with colored lights. This makes the walls appear to "move back," enhancing the attraction in the middle of the floor.

Ambient lighting can also include the use of chase or flashing lights, mirrored balls to reflect pinpricks of light, and revolving color wheels. It can consist of an outlined entrance in Tivoli lights (small, clear, decorative globe-shaped lights of low wattage), or neon tubes twisted into graphic shapes or signs.

Black light is gimmicky, but can be effective at times. This is special ultraviolet light that will cause surfaces that have been treated with ultraviolet paint to glow in the dark. Darkening an area between two different parts of an exhibit can be an interesting and skillful way of bridging the change. The copy or graphics glowing in that darkness, under the black light, will make a strong statement as well as create a change in mood.

Task Lighting

Task lighting is the all-important spotlighting and highlighting of an exhibit. This puts the light where it really counts and makes the items stand out and show up at their very best. Some exhibit areas or rooms are equipped with ceiling track lighting which can facilitate the spotlighting and floodlighting of a show. In this setup, the designer may be in control of both the general lighting and the special lighting.

Small objects in cases can be lit with miniature pinspots of bright incandescent light, tubular lights or even pencil-like fluorescent lamps. Some objects are especially attractive when lit from behind or below. Frosted glass panels and shelves are good to use in these instances. Wherever and whenever possible, the designer should try to hide the source of light. No matter how attractive the lamp or the lamp holder, it might compete for the viewer's attention. Not only might it detract from the subject on view, it could prove to be an irritant to the viewer.

Special Lighting

Backlighting objects or photographic transparencies can be especially effective when the area in which they are to be used has low-level lighting. Illuminated cases appear more brilliant when the surroundings are darkened. Rear projection and slide shows need controlled general lighting to work. The use of "dissolves," where one object seems to fade away and another object takes its place, requires a timer device.

Thus, lighting can help tell the story, set the scene, and emphasize or enhance an object. It can isolate one item or unify a group of unrelated pieces. It can create the mood or ambience, add drama and excitement. Lighting can create a sense of direction, a path for traffic to follow, and set a pace and tempo. On a trade show floor, with dozens or hundreds of exhibits vying for attention, good lighting can be the beacon that brings in the crowds.

SPECIAL EFFECTS

In addition to lighting, color, line, texture, and graphics, the designer can add touches of unique excitement to an exhibit which will increase the viewer's enjoyment of the show and his or her comprehension of what is being presented.

Movement and/or Animation

Motors—Just as flashing lights are more emphatic and attention-getting than a constant glow from a lamp, so is animation more eye-catching and startling than a stationary display. The movement can be smooth and subtle, such as a turntable slowly rotating and showing an array of items or a complete back-to-front display of a single item. The turntable may be a heavy-duty floor unit made to sustain a great weight, a tabletop unit for smaller and lighter pieces, or one that is suspended from above to put a graphic mobile into a spin or to activate a flutter of ribbons. Ceiling motors can be used for a variety of motion effects.

Conveyer belts bring an exhibit to a stationary audience. The conveyer belt works like a track that goes around the exhibit area and brings a continuous display of material before the viewer who remains in one place. This is easier on the viewer, but much more complicated for the display designer and the construction of the exhibit. Crowds will always collect around a display of miniature trains that circle around and around the tracks, winding its way through a set but convoluted pattern. In its simplest form, the "train and tracks" can be a relatively easy yet eye-catching device—if it goes with the theme and tone of the exhibit.

Models and Miniatures—Every Christmas

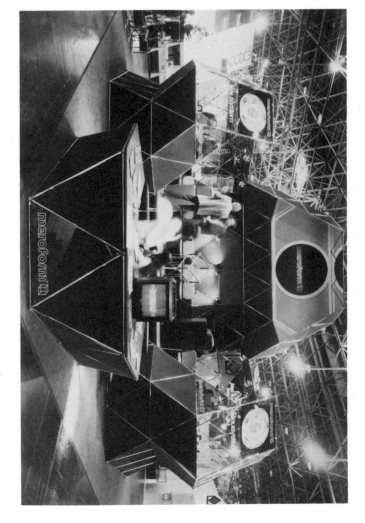

Figure 22-10. Meroform creates a series of islands with its system of ball joints and precut lengths of tube. The shapes rise up to get attention. The center unit (the tallest) is further highlighted by the lighting used over the seats, where the business of the exhibit is done. The counter, in the foreground, displays the free brochures for distribution. There is a lamp for extra light and a television monitor to help "sell" the passerby. The blowup of the ball-like design featured in the upper section of the two end structures is the logo for the system being demonstrated. *Meroform, Wurzburg, West Germany.*

there are long lines stretching around department stores featuring animated windows. The stuffed animals jerk right and left and the pixies move up and down. The simplest actions and movements please millions. Even without the animation, miniatures attract and fascinate audiences. Scaled models are informative as well as intriguing and might do a better job of instructing than a full-size replica. For the exhibit designer faced with space restrictions and traveling and shipping schedules, the model setup and the use of miniatures can be extremely useful.

Lighting

As discussed earlier in this chapter, flashing and chasing lights can also supply "motion" to an exhibit. A light going on and off behind a transparency set into a light box will get attention. A motion message, as the name implies, is an electrified billboard on which the message runs across the board and can be changed by a keyboard programmer. This is a rather new entrant into the exhibit and display field, and is actually a miniature version of the famous, outdoor, multibulb signs used in New York's Times Square.

Audio-Visuals

Television screens and monitors are always noticed and watched. People will stand outside a display window to watch the flickering figures on a silent screen, or line up in a store to see five or six screens showing the same program.

When the designer and the exhibitor decide on a slide or film presentation which may take several minutes to view, they might want to consider setting it up somewhere beyond the main flow of the show. A piece of film or a slide show played and viewed on a screen, may cause a tie-up in the traffic flow, unless space is provided for the group as it gathers to watch.

TV monitors can also be used as directories to tell what is going on and where the action is taking place.

Live Actors and/or Animals

Live action must be carefully planned. A live demonstrator can quickly draw an audience, but just as quickly lose one. People will stand around, intrigued and delighted, watching a mime, a magician, a puppeteer, or performing animals, but will lose interest completely by a poorly delivered sales pitch.

Some exhibitors still feel that a scantily clad young woman will draw an audience, and they will depend on her charms to get attention. She may draw an audience, but does she necessarily sell the product or deliver the message? Is the audience she draws, the

right audience for the product being shown? A person in an animal suit can be fun, but is this in keeping with the image of the exhibitor?

Greater anticipation and excitement is generated when the live performer is not always "on," but makes scheduled appearances. In this way, the exhibitor can gain an audience in the exhibit area and "sell" the product or idea to those who are waiting to be entertained or to those who have just been amused. It can also be used as a means of controlling traffic.

Audience Involvement

More and more exhibit designers are finding that an exhibit or display that involves the viewer physically is very effective and leaves a long-lasting impression on the participant. When a person makes contact with the materials on view, turns a crank, pushes a button, switches on sound recording, changes the location of an object, tastes, smells, touches, or in any way makes actual contact with the material—he or she becomes personally involved with the display, and the displayed items become part of his or her experience.

Children's museums are doing more "hands-on" exhibits than ever before. The hands-on experience allows the observer to pace the show according to his or her own level of interest. The participant will spend more time at some displays and less at others.

Computerized material, involving keyboards and video terminals, is also becoming increasingly popular. People enjoy testing themselves or challenging the "unknown brain" within the machine.

Optical illusions are even more dazzling when the visitor can create them by moving his or her own vantage point or actually moving the object. As in most displays, when the presentation appeals to more than the sense of touch alone, the efficacy of the display increases.

The problems inherent in the "hands-on" approach are many. A particular display may be such fun that people will gang up to "play" with it. The net result can be a traffic jam. Some viewers play roughly and can break or foul up a machine or keyboard. Other viewers may pass up pertinent material in favor of the "fun and games," not getting the full value of the total exhibit. Also, special lighting requirements may be necessary. It is not unusual for displays with screens to require darkened areas.

Because of traffic flow and the lighting requirements, "hands-on" displays could be set up in bays or culs-de-sac, out of main traffic aisles. They could also be planned as terminals for aisles. If the units were set up as island displays, the surrounding aisles would need to be made wider so that traffic could move without any impediment. Extra security guards might be re-

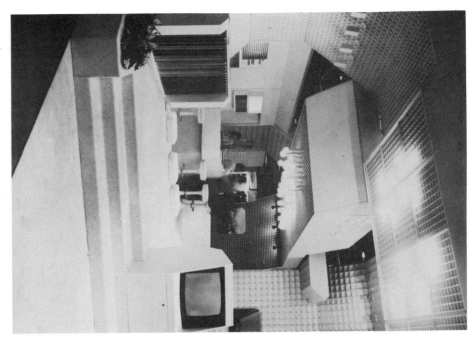

Figure 22-11. PAG of West Germany presented their Pagolux Light and Acoustic System in this exciting, architectural exhibit, rich in diagonals. They showed the range of their molded plastic panels both at eye level and above, on the ceiling. The area was separated from the rest of the trade show floor by the light-colored, soft carpeting that covered the stairs and the planters. A television monitor "sold" those who opted for sitting it out on the carpet-covered benches built into the exhibit. In the rear, the exhibit contains an entertainment area for "special" customers. *PAG, Essen, West Germany.*

quired to control the time each viewer spends at a particular device, especially if queues begin to form.

Today's display designer has to be aware of the many miracles of modern technology in order to produce exhibits that not only attract but impress.

MAKING THE EXHIBIT SPECIAL

Throughout this book, the word "image" has appeared over and over again because it is an essential part of the personality of an organization. It is what makes one group or store different from another, even though the product or idea offered may be almost the same. It is the "packaging" or "gift wrap" of an organization that makes the consumer reach out for its product. In being special or getting attention, the image must always be considered. A person hanging from the edge of a roof will gain attention, as will wearing bright red satin to a graduation ceremony. Filling an exhibit with lively piglets will draw crowds, but what does it say about the sponsor of the space?

In keeping with the tone, style, tradition, and position of the exhibit sponsor in the business community, the designer has to plan carefully for "special attention." Many of these attractions are the "amenities of design," the gracious, nonselling aspects of the setup and the surroundings, those features that satisfy the aesthetics or personal comfort of the viewers.

The Amenities

Plants and Flowers—These are obvious "audience pleasers," and yet, often omitted. The greenery adds life and sparkle to an inanimate presentation, and in its naturalness of form, can break up a stiff, regimental presentation of straight lines, angles, and rectangles. Plants will do well for a limited showing under what can become adverse conditions: no sunlight, too much heat from strong lights, lack of air, too much smoke, and friction from passersby. Artificial plants will also work, but many people do not find them satisfactory substitutes.

Designers may also use branches and twigs to introduce a sense of freedom and movement to an exhibit that is all straight lines and sharp angles. In water-filled containers or set into moistened florist foam, the leafy branches will do quite well for a short time. Flowering plants can add a lovely touch of color to a showing. The cost may be negligible in comparison to other expenditures, and worth it for the effect they produce. Cut floral arrangements can be luxurious and eye-filling, but require more tending and will need replacing if the show lasts more than a few days. Though in the long run, it may be more expensive than an outright purchase, plants can be rented. Some florists will come in and "care" for their charges while the plants remain on view.

As previously stated, plants not only add color and free form, they can be used as screens, dividers, and backgrounds for dimensional objects such as sculpture and crafts. An oasis of greenery can be a focal point in an exhibit or indicate a change in direction. Plants and flowers also mean that the exhibitor is thinking of the visitors, providing them with this extra treat. It is not something the exhibitor is "selling"; it is being offered as goodwill.

Seating—Unless this is an exhibit that will draw large crowds and must be scheduled to get people in and out within a particular time frame, it is a nice and friendly amenity to provide some form of seating. At a trade show, where space is at a premium, some exhibitors, nevertheless, will arrange for seating within the exhibit area. It is easier to sell someone who is seated than a "person-on-the-run." The longer the exhibitor can keep a potential customer within the confines of the booth, the greater the potential for making a sale. (Where order writing is anticipated, tables may be necessary.)

In other exhibits, benches set along the way can provide happy rest stops. The designer can plan these islands of seating in relation to the presentation and the general traffic flow. Some pieces or items need to be studied more than others, and a conveniently located seating arrangement allows those who would like to sit and observe the piece, to do so. In a large exhibition hall where a single exhibit is on view or where the exhibit may cover several salons or floors, the designer may break up the showing with rest areas. Some persons may find it too exhausting or strenuous to cover a big show without an occasional rest. A large corporation sponsoring an institutional type of display may provide the seating as its contribution to goodwill. By doing so, it may not be selling a particular product, but it will be selling its name, its reputation, and its image.

Refreshments—A coffee cart or wine bar is a deluxe addition to an exhibit and will pay off in its ability to "hold" a viewer in an exhibit area. This is especially true at trade shows. Refreshments relax the viewer and offer an essential change of pace. They can be as varied as a sampling of an exhibited food product, canapés, cheese and crackers, cookies, jars of hard candies, and assorted hard or soft drinks.

At some trade shows, there are regulations about what may or may not be served in display booths. The show management may opt for setting up its own hospitality booths which will supply or sell food to the show visitor. To the viewer who plans to spend several hours in the exhibit hall, this is important.

Movable Paths—This is a bit extreme and very much a "super production," but some exhibitors may wish to actually move visitors through the exhibit. The visitor steps onto a moving ramp and then is transported around the show just as a traveler in some airports is moved through miles of passages.

With this type of arrangement, the designer is completely in control of the traffic flow and visitor movement. There is no bunching, no crowds, and no confusion. The viewer gets to see what is to be seen, and the moving path is paced to accomplish a complete tour of the show in a given amount of time. In this way, people are admitted at one end and exit from another, making it possible to keep feeding more and more people into the show.

The great disadvantage is to the viewer. He or she is limited in the amount of time allotted for viewing and cannot remain to study any one item more fully. If another viewing is desired, it means going back and starting all over again. The movable path can be a great advantage for the very young, the elderly, and the handicapped. It does take the strain out of "doing" a show. This exhibit extravaganza is generally associated with "World's Fairs" and large permanent exhibits.

Tie-ins

To make an exhibit especially memorable or special, one must go beyond the confines of the actual showing. It has already been mentioned that an exhibit has to be produced, packaged, and sold. Sometimes, it is the packaging and salesmanship, more than what is being shown, that makes a show successful. Many shows succeed, in large measure, because of their tie-ins.

The production and promotion of an exhibit often requires posters, mailings, catalogues, publications, and a long list of souvenirs. Today, the poster is not simply a card to include in a display window; it has become a piece of graphic art, to frame and hang. The effectiveness of the show's logo or design and the poster can sometimes "make" the show. A good display designer should be aware of the advertising requirements for promoting a show and be ready to assist with concepts and tangible product ideas.

Community involvement is very important, too. It is advantageous to be able to tie in with other groups or products. If it is an artistic or cultural promotion, department and specialty stores may become involved in promoting the show. They may devote valuable window space to the exhibit and even use posters and the show logo as part of their presentation. Local "talk shows," both on radio and TV, are always looking for interesting and timely subjects to discuss and show. An exhibit can get free advance publicity more easily if there is a gimmick or handle to work with.

T-shirts, banners, bumper stickers, and shopping

bags are only a few of the identifiable objects that can be used to promote a show once it has begun. The materials the viewers take away with them will proclaim the show to others who have not yet been there. These are the most effective "ads." They are "testimonials" from satisfied customers. A shopping bag or tote with a logo imprint can start a kind of self-interrogation: "What kind of show is it? Why is everybody going to see it? What am I missing?" Many people want to be where "everybody" is and doing what "everybody" is doing. These tie-in concepts reinforce the poster, the fliers, and the mailings.

The trade show exhibitor can also gain from tie-ins and giveaways. The silk-screened plastic bag is always a show favorite. It is lightweight, reusable, and great for carrying the brochures and samples the visitor accumulates during a tour through the show building. The logo or trade name emblazoned across the bag advertises the sponsor and his or her product, and suggests a visit has been made to the sponsor's booth, even if it was only to pick up a bag.

Americans are button collectors. Pin a button on trade show visitors, and they will very likely remain wearing it all the time they are on the show floor. In this way, the show visitor becomes a walking signboard. Flowers, live or artificial, are always popular. Tags and balloons are eye-catchers and not expensive to have produced in volume. Imprinted ball-point pens and pencils will be picked up and carried away. They will keep selling weeks later, far away from the show.

The ideal giveaway should be lightweight, compact, practical, reusable, and long-lasting. From the exhibitor's point of view, it should be inexpensive and imprinted with his or her logo, name and, possibly, the address. The more discreet the imprint, the more likely it is that the giveaway will be kept and used. There are many manufacturers of such souvenirs, but since the exhibitor's name will appear on it, it is up to the designer and the exhibitor to make sure that the "giveaway" is worthy of their image.

"SELLING" AN EXHIBIT DESIGN

In order to cover as many of the points outlined and suggested in this chapter, the designer should go beyond scaled floor plans and elevations. It is recommended that the designer prepare a "mock up" or scale model of the proposed exhibit. It could be made of cardboard, lightweight wood, wire, or whatever would best simulate the actual design.

This model could then be set into a box or onto a larger floor, also in scale, which would suggest the relationship of the exhibit or booth to the total space of the exhibit hall. If the exhibit is a booth in a trade show, it would be beneficial to mark off, on this total display "floor," the location of the neighboring booths and the general traffic aisles of the entire show. This will help the designer to orient the entrances and exits to the traffic flow. It will also allow the designer to take advantage of those neighbors who ordinarily draw a large attendance, either because of their reputation or because of the size and extent of their exhibit.

The designer can use cutout, self-standing, silhouettes of people, also in scale, to get a sense of eye level, and aisle and space arrangements. The model will provide the designer with the opportunity to consider the flexibility of the exhibit's proposed design; to stretch it or condense it as the available space may require. This is especially valuable when the exhibit is collapsible and must travel from one exhibit hall to another. The designer can pretest the adaptability of the panels and the frames in other configurations.

If the designer is planning a maze, the model will show exactly how it works and where traffic tie-ups may occur. A proposed supergraphic design that is meant to move the viewer along from subject to subject can be tested in model form. The use of buildups, platforms, risers, etc., can also be tried out in miniature. The model will point out where a touch of color will work, where greenery could be best used, and where seating can be included.

If the designer is working for a large corporation or must make a presentation to a committee, the model is an excellent selling tool. It also provides the exhibitor, the people who will pay for the exhibit, with the opportunity to see what is being planned, to make suggestions, and to move around some pieces of the model. Perspective drawings are effective, but can be misleading because of the forced depth perception.

The model can be as simple as a cardboard construction with little or no color or detail, or very realistic and minutely detailed. The designer's efforts will be determined by time, budget, and complexity of design.

Exhibits are displays with a difference. They are still promotional presentations. A good exhibit design solves a space problem, but must also sell a concept or a product. If the theme or product is not "sold," the design may be an artistic achievement, but it would not necessarily be a good exhibit design.

23 Fashion Shows

A fashion show can be enhanced by display techniques, but it is a different kind of "theater." The major differences between a fashion show and display are the movement, the animation and the choreography which are essential to a fashion presentation using live models. If there is no movement, why use live models? The movement of a line of models requires timing, planning, and pacing.

It is essential to provide room for the model's movements (i.e., stages, runways, walkways, aisles, and so on). Not only do the models need room in which to move, but the clothing being modeled does also. A cape may be "flung," a skirt swirled, or a jacket removed.

The fashion show should have a theme, a central basic idea on which the show is built. The theme will suggest the type of merchandise being shown and the audience for whom it is being prepared. The store could do a "Back to College" show for high school and college students, a bridal show for prospective brides and the all-important mother of the bride, or a fall showing of new fabrics and trends for the store's special customers. In any and every case, there should be an idea, a "handle," gimmick, catchline, or phrase that will not only "set" the show, but suggest the signs to be used, the advance publicity, and the printed programs.

In some ways, a fashion show is like doing a window display as part of a promotion. The setting of the fashion show can be compared to the background of the window display. (Basically, the main difference is the length of time the shopper is involved with each. The fashion show can even last for a half an hour or more.) If the background setting makes too strong a statement, it can get in the way of the proceedings.

If a setting is used, it should be open and neutral; pleasant, suggestive, but not intrusive. It should say "something," but not too definitively. A skyline, if it is semiabstract or stylized, can suggest city clothes, career fashions, and even "after-dark" styles. A balustrade with a garden beyond could suggest formal wear, a garden wedding, daytime dresses, even "Tennis, anyone?"—if done properly. Ideally, the background can be a vignetted drawing or painting that sits well back on the stage and does not try to upstage the merchandise being paraded in front of it.

A series of curtains on a track (*travelers*) can be used to set an entire show with six or seven "scenes." A variety of blinds that can be rolled up or down could also be used to set a show: bamboo blinds for beach and resort wear, Austrian blinds for formals and bridals, Roman shades for daytime and dress-up, colored venetian blinds for career fashions and even sportswear or separates. A few potted plants, center stage, rear, or to mask the entrance or exit of an impromptu stage, can be effective without being distracting. The live green plants or the colors of flowering plants can create a setting, completely camouflaging an open space on the selling floor or brightening up a community room.

Certain devices will always work in a fashion show setting. They say, quickly and effectively, what has to be said. Stairs, ramps, platforms, and risers are always good, but can be dangerous if not used properly.

A well-designed staircase provides a dramatic entrance because there is sweep and movement in the model's descent. If the steps are too deep or too high, however, the model will look awkward walking up and back. A ramp with a gentle incline can also be effective, but rushing down because the incline is too steep, or trudging up a ramp can make even the most graceful model in the loveliest outfit look ludicrous. A platform or two can be used to step onto, turn about on, and step down from. This makes for good choreography, while allowing the garment to be shown to its best advantage. Turntables can be used effectively, especially as an "entrance," where the model goes from an almost back view into a front view before stepping off.

Archways, doorways, beaded curtains, the opening of curtains, etc., will all work when the models make their entrances. They can also be used effectively in combination with steps, ramps, and turntables.

Settings or props that take up too much stage or runway space can be a problem. The designer can emulate Japanese theater techniques, and have specially dressed, "invisible stagehands" dress and redress the stage with each change of merchandise. It does, however, require special props, and the movement of the stagehands can clutter and detract from the fashion showing.

Often, the best props or scene-setters are the ones the models bring in and take off with them. A model carrying a beachball, an umbrella, a book or newspaper, a camera, an attaché case or an artist's portfolio, a hat box, a bunch of flowers or a fan, a bunch of balloons, a big stuffed animal—any of these can set the scene. The prop also adds sparkle or serves as an accessory to the costume, whatever it might be. With one of these props, the model also has some "business" to do that will play up the costume, and humanize his or her actions. Also, this portable prop does not take up performing space or slow down the pace of the show.

Lighting is most important. In a window or ledge display, the displayperson arranges the lights for shadows as well as highlights. The object that is being lit is fixed in one place, and the lights are fixed on that location. In a fashion show, it is desirable that the light follow the model, keeping the model in the spotlight. If that is not possible, then the traffic route—the stage or runway or both—should be bathed in strong light and the audience left in the shadows. This is especially true when the "runway" is really not much more than a path on the floor and the seated audience is almost at the same level. In such a situation, unfortunately, the patrons on one side can be a distraction for the patrons on the other side and, as in an open-back window, they can conflict with the featured performers.

If the show runs longer than fifteen minutes, it is desirable to have some lighting changes. These changes may consist of filter colors, the degree of whiteness, the direction of the light. Prolonged exposure to the same degree of brightness can render the viewer insensitive to what is going on.

Different types of merchandise can be "explained" by different colored lights on the background: yellow for sports and swimwear, blues and violets for formalwear, pinks and reds for lingerie and intimate apparel, and cool blue light for outerwear. The use of colored light to bathe or wash the background can actually set a scene without a prop.

Most shows today use music, live or taped, to create the tempo for the showing. It gives the models a beat to move to, and it takes the viewer along with the sound. A change of tempo is effective in delineating "scenes" and merchandise groupings. The music and the lights are basic requirements for a fashion show, and the decor and props are extras.

As previously noted, there should be a theme, a logo, a concept, or a symbol which is carried through the whole show—from the preliminary announcements until the finale. If the store were doing something as simple as "New Directions for Spring," for example, the logo could be a weathervane, a windmill, a street sign, a take-off on the engraved Victorian hand with the pointing finger, or a montage of arrows. The design logo could then be used on posters, mailings, and programs (if any are printed). A giant blowup or a simple, overscaled construction of that logo could be the "setting" for the show. The scenario or commentary for the show could include: "Trends from the east," "Traveling south," "When the sun sets in the west," "Should the winds blow in from the north," "Tomorrow's forecast," or any other words or phrases indicating direction. The models could carry pinwheels, balloons, umbrellas, or ribbon streamers on a stick. If the store has a store-wide promotion going on and the fashion show will tie in with it, the theme, logo, etc., of that particular promotion should be elaborated on in the fashion show.

24 Store Planning

"Interior designers" have probably been plying their trade as far back as when exotic bazaars and old Persian markets were the shopping centers that attracted the bargain shoppers of days gone by. Someone had to have selected the rugs and tapestries that supplied the rich and colorful ambience. Someone must have decided that raising certain merchandise off the sandy ground and onto a rug-covered platform would make it more visible and more desirable. Where the brass lanterns were hung and where the encrusted candelabras were set did affect the highlights and shadows on the buffed and gleaming merchandise. The casual but carefully orchestrated tumble of merchandise from baskets, barrels, and brass bowls, however, must have been left to the "displayperson." Thus, for a long, long time it was the interior architects and designers who created the retail space and supervised its decoration.

In the past few decades, a new breed of architect/designer has appeared on the scene, the store planner. This new designer is more than a space planner, decorator, a divider of the selling floor space. This is a designer who is also a merchant and a merchandise presenter. Today's store planner is a designer, an architect, a space "surgeon," a lighting expert, a colorist, and a visual merchandiser with a knowledge of mannequins, fixtures, furniture, and forms, and the "know-how" to sell the merchandise. Most of those we now call store planners have a background in architecture or interior design, but more and more visual merchandisers are bringing their special talents into the store planning field.

It began late in the 1960's when the large department stores were caught up in the "boutique blitz" that exploded in retailing. Management wanted to subdivide the large, open, selling spaces into intimate and exciting minishops, rich in personality and unique flavor. Budgets were barely sufficient for the transformations into these seasonal shops and environmental selling experiences. Thus, the assignments were often turned over to the existing "display departments" with the order to: "Make a miracle happen, but don't spend any money!"

Miracles did happen. Fresh, innovative, and intriguing shops and boutiques did appear on the vast, high-ceilinged, and often impersonal floors. They created warm and charming boutiques filled with special merchandise and spilling over with new and inexpensive methods of housing and displaying that merchandise. Never did so many improvise with so little. It did not take long for the more progressive minds in merchandising to realize that some displaypersons or visual merchandisers had something extra to offer store planning.

Here were talented and imaginative people that

199

Figure 24-1. Bright colors; an amusing display right on the aisle, raised up on a strongly patterned platform; and a fun department name—turn a bland area into a swinging, trendy shop. The display department added topical posters and prints on the back wall area amid the already brightly colored merchandise—and the whole tucked-away corner of the store comes to life. *Macy's, New York.*

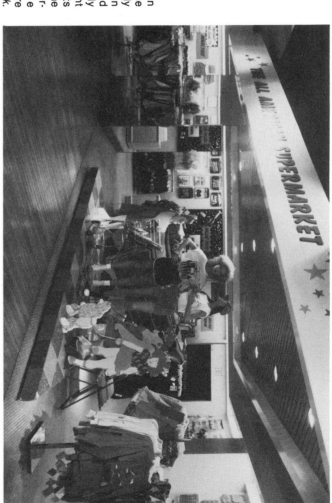

could see beyond the traditional round racks and tired and trite, overexposed methods of merchandising. The visual merchandisers, who became the store planners of the 1970's and the 1980's, have attempted to enhance the merchandise, making an art out of even housing and stocking it.

FUNCTIONS OF THE STORE PLANNER

The following are the functions of the store planner involved in store design today:

1. To design an efficient and attractive selling environment that will promote maximum sales and savings in labor and energy.

2. To combine the selling space with the "behind-the-scenes" service area where stock is maintained and the nonselling activities of the store are carried on.

3. To set up traffic patterns that will promote customer movement from areas that get the greatest exposure (near entrances, elevators, and escalators) to remote corners and back areas where the more expensive items are usually located.

4. To promote and sell. To stock and show. The store planner selects the selling vehicle for the specific merchandise being offered.

5. To enhance the store's image and, thereby, add stature to the merchandise being offered.

The store planner works closely with the architect (if there is one), the store management, the merchandisers, and the buyers. Based on previous sales figures, or on projected or anticipated sales figures, the store planner, together with the executives, will prepare a *block plan.* This is the first allocation of space on the ground plan and the designation of selling areas on that selling floor. This apportionment of space is based on the merchandising needs, proposed traffic patterns, proximity to related merchandise, and anticipated sales. By roughly blocking in the areas, management gets a visual picture of how much space is actually needed and how much is left for growth. The "behind-the-scenes" areas (service elevators, storage, employee's changing rooms, toilets, offices, etc.) and the social amenities (rest rooms, vistas, galleries, restaurants, meeting or community rooms, etc.) will then be fit into the remaining space. The floor plans are then redrawn, always in scale, with more and more details and specifications added on.

The final floor plan will have all the counters, cases, tables, and free-standing floor fixtures (round racks, quad racks, T-stands) drawn in place, and will show the aisles, passageways, dressing rooms, exits and entrances, escalators, elevators, and more. Islands will be indicated for display arrangements, platforms located for mannequins, and T-walls to separate areas. The store planner will locate the "impulse items" (merchandise purchased on impulse rather than by plan; e.g., cosmetics, candy, inexpensive but faddish novelties, etc.) in the high-traffic areas, leaving the customer to find his or her way to the "demand merchandise" (the necessities: household goods, appliances, and so on).

Figure 24-2. The escalator often becomes the focal point of a store's interior as it soars three or more floors through an open space with light flooding in from above. The areas closest to the escalator have the greatest traffic; therefore, those areas will often feature "impulse items." The same holds for the walk-around areas around the escalators or stairways. *Abraham & Straus, Eatontown, New Jersey.*

The effective store planner directs the shopping drama which starts right at the entrance. He or she plots the lighting, creates the changes in color and texture as the shopper moves from area to area, and is responsible for the raising or lowering of ceilings over aisles or boutiques. It is also his or her responsibility to place mirrors for reflection or glitter, to suggest changes in flooring materials between aisles and shops, and to arrange for dividers, screens, plants, and art-work. Also, related merchandise is placed close together so, for example, shoes can be matched to a handbag, or skirts to sweaters.

Whether the store planner is designing a small speciality store or dividing up floors or areas in a large department store, the basic responsibilities, as enumerated above, are still the same. However, the small store presents particular problems since space is especially precious and each cubic foot is expected to earn a certain amount of dollars in gross sales. In the larger operations, this is still a factor to consider, but sometimes the gracious sweep of a wide aisle or a vista is worth the expenditure of space in favor of store image and the ambience that is achieved.

REHABILITATIONS

Not all stores are built from the ground up, all new and ready to accommodate the needs of a particular retail operation. Some merchants seem to find it more economical and desirable or, for the sake of a "different" look, more advantageous to start with an existing structure and restyle it to their own requirements. Many department and specialty stores discover that after some years their operations have become dull, dingy, and dated, and they no longer function as efficiently as they did twenty or thirty years earlier. New fashions just do not look "new" in an area whose decor is passé.

When an existing structure is restyled, redecorated, and rearranged, but not necessarily gutted and rebuilt, the store planner/architect is involved in rehabilitation, or "rehab." Rehabilitation is the remodeling, redecorating, and refixturing of an existing structure, often by the store planner. The "rehab" will still have the interest, the spirit, and the architectural details and flavor of what it once was, but it comes out fresh and ready to function for today's fashions.

STORE PLANNING AS A CAREER

This chapter is intended to show that store planning is a growing field that visual merchandisers can enter. There is no way that one chapter or even an entire book will create a store planner, but many of the

Figure 24-3. The change of floor level will often indicate a change in the type of merchandise being presented. Mannequins, plants, and an occasional prop will fill in the odd angles, while mirrors can be used to reflect the merchandise and the light—and the shopper gets new vistas and views with the twists and turns of the stairway. *Bonwit Teller, New York.*

Figure 24-4. The ground floor of an old loft building becomes an attractive up-to-date shop. This "rehab" features refinished oak floors, exposed brick walls, and embossed metal ceiling. Although visible, the pipes and ducts, along with the ceiling, have been painted in black to help make them disappear. The height of the ceiling is enhanced by the unusual middle-of-the-floor fixtures and the tall wall shelf units. Spotlights light up the selling floor and the merchandise. *If...Boutique, New York.*

techniques that store planners use have been discussed in this text.

A knowledge of mechanical drawing and drafting (Chapter 15) is essential. The store planner must be able to communicate in the language of plans and elevations—and all in scale. The awareness of the importance of color and texture (Chapter 5) and the impact of light and lighting (Chapter 6) on color and on the merchandise are essential to the store planner. He or she must understand also how color, light, and texture will suggest certain "clichés" of ambience (Chapter 19).

Fixtures are the "furniture" of the store (Chapters 11 and 12), and the store planner must know the various types that are available and what they will do for the merchandise and the store's image. It is a function of the store planner to use the floor space—and the air space—to their fullest. He or she must devise economical and creative methods for housing stock and highlighting displays. Sometimes, the store planner will use real furniture and antiques (armoires, chests, period cabinets, for example) as fixtures or props in order to get a desired effect for a unique shop or department.

Mannequins and forms (Chapter 8) are the "hand-maidens" of display and they serve the store planner well. They can be used instead of signs to designate what is being sold in an area, or to add a high point in an otherwise flat merchandise presentation. Mannequins add drama as aisle liners or as centers of interest in island presentation; they are invaluable to the store planner, especially where a store has no display windows.

Any displayperson who wishes to become a store planner should consider studying, in depth, interior design, materials and methods of construction, perspective rendering, the history of furniture and decoration, furniture construction, and lighting techniques. There are some schools that do grant degrees in store planning. This is a relatively new field and one that has much to offer the displayperson who wants to advance in retailing. Individuals interested in store planning might contact the local chapter of the Institute of Store Planners (ISP) or the American Society of Interior Designers (ASID) for more information on schools with store planning curricula.

25 Trade Organizations and Sources

Though visual merchandisers are often artists and craftspersons involved in aesthetics and the arts, they are also essentially businesspeople. They are in the business of presentation, and their purpose is to sell the store and the merchandise within it. As businesspeople and craftspeople with specific talents, there are "guilds" available to them. The guilds are different from trade unions. While unions might have a widely diversified membership, the organizations to be discussed here, were formed specifically for the creators and/or the end users of the mannequins, fixtures, props, decoratives, foliage, point-of-purchase displays and displayers, store furniture, and so on.

Most of these organizations sponsor trade shows once or twice a year. The trade show is an exhibit of basic products as well as the new products conceived by designers who are employed by the manufacturers. These products and concepts, hopefully, will enhance the presentation of merchandise, suggest new trends in store fixturing, and/or reinforce an advertising campaign. These shows are generally scheduled for those times of the year that are convenient for the supplier and the buyer, while still allowing the end user sufficient time to order for an upcoming season, a store opening, or a new promotional year.

Very often, buying offices, resident buyers, and fashion forecasters will plan group meetings for these show times. Visual merchandisers and their staffs as well as store planners will be invited to attend these industry meetings in the same city, at the same time. It adds another dimension to the trade show and makes attendance even more worthwhile.

MAJOR ORGANIZATIONS

Described below are some of the major organizations that are essential to the craft and profession of visual merchandising. They are presented in order of their seniority—the length of time they have been effectively serving the industry and the people in that industry.

Point of Purchase Advertising Institute (POPAI)

The Point of Purchase Advertising Institute (POPAI), headquartered in New York City, was formed as a nonprofit organization in 1938. It was created to serve those who make and utilize advertising and merchandising units used at the point where a sale is made. The Institute's membership includes the designers and producers of the displays and fixtures as well as the advertisers who order these pieces and the retailers who use them. Today, the POPAI is an international organization and one of the most active and aggressive trade associations in the marketing field.

Among the many services offered by this organization to its membership are workshops and seminars which deal with problems and new trends that develop in the field. They also sponsor research studies on buying habits, customer reactions to advertising, and techniques and current practices in the marketplace.

An annual trade show is sponsored by the POPAI, in which the latest and most innovative concepts in signing and display are shown, and new materials and techniques are introduced. Top marketing executives as well as display producers visit this exhibition. The organization also makes awards to the outstanding signs and displays of the year and they publish an annual *Merchandising Awards Yearbook*.

The POPAI maintains an information center which distributes many publications of interest to advertisers and marketing people. They publish *POPAI News* and prepare operating guidelines and bulletins to keep their membership informed on current matters of importance to them. There is also a public relations program, a speaker's bureau, and an active educator membership. The group is most cooperative with schools where advertising and display is taught and actively promotes the career openings in the point-of-purchase field.

National Association of Display Industries (NADI)

The National Association of Display Industries (NADI), headquartered in New York City, was organized in 1942 by leading manufacturers, designers, distributors, and importers in the visual merchandising field. It was conceived as a viable source for creating new business for the industry and to arrange a showcase for all that is new and innovative.

Twice a year, traditionally in June and December, the NADI sponsors a "market" or trade show held in New York, which attracts thousands of displaypersons and store planners from all over the world. The June market is referred to as the "Spring Show," and the December show is known as the "Christmas Show." The descriptive title goes back to the 1950's and 1960's when decorative seasonal props were the major business of trade shows. Some manufacturers display their wares in their own showrooms, while others, mainly those located outside of New York City, show at a designated and well-advertised and promoted central location.

Though its membership consists almost exclusively of the producers and distributors of visual merchandising and store planning materials, the NADI does participate in research programs intended to benefit the customers of their products. It has recently formed an Education Advisory Board which is working closely with schools that offer visual merchandising curricula. There are scholarships and grants as well as a cooperative work plan which is designed to foster closer relations between the manufacturers and the future displaypersons.

In addition to maintaining the most accurate and complete mailing lists in the industry (available only to its members), it offers a free employment information exchange which can be used by store management, visual merchandisers, and manufacturers.

The NADI feels that a strong industry organization will not only benefit the producers, but strengthen and assist the visual merchandisers in their quest for stature and greater recognition in the retailing industry. It enables them to do their jobs more effectively by having better fixtures, mannequins, and props with which to work. The NADI presents the Annual Display Awards (ADA's) to the most outstanding persons in the visual merchandising industry. It also honors the greatest names in retailing by induction into the NADI Hall of Fame.

Institute of Store Planners (ISP)

The Institute of Store Planners was formed in 1961 to gain professional recognition for persons involved in the business of store planning and design. Professional membership is granted to persons twenty-five years of age or older who have been working a minimum of eight years as full-time store planners. They are expected to be able to assemble and analyze merchandising data and be capable of applying this information to a working store plan. The store planner should be able to create and/or supervise the execution of the interior design: prepare the necessary drawings, establish budgets, and work with architects and engineers on the structural and mechanical elements of the job.

An associate member has to be twenty-one years of age or older and have had at least three years of full-time employment and experience as a store planner. The individual has to be professional, capable of reading and interpreting plans and seeing them through to completion. Trade membership is open to any reputable industrial concern that supplies either the materials or services necessary to the store planning profession. This would include manufacturers of fixtures, merchandisers, woodworking, store furniture, interior design materials, and so on.

The professional membership includes architects, store planners, and interior designers. Some of these professionals work for a department store, on staff, and are actively involved in the daily changes and alterations in the store as well as advance planning on new stores to be built or rehabilitated. Others are either self-employed or work as part of a design office or an architectural concern.

The ISP has an active education program, sponsoring scholarships for students in store planning programs in schools across the country. There are also newsletters, publications, and many regional and joint meetings which are often combined with presentations by trade members. There are several local chapters which plan special programs for their groups.

Western Association of Visual Merchandising (WAVM)

The Western Association of Visual Merchandising was formed in 1972 in San Francisco as a nonprofit organization whose original purpose was to sponsor a California visual merchandising show. The membership has grown dramatically and is composed of manufacturers, producers, distributors, and representatives for established lines. They exhibit at an annual display show (usually held in May). Membership is not a condition for participating at the exhibitions, and as many as two hundred exhibitors have shown their products at the annual showing, all under one roof in San Francisco.

The Retail Advisory Board of the WAVM, comprised of fifteen visual merchandisers from all over the country, gives advice on what can be done to improve the standards of the annual show, as well as on the other diversified activities of the organization.

The WAVM bestows the Golden Purchase Award on the "Salesperson of the Year" (in the field of visual merchandising). A Presentation Award for Creativity and Originality (PACO) is judged and presented by the Retail Advisory Board to encourage manufacturers to produce and present their products better and more imaginatively.

Another branch of the WAVM is the Retail Design Education Institute (RDEI). This is WAVM's effort to strengthen and encourage ties with the area of education. They have long-term goals for the teaching of visual merchandising, the presentation of scholarships, and the opening of employment opportunities to young persons entering the field. Direct annual grants are made to schools teaching visual merchandising.

SOURCES OF INFORMATION AND IDEAS

Trade Shows

The displayperson in search of mannequins, fixtures, or props would do well to visit New York City during the two annual trade shows of the National Association of Display Industries. If the West Coast is closer or more convenient, the trade show held under the auspices of the Western Association of Visual Merchandisers (WAVM), in San Francisco, would be the place to see the best representations of what is new and current in merchandise presentation materials.

Even if store planning is the activity that the visual merchandiser intends doing, these are still the trade shows to see. The displayperson can write to either the NADI in New York or the WAVM in San Francisco for the dates of the upcoming shows. Both groups will supply a list of the names and addresses of manufacturers and distributors of mannequins, forms, fixtures, and decoratives. Also, the trade show booklets are invaluable listings of who's who in the field, what is available, and where it can be obtained.

Trade Magazines

The visual merchandiser should subscribe to *Visual Merchandising* magazine, published in Cincinnati, Ohio. In this monthly magazine, in addition to articles relevant to merchandise presentation and store planning, there are dozens of advertisements for the many elements necessary for the successful installation of windows and interiors. By filling in the numbers on the request card that is inserted at the back of the magazine, the displayperson is assured a steady flow of brochures, booklets, and illustrative material on new products and designs.

The same sources (the trade shows and *Visual Merchandising*) are excellent places to secure information on fixtures, lighting devices, printing machines, cutout letters, and all the other items that can add to the effectiveness of a display.

Research

The visual merchandiser should keep an active research file of booklets, brochures, photographs, ads, swatches, and any other bits and pieces that will someday make the designing or installation of a display better and simpler to execute. It is never too soon to start amassing this type of material.

Since this is an ongoing sort of collection, it should be reexamined often, updated, and kept viable. With outdated material weeded out, an "idea" that was filed away might stimulate a whole new set of promotional concepts. Photographs from fashion magazines can often suggest new arrangements for mannequin groupings, color schemes, or even fashion accessorizing. A postcard from some exotic, faraway place in the tropics may become the starting point for a display—as a background for a swimwear presentation, for example.

Keeping a reference file is an absolute "must." It gives the visual merchandiser/displayperson a place from which to start. Ideas evolve from other ideas.

26 What Is a Visual Merchandiser?

To a person who has selected visual merchandising as a career, it too often implies merely doing displays in a department or specialty store. Visual merchandising, or display, is much more than that. The career possibilities and the fields in which one can practice the techniques of "showing" and presentation are myriad. Though trends in fashion are a great influence on what the visual merchandiser/displayperson is showing, be it books, luggage, or even auto tires, visual merchandising is more than fashion and fashion accessories.

Visual merchandisers (V.M.) can find careers in the field of commercial exhibiting, museum and graphic art exhibiting, the staging of fashion shows, point-of-purchase design, store planning, and packaging. Displaypersons may work as trimmers, decorators, or designers in a department or specialty store, or for a manufacturer of display fixtures or props. Or, they may work as free-lance trimmers for individual stores. With trade shows becoming more and more important and appearing with greater frequency in more cities and in specially built exhibit centers, this too has become a lucrative field for the adaptable and capable displayperson.

One should select the direction or field that seems to offer the greatest potential for personal development and financial gain. This decision should take the following into consideration: the individual's temperament and talent, his or her degree of creativity, willingness to interact with people, and ultimate goals and ambitions.

Some people want to lead or direct. They are organizers and administrators. The visual merchandising field needs people who can organize, arrange, plot, and plan in an orderly manner with one eye on the budget and the other on the calendar and the time schedule. These talents are necessary to the creative process of display.

Some displaypersons, on the other hand, have "star" personalities. They need to razzle-dazzle, to sparkle, and erupt in creative outpourings. They are filled with imagination, touched with flair and atingle with excitement. For them, the planning, scheduling, bookkeeping, and nitty-gritty of following the "book" can be utter torment. It would be a waste to misuse or misdirect their unique talents.

Other displaypersons may find the mechanical aspects of drafting and the specifics of space and layout more to their liking. They could be in tune with interior design and all it entails. For them, a career in store planning or the designing of commercial interiors might provide the greatest satisfaction.

Personal gratification is most important in the development of a career. Since so much of our time is spent on the job, it is imperative that we like what we do, that we are happy and enthusiastic doing it. With so many diversified and fascinating areas from which to choose, no displayperson should ever be bored or unhappy.

No matter in which direction he or she goes, first and foremost, a visual merchandiser is a merchandiser, a person whose business it is to sell or promote by means of presentation. Whether presenting a garment, an organization, or an idea, we expect a displayperson to be an artist and/or a designer. Creativity and imagination are his or her major attributes. Most people not involved in the industry tend to take window and interior displays for granted. They do not realize the time, thought, planning, and preparation that go into creating a display. It takes talent to dress a mannequin or rig a form, to create the semblance of life, or to create animation in nonanimated objects.

The displayperson is a fashion coordinator—should be *au courant*, knowing the trends, the looks, the newest styles. He or she needs to know from where, in the long history of fashion design, these "new" designs evolved. He or she must find the settings, props, and accessories that will enhance these new trends.

The visual merchandiser should be a connoisseur, a collector, and an avid reader; a student of the world, past and present. In trash heaps, in second-hand stores, and at house razings, he or she may find tomorrow's display setting or a prop or a fixture that was not originally designed to be a fixture. The visual merchandiser should be able to see beauty where others may not, and then be able to make that beauty visible to all.

A good displayperson should be an interior designer, a space planner, a lighting expert, a landscape gardener. The displayperson may even be called upon to brighten up and lighten up an architectural colossus perpetrated by an architect with an "edifice complex." Some builders have been known to construct monuments rather than market places. They build in and leave little room for change, and change is the life force of fashion.

The store planning and display departments are called upon to do seasonal shops and special selling environments. They are expected to come up with clever, bright, and inexpensive ideas that change a "blah" department into a stimulating selling ambience. The ebb and flow of the traffic within the store, and the direction of that traffic past the eye-stopping displays and into sales areas, are part of the store planner's art form.

The visual merchandiser must be involved in a store's advertising, copywriting, signage, and graphics. He or she must be able to communicate with coworkers, management, and potential customers. This communication is written as well as oral. The displayperson should be able to write simple, direct, understandable sentences. Often, the visual merchandiser is called upon to write the copy-line or card heading that adds meaning, and sometimes humor, to the merchandise presentation.

And always, the good visual merchandiser is learning. He or she is always studying the world around, past the display window, outside the store, and beyond the parking lot. It requires constant preparation to do a good and thorough job.

Let us assume now that you already are a displayperson. You have selected a particular field in which you feel comfortable, happy, and fulfilled. What are you going to do to maintain that feeling? Are you still growing, learning, and stretching your talents? Here is a checklist for you to consider every once and a while, especially when you feel your job is not quite what you think it should be.

1. When is the last time you read a book that really stimulated you to think? When did you last feel that you learned something and expanded your horizons?

2. How long has it been since you have been to a museum, a gallery, an art show? Have you been keeping up with what is new in the world of art, or what was very old but is suddenly new and fashionable? Are you keeping up with the new media, new techniques, new approaches to presentation?

3. When did you last involve yourself with the new directions in the field of graphics, with posters, layouts, signage techniques and devices, and with new typography and methods of graphic reproduction? Are you keeping up with the advances in photography, holography, and calligraphy?

4. Do you remember the last experimental play or movie you saw? Even if you hated it or were totally confused by it, did you try to get something out of it?

5. If you have traveled, what have you seen and absorbed that you cannot get from a picture postcard or a guidebook? Did you wander through foreign streets picking up sounds, smells, and sights that someday may serve as inspirations for displays? Are you really looking, or are you just sight-seeing without really absorbing the sights?

6. Have you taken any school courses lately? Not simply for credit, but just because you wanted to know more about something—anything? Are you still growing intellectually? Are you learning more about your profession and the world?

7. What does your reference library look like? Are there cobwebs spread over two or three dusty and neglected books, or is it continually growing, constantly in use, a viable shelf of wonders? Do you allow yourself to get "lost" in these books? Do you use your dictionaries and learn to delight in language so that you may communicate better with those around you?

8. Look in the mirror—the full-length one! Take a real, long look. Do you look like a person who is involved with fashion and with the presentation and promotion of new looks and ideas? Do you look, feel, smell, act and react like a person who is a trend-setter? Are you enthusiastic, and does the enthusiasm (quiet or effervescent) come across and touch those near you? Are you sending off "sparks"? Are you sending out messages? Are you communicating?

9. And, in a quiet moment, think about this: Are you growing as a person? Are you honest, ethical, and sincere in what you do?

Check your score and see how you rate. You may find some of the "problems" with your job are really problems within yourself. You are in the "*Showing Business*." You are supposed to be an "image maker," but your own personal image must also be created, fostered, and developed.

Selected Bibliography

History and Background

Artley, Alexandra, ed. *The Golden Age of Shop Design: European Shop Interiors, 1880–1939.* New York: Whitney Library of Design, 1976.

Emory, Michael. *Windows.* Chicago: Contemporary Books, 1977.

Gaba, Lester. *Art of Window Display.* New York: Studio Publications/Crowell, 1952.

International Window Display. New York: Praeger, 1966.

Joel, Shirley. *Fairchild's Book of Window Display.* New York: Fairchild Publications, 1973.

Kasper, Karl. *Shops and Showrooms: An International Survey.* Translated by Lieselotte Mickel. New York: F.A. Praeger, 1967.

Marcus, Leonard. *The American Store Window.* New York: Whitney Library of Design, 1978.

Color and Light

Birren, Faber. *Color and Human Responses.* New York: Van Nostrand Reinhold, 1978.

_____. *Color in Your World.* New York: Collier Books, 1978.

_____. *Creative Color.* New York: Reinhold, 1961.

_____. *Principles of Color.* New York: Van Nostrand Reinhold, 1969.

_____. *Selling with Color.* New York: McGraw-Hill, 1945.

Judd, Deane Brewster. *Color in Business, Science and Industry.* 3d ed. New York: John Wiley & Sons, 1975.

Mechanical Drawing and Drafting

Dalzell, James Ralph. *Plan Reading for Home Builders,* 2d ed. rev. New York: McGraw-Hill, 1972.

Gieseke, Frederick Ernest. *Technical Drawing.* 7th ed. New York: MacMillan, 1980.

Spence, William Perkins. *Drafting Technology and Practice.* Peoria, Ill.: C.A. Bennett, 1973.

Display Techniques

Allport, Alan. *Paper Sculpture.* New York: Drake Publications, 1971.

Buckley, James. *The Drama of Display.* New York: Pellegrini & Cudahy, 1953.

Carty, Richard. *Visual Merchandising, Principles and Practice.* New York: MPC Educational Publications, 1978.

Coutchie, Marianne. *Jewelry on Display.* Cincinnati: Signs of the Times Publishing Co., 1972.

Hayett, William. *Display and Exhibit Handbook.* New York: Reinhold, 1967.

Kretchmer, Robert. *Window and Interior Display.* Scranton, Pa.: Laurel Publications, 1952.

Mills, Kenneth, and Judith Paul. *Create Distinctive Displays.* Englewood Cliffs, N.J.: Prentice-Hall, 1974.

Mitchell, R.F. *Rigging and Forming Men's Wear.* Cincinnati: Display Publishing Co., 1956.

Pegler, Martin M., ed. *Store Windows that Sell.* Vol. I. New York: Retail Reporting Bureau, 1980.

_____. *Store Windows that Sell.* Vol. II. New York: Retail Reporting Corporation, 1982.

Randall, Reino, and Edward C. Haines. *Bulletin Boards and Display.* Worcester, Mass.: Davis Publications, 1963.

Rowe, Frank A. *Display Fundamentals.* Cincinnati: Display Publishing Co., 1965.

Samson, Harland E. *Advertising and Displaying Merchandise.* Cincinnati: South-Western Publishing Co., 1967.

Smith, Gary R. *Display and Promotion.* 2d ed. New York: Gregg Div./McGraw-Hill, 1978.

Visual Merchandising: Chapters by 24 Display and Store Design Professionals. New York: National Retail Manufacturers Association, 1976.

Display Ideas

Barber, Bruce T. *Designer's Dictionary:* Vol. I. Lockport, N.Y.: Upson Co., 1974.

———. *Designer's Dictionary:* Vol. II. Lockport, N.Y.: Upson Co., 1981.

Pegler, Martin M. *Show and Sell.* 2d ed. Cincinnati: Signs of the Times Publishing Co., 1979.

———. *Tell and Sell.* Cincinnati: Signs of the Times Publishing Co., 1979.

Trout, Joseph J., ed. *The Progressive Grocer's Display and Merchandising Idea Book.* New York: Progressive Grocer Magazine, 1968.

Store Planning and Design

Carney, Clive. *Impact of Design.* New York: Architectural Book Publications, 1960.

Hornbeck, James S. *Stores and Shopping Centers.* New York: McGraw-Hill, 1962.

Interiors Book of Shops and Restaurants. New York: Watson-Guptill Publications, 1981.

Ketchum, Morris. *Shops and Stores.* rev. ed. New York: Reinhold, 1957.

Mang, Karl, and Eva Mang. *New Shops.* Cincinnati: Signs of the Times Publishing Co.

Novak, Adolph. *Store Planning and Design.* New York: Lebhar-Friedman Books, 1977.

Pegler, Martin M., ed. *Stores of the Year 1979/1980.* New York: Retail Reporting Bureau, 1980.

———. *Stores of the Year.* Vol. II, New York: Retail Reporting Corporation, 1981.

———. *The Language of Store Planning and Display.* New York: Fairchild Publications, 1982.

———. *Dictionary of Interior Design.* New York: Fairchild Publications, 1983.

Exhibits and Trade Shows

Best in Exhibition Designs. 2d ed. Washington, D.C.: R.C. Publications, 1977.

Carmel, James H. *Exhibition Techniques: Traveling and Temporary.* New York: Reinhold, 1962.

Clasen, Wolfgang. *Expositions, Exhibits, Industrial and Trade Shows.* New York: Praeger, 1968.

Franck, Klaus. *Exhibitions: A Survey of International Designs.* New York: Praeger, 1961.

Hanlon, Al. *Creative Selling through Trade Shows.* New York: Hawthorne Books, 1977.

Lewis, Ralph H. *Manual for Museums.* Washington, D.C.: National Park Service, U.S. Dept. of Interior, 1976.

Neal, Arminta, *Exhibits for the Small Museum: A Handbook.* Nashville: Amer. Assoc. for State and Local History, 1976.

Point of Purchase

Offenhartz, Harvey. *Point of Purchase Design.* New York: Reinhold, 1968.

Point of Purchase Advertising Institute. *Point of Purchase Advertising Institute's Annual Award Winners.* New York: Point of Purchase Advertising Institute, published annually.

Packard, Sidney, and Abraham Raine. *Consumer Behavior and Fashion Marketing.* 2d ed. Dubuque, Iowa: W.C. Brown, 1979.

Roth, Laszlo. *Package Design.* Englewood Cliffs, N.J.: Prentice-Hall, 1981.

Scott, Walter Dill. *Psychology of Advertising.* New York: Arno Press, 1978.

Signage and Silk-Screening

Biegeleisen, Jacob Israel. *The ABC of Lettering.* 5th ed. New York: Harper & Row, 1976.

———. *Art Directors' Workbook of Type Faces for Artists, Typographers, Letterers, Teachers and Students.* 3d ed. New York: Arco Publishing Co., 1976.

———. *Design and Print Your Own Posters.* New York: Watson-Guptill Publications, 1976.

———. *Screen Printing: A Contemporary Guide to the Technique of Screen Printing for Artists, Designers and Craftsmen.* New York: Watson-Guptill Publications, 1971.

Claus, Karen E., and James Claus. *The Sign User's Guide: A Marketing Aid.* Palo Alto, Calif.: Institute of Signage Research, 1978.

Follis, John, and Dave Hammer. *Architectural Signing and Graphics.* New York: Whitney Library of Design, 1979.

Gregory, Ralph. *Sign Painting Techniques.* Cincinnati: Signs of the Times Publishing Co.

Kosloff, Albert. *Photographic Screen Printing.* 4th ed. Cincinnati: Signs of the Times Publishing Co., 1972.

Turner, Silvie. *Screen Printing Techniques.* New York: Taplinger Publishing Co., 1976.

Fashion Shows

Corinth, Katherine. *Fashion Showmanship.* New York: John Wiley & Sons, 1970.

Diehl, Mary Ellen. *How to Produce a Fashion Show.* New York: Fairchild Publications, 1976.

Goschie, Susan. *Fashion Direction and Coordination.* Indianapolis: Bobbs-Merrill, 1980.

Shirley, Thelma H. *Success Guide to Exciting Fashion Shows.* Chicago: Fashion Imprints, 1978.

Index

About the Author

Martin Pegler is an author in a hurry. And no wonder. During the past year he has:

- Taught full-time at Fashion Institute of Technology, State University of New York, on display and related subjects. He has also taught at the Barbizon School of Fashion Merchandising. Both are located in New York.
- Served as a consultant in the display field as well as an interior designer of commercial spaces.
- Toured Europe with twenty-five students studying fashion merchandising and display—with a healthy dose of European culture tossed in by guide and teacher, M. Pegler.
- Wrote articles on a regular basis for the magazine, *Visual Merchandising*, and contributed to other fashion publications.
- Wrote scripts and selected color slides for several audio-visual programs.
- Traveled the lecture circuit, including an overseas stop in England. (He has been invited there again for four talks in 1983.)
- Worked on two books for Fairchild Books, one a new edition of his *Dictionary of Interior Design*, and this text for students and professionals, *Visual Merchandising and Display*.

And during his free time, to get away from it all, there is the community work in Rockville Centre, New York, where he offers lectures on design history and builds sets for the town's theater.

Martin Pegler has been able to have his cake and eat it, too, for as long as he can remember. Following a stint in the army during World War II, and a brief fling as a pre-med student, he decided he really liked display and design. He earned degrees in fine arts from New York University and Columbia, and went to work for a company, but always intended to go it alone. Even in his early jobs, he took one day off each week to teach, and on weekends he looked for free-lance clients. Along the way, he joined the important professional groups, ASID and ISP.

After his marriage, the children arrived, three all told, and when he baby-sat, he worked on free-lance assignments. The word to his offspring: "Play nicely, but don't bother me." It didn't hurt their upbringing. All three are individual and creative. Wife Suzan remains his confidante, chief critic, and all-purpose sounding board after almost forty years of collaboration.

In his eight-room home, he has liberated three as dens. One serves as a library where he can escape and contemplate. A second is an office where he does his writing. The third, in the attic, is a workroom where he can convert display ideas into reality.